Passions in Print

PRESS OF THE PALACE OF THE GOVERNORS

New World Saints, hand-colored image and portfolio box, Press of the Palace of the Governors, 1995.

PASSIONS *in* PRINT

PRIVATE PRESS ARTISTRY IN NEW MEXICO

1834–Present

PAMELA S. SMITH

with Richard Polese

MUSEUM OF NEW MEXICO PRESS SANTA FE

CONTENTS

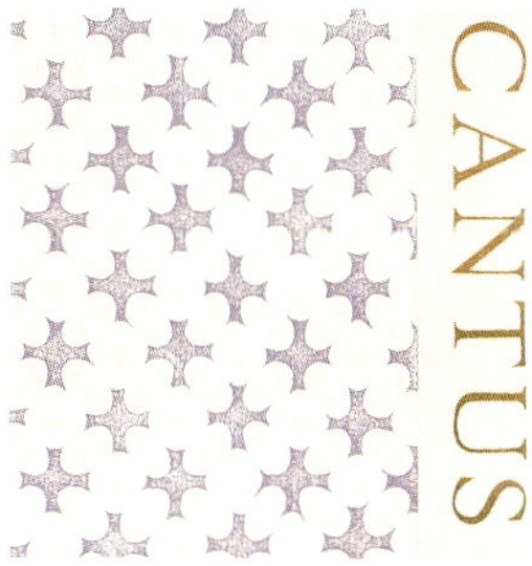
CANTUS

Based on the exhibition *Lasting Impressions: The Private Presses in New Mexico, 1834–2003* at the Palace of the Governors, Museum of New Mexico, Santa Fe, February 18, 2005–February 4, 2007.

Funding for this publication was generously provided by the Lannan Foundation.

Project editor: Mary Wachs
Design and production: Deborah Flynn Post
Composition: Angela Taormina
Principal photography: Blair Clark

Manufactured in Singapore
10 9 8 7 6 5 4 3 2 1

Library of Congress Cataloging-in-Publication Data

Smith, Pamela S.
Passions in print : private press artistry in New Mexico / by Pamela S. Smith, with Richard Polese.
p. cm.
Includes bibliographical references and index.
Contents: The church and the press : nineteenth-century beginnings — Artists, writers, and the private press golden era, 1920-1940 — The war years and beyond, 1941-1955 — Vigor and variety : a small press revival, 1960-1975 — Past meets present in the age of technology, 1976-2005.
ISBN 0-89013-479-0 (alk. Paper)
1. Private presses - New Mexico - History. 2. Publishers and publishing-New Mexico-History. I. Polese, Richard. II. Title.

Z231.5P7S655 2006
070.5'93'09789-dc22 2005019507

Museum of New Mexico Press
Post Office Box 2087 Santa Fe, New Mexico 87504
www.mnmpress.org

Front cover: Woodcut illustration by Willard Clark, ca. 1939. See page 28.

For New Mexico's private press printers,

whose passion and dedication to the art of the book

have enriched the lives of generations of readers.

The Press of Gustave Baumann

Frijoles Canyon Pictographs, 1939, featuring Baumann's woodcut illustrations.

Preface

CHANCES ARE you have seen their books, felt the sumptuous handmade papers, admired the lavish artwork and rich textures of a crafted binding but perhaps knew little about the making of these literary treasures. Fine printers and their collaborators are as rare as the editions they produce and seldom recognized outside their specialized field. Exploring the little-known but remarkably rich realm of private press printing and publishing in New Mexico, this book sheds light on a group of artisans—printers, bookbinders, illustrators, and designers—that independently produced some of the region's best-known literary treasures. Set against the southwestern landscape and threaded with elements of New Mexico's unique cultural heritage, it tells the story of a private press movement unlike any other.

The narrative moves through a series of chronologically arranged biographical sketches in which I have attempted to show how individual talents and unique personality traits, along with the influences of time and place, all contributed to the shape of New Mexico's handmade books.

The story begins in the nineteenth century where it focuses on two private printing efforts closely allied with the church, then moves on in Chapter Two to what is often considered the "Golden Era" of New Mexico private presses, 1920 through 1940. Included is a highly creative group of artists and writers that involved itself in private publishing efforts. Chapter Three covers a transitory period from 1941 to 1955 and the presses that struggled through the war years, while Chapter Four, 1960 through 1975, surges with the enthusiasm of a small press revival. The story concludes in Chapter Five as it moves from the mid-1970s into the present, a period marked both by technological advances and nostalgia for the past.

To suit a widely varied and creative effort, the term "private press" is loosely applied throughout the book and interchanged with "fine press" and "small press." Although a simple and concise definition of the terminology has escaped writers for centuries, a private press is generally accepted to be a small publishing house, operating outside the realm of the commercial book trade, where personal literary interest and aesthetic supersede financial gain.

The publishers included in the book were selected because of the independent nature of their work, their dedication to handcrafts, and their track records for producing books rather than ephemeral material. Based on these criteria, I have attempted to present a thorough picture of the private press movement in New Mexico. Undoubtedly some worthy efforts have eluded my investigations. What emerged, however, is a colorful and eclectic group of book artists.

Acknowledgments

RESEARCH FOR THIS BOOK began more than thirty years ago with my induction into the world of fine printing in New Mexico. From a privileged vantage point — proprietress of a working historic print shop at the state museum — I acquired a wealth of inspiration and information from a steady flow of museum visitors. Tips came from fellow printers like "Hair Register Mike," from an occasional publishing industry notable like Boston's David Godine, and from book lovers in all shapes and sizes. To this multitude of mostly nameless enthusiasts I owe a great debt of gratitude.

As the idea for a book and exhibition on private presses began to germinate several years ago, it received support and encouragement from Mary Wachs and Mimi Roberts of the Museum of New Mexico, along with Barbara B. Hagood, then deputy director of the museum. I am grateful to these three for their ability to see the potential in the subject and for the work they put into getting the project up and running; and to Dr. Frances Levine, director of the Palace of the Governors, who helped generate funding to make the book a reality.

To librarians and archivists who patiently guided my search through hidden corners of their collections, I am indebted as well. In particular, I would like to acknowledge Museum of New Mexico librarians Hazel Romero of the Fray Angélico Chávez History Library, Mara Yarbrough at the Museum of Indian Arts and Culture/Laboratory of Anthropology Library, and Mary Jebsen at the library of the Museum of Fine Arts.

It was my privilege in writing this book to work with an extraordinary group of printers and publishers. They deserve sincere thanks for sharing their fascinating lives in hours of interviews that make up much of the book's text. I would like to pay special tribute to Paula Hocks of Running Women Press and Andy Gregg of Vinegar Tom Press, who died before they could see their publishing efforts honored here.

Work on the book never could have been completed without the help of friends — Priscilla Spitler, who was always willing to lend an intelligent ear no matter what she was in the middle of; Sarah Laughlin, who fine-tuned the manuscript; and my collaborator Richard Polese, whose confidence and encouragement made it all possible. I am grateful, as well, to Leonard Jaffe and Dr. Marta Weigle, who lent their expertise as readers.

Finally, I would like to express my appreciation to designer Deborah Flynn Post and photographer Blair Clark, who was always willing to take "just one more" shot. The fine quality of this book is due in part to the generous support of the Lannan Foundation.

Pamela S. Smith
Abiquiu, New Mexico

Margaret Hale and Joseph O'Kane Foster at the etching press,
Vancil Foster Greeting Cards, ca. 1924.

Introduction

Fine Printing involves an aesthetic dedication. It is an expression of the human spirit which, through the arrangement and presentation of the printed word, reaches toward order and harmony and beauty.

—Joseph Blumenthal, *The Printed Book in America*[1]

THE HISTORY OF THE PRIVATE PRESS winds through centuries of finely printed books that may not have seen the light of day had it not been for the efforts of a single press owner. Risk and adventure, the suspense-filled anticipation of introducing an unknown author or an untried piece of literature, are all part of the attraction of independent publishing.

In 1744 Benjamin Franklin's love of the classics inspired his printing of America's first translation of Cicero's *Cato Major*. William Blake produced his own beautifully "illuminated" poetry by means of relief etchings, completing the book *Songs of Innocence* in 1789. More recently, the American West's best-known independent publisher Alan Swallow premiered Frank Waters's *The Man Who Killed the Deer* in 1942.

The work of the private printer is guided by personal taste and aesthetics and is fired by a do-it-yourself philosophy that includes everything from editorial and press work to design, typesetting, illustrating, binding, and even the marketing of books. Combining technical skill with a love of literature and artistic talents, private printers have produced limited-edition publications valued as much for their beauty as for their content.

Standards of private press craftsmanship harken back to the late nineteenth century when the idea of books as an art form evolved as part of the Arts and Crafts Movement. In response to the industrialization of Victorian

England and the poor quality of mass-produced printed material, the multitalented British designer William Morris established the Kelmscott Press in the early 1890s. Beautifully crafted books, inspired by meticulous medieval workmanship, became the hallmark of his publishing house and further influenced the fine printing world.

Chicago small presses emerged amid the city's booming printing industry and benefited from schools, such as the Art Institute of Chicago, that offered training in the industrial arts. In California a proud tradition of fine printing has been passed along from one generation to the next by notable craftspeople, such as John Henry Nash, Edwin and Robert Grabhorn, Saul and Lillian Marks, and William Everson.

Devoid of any such tradition and training ground, New Mexico's fine printers have relied on resourcefulness, embracing standards of craftsmanship along with their own frontier inventiveness. The majority were immigrants, drawn here from all parts of the country by the very imagery they then lavished in their books. Rich southwestern lore has inspired private publishing efforts in New Mexico for nearly a century, along with other subject matter as varied as the group that fashioned the material into books. Religion, poetry, politics, history, linguistics, theater, and environmental issues all found their way into the pages of the region's privately printed works.

Most of these artisan printers came with developed skills and experience. Renegades of the publishing industry, they sought to do the job themselves, to maintain artistic control over the entire process. With this aim, many opted to do the work on hand-operated letterpress equipment. A form of raised surface printing going back to Gutenberg in the fifteenth century, this method makes use of moveable metal type and relief printing blocks to yield a carefully crafted product.

The use of a wide range of imaginative approaches and unconventional materials separates New Mexico small press production from the more classic works done elsewhere in the country. There are editions bound in floral wallpaper and plywood, as well as snakeskin, buffalo hide, and colcha-stitched fabrics, reflecting the textures of the region. There are whimsical woodblock illustrations spontaneously carved from discarded orange crates and a rainbow of colored text papers to replace subdued tones of white and cream.

Without the constraints of tradition, a variety of uncommon printing equipment was put to use along with the usual letterpress machinery. Outmoded mimeograph machines, photo duplicators, and an A. B. Dick offset press all have played a role in producing limited-edition books here. Recently added to this list are electronic innovations—computer typography and digital imagery—used in combination with handcrafted techniques.

Quality of work varied significantly throughout the years, from the ephemeral to the precious, from crude folk charm to sensitively rendered typography. Despite a certain unevenness, New Mexico's privately printed books and portfolios have captured national attention as recipients of awards bestowed by organizations such as the American Institute of Graphic Arts.

The work comes at a price. Fine printing is a labor of love rather than a source of lucrative income. The challenges of keeping a small press going in the hardscrabble New Mexico economy bested many enthusiastic efforts. Some kept their small publishing houses afloat with the fruits of their physical labor, driving fence posts, raising hogs, and doing double time as pressmen at local newspaper plants to support their fine printing endeavors. Despite these valiant efforts, the average lifespan of a New Mexico private press is about seven years.

How is it, then, that private printers and publishers persist? Perhaps the answer lies in passion rather than in reason. Jetta Carleton Lyon referred to the Lightning Tree publishing enterprise she owned and operated with her husband Jene as "an affair of the heart" where the satisfaction of keeping the printed book alive was reward enough.[2] Running Women Press proprietor Paula Hocks spoke of the intimacy of the handmade book and the importance of creating a work of art that can be held in the hands. And Clifford Burke of the Desert Rose Press stated eloquently, "To see the labor, all of the pieces evolve into a work of art, that first proof, or the first finished copy of a book: there's nothing quite like it that I know of. I have lifted every letter, caressed every word; much of what I know of a poem is in my hands. I have birthed it."[3]

All have shared a love of the book and a commitment to time-honored printing techniques. In the pages of their enduring works, they offer an opportunity to see, feel, and touch the literature of the Land of Enchantment.

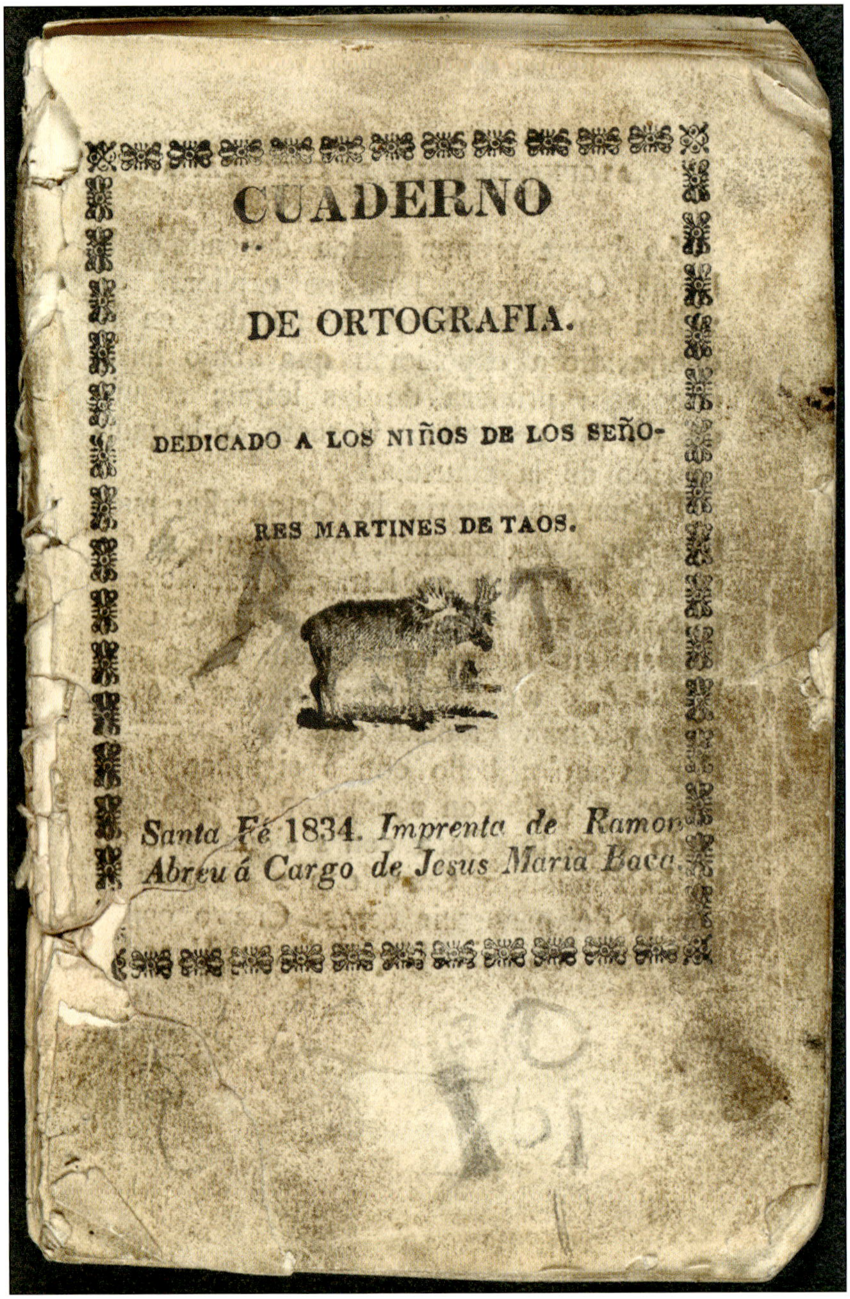

The Press of Padre Martínez
Cuaderno de Ortografía, title page, 1834, attributed to Padre Martínez.

CHAPTER 1

THE CHURCH AND THE PRESS: NINETEENTH-CENTURY BEGINNINGS

THERE WAS NO PRINTING PRESS in New Mexico prior to 1834. Claimed by Spain in the sixteenth century, this northernmost outpost of the Spanish New World empire remained little changed and badly neglected by the European monarchy for more than two centuries. Landlocked by vast prairies and towering mountain ranges, the area was further cut off from technological advances and economic developments by the government's tight control of trade routes. Printed materials arrived from Mexico via the Spanish-controlled Camino Real.

A scant population of colonials clustered around Santa Fe and Taos and was scattered throughout rural villages, where most eked out a living from subsistence farming while fending off attacks by marauding Indian tribes — a life that left little time for the pleasures of formal learning and reading.

For those who sought a scholarly path, there were few opportunities. According to his *Exposición*, which Pedro Bautista Pino presented to the Spanish government in 1812, education in New Mexico was limited "only to the children of those who are able to contribute to the salary of the school teacher."[1]

Twenty years later little had changed. In his comprehensive survey of conditions in the territory, Mexican lawyer Antonio Barreiro once again drew attention to the poor quality of public education. *Ojeada Sobre Nuevo México* (*An Overview of New Mexico*) points out the scarcity of books and underscores New Mexico's need for a printing press.[2] Despite efforts to expose the problem, schooling remained out of reach for most citizens of the territory well into the nineteenth century, and illiteracy was widespread.

In short, there was little demand for a printing press until the early 1830s, when profound political and economic changes began to unravel the edges of New Mexico's isolation. Spanish rule ended in 1821. Under an independent Mexico, trade sanctions were lifted, making way for an influx of foreign goods, ideas, and settlers. Over the Santa Fe Trail came manufactured cloth, clothing, coveted ironware, and in 1834 the tools that would launch New Mexico's private press movement.

The nineteenth century spawned two important private printing efforts guided by Padre Antonio José Martínez, the curate of Taos, and Presbyterian missioner John Menaul. Although their work was separated by nearly four decades, the two shared common objectives: using their printing presses to educate and to Christianize, much as the church had been doing since the invention of printing. Padre Martínez introduced locally published primers, including the *Cuaderno de Ortografía* (1834), New Mexico's first printed book, while Menaul's passion for linguistics led to the first printed materials in the Keres language at Laguna Pueblo. Both men made an indelible mark on a century characterized by change and upheaval.

The Press of Padre Antonio José Martínez

PADRE MARTÍNEZ was born in 1793 to Severino and María del Carmel Martínez in the northern New Mexico village of Santa Rosa de Abiquiu. There, in rare exception to the uneducated majority, he began his studies at age five. After the family resettled in Taos in 1804, he continued to develop the knowledge he had, despite a lack of established schools. Several years later, spurred again by his thirst for learning, he entered a seminary in Durango, Mexico, where he remained studying for the priesthood for nearly six years. He was ordained in 1822 and returned to New Mexico, where four years later he was made curate of Taos.[3]

As a priest and one of New Mexico's educated elite, Martínez was invited to participate in political activities, which he did with great vigor. Between the years 1832 and 1838, he served as one of seven elected deputies to the Departmental Assembly. After New Mexico fell to American forces in 1846, he played a role in setting up the new government and developed a strong voice in the affairs of the territory, a voice which brought him trouble along with renown.

Padre Antonio José Martínez, ca. 1848.

Early in his priesthood he placed himself at odds with the Church regarding heavy obligations of tithes on the poor. In 1837 his name was linked with a popular uprising near Santa Cruz,[4] an outcry against government and taxation, and a decade later rumors again identified him as one of the instigators of the Taos Rebellion.[5] His long-standing differences with Archbishop Jean Baptiste Lamy resulted in his suspension from office in 1856; their disputes were fictionalized in the pages of Willa Cather's 1926 novel *Death Comes for the Archbishop.*

Although a controversial figure, Padre Martínez became a favorite of the poor people of New Mexico. He championed their rights, became their voice in the forum of changing governments, and led the way in spreading public education. In 1826 he opened his first school in Taos, offering both primary and higher-level classes for boys and girls.[6] Later he took on clerical students and helped to prepare them for seminary studies.

By the early 1830s New Mexico was long overdue for the services of a printing press, and Padre Martínez, with his interest in education and political involvement, was a prime candidate for ownership. The press came in July of 1834, brought by Josiah Gregg and his partner Jesse Sutton on a wagon train from Missouri.[7]

According to Lucian J. Eastin, a soldier under Gen. Stephen Watts Kearny who later used the press in Santa Fe to print the laws of a newly established American government, the wood and iron hand press was less than impressive. He identified the machine as a Ramage press and dismissed it as "a very small affair."[8]

Once the printing press arrived in Santa Fe little time was wasted in putting it to work. By August, secretary of the legislature Ramón Abreú had issued an *aviso* announcing the opening of the press,[9] as well as the newspaper *El Crepúsculo de la Libertad.* Edited by Mexican lawyer Antonio Barreiro, the publication was a campaign device to facilitate his election to the Mexican Congress.

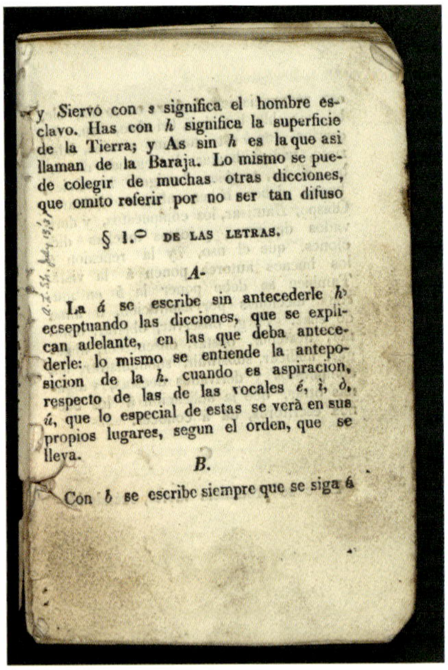

y Siervo con s significa el hombre esclavo. Has con h significa la superficie de la Tierra; y As sin h es la que asi llaman de la Baraja. Lo mismo se puede colegir de muchas otras dicciones, que omito referir por no ser tan difuso

§ 1.° DE LAS LETRAS.

A.

La á se escribe sin antecederle h: esceptuando las dicciones, que se esplican adelante, en las que deba antecederle: lo mismo se entiende la anteposicion de la h. cuando es aspiracion, respecto de las de las vocales é, ì, ò, ú, que lo especial de estas se verà en sus propios lugares, segun el orden, que se lleva.

B.

Con b se escribe siempre que se siga á

THE PRESS OF PADRE MARTÍNEZ
Cuaderno de Ortografía, 1834, attributed to Padre Martínez.

THE PRESS OF PADRE MARTÍNEZ
Leather binding on *Ortografía de la Lengua Castellana*, 1837, book printed on the Martínez press.

Padre Martínez soon became associated with the publishing effort. Before the year ended, the Abreú press issued what has been heralded as New Mexico's first printed book—a little twenty-two-page primer titled *Cuaderno de Ortografía*. Though authorship of the book is obscure, it is dedicated *"a los niños de los Señores Martines de Taos"* and is commonly thought to be the work of Martínez, who purchased the press the following year and moved it to Taos.

Padre Martínez became a private press publisher whose strong viewpoint shaped editorial content and whose personal preferences determined titles to be issued. His printer was Jesús María Baca, whose name or initials appear on imprints from the time the press was set up in Santa Fe until 1857, when Baca's failing eyesight caused him to retire.[10] A native of New Mexico, he studied his trade in Durango, where some speculate his working relationship with Padre Martínez may have begun.

From 1835 until 1844, Padre Martínez produced Spanish language primers and religious instructional material, along with some autobiographical and political works. In response to the needs of his students, he completed in 1836 an arithmetic book titled *Cuaderno de Cuentas*, in 1837 the grammatical study *Ortografía de la Lengua Castellana*, and in 1841 another speller called *Corto Compendio*, along with *Algunos Puntos de Lógica*. At least two of these were extracted or translated from previously published books.

In an attempt to clear himself of any blame for the Santa Cruz uprising and restore his good name, Padre Martínez elaborated on his own virtues in an autobiographical work he published in 1838 titled *Relación de Méritos del Presbítero Antonio José Martínez*. Four years later he produced a book for use in classes he had established in Spanish and Mexican law. *Instituciónes de Derecho Real de Castilla y de Indias* was excerpted from a four-volume series written by José María Alvarez and published in Guatemala under the same title. An *Exposición* documenting the conditions of Indians living in the area and directed to government officials followed in 1843.

The exact output of the press is not known. The most recent bibliography, compiled by Henry Wagner more than sixty years ago and published in the *New Mexico Historical Review*, lists some ten books along with a few broadsides, notices, and proclamations. Martínez himself cited nine items in an advertisement on the back of his *Discurso Político* title page, an 1839 tract on the political obligations of Christians.

Because of the scarcity of extant copies it is likely that editions produced at the press were fairly limited. The books themselves are small in format, owing to the limitations of the Ramage press. Each measures about 4 × 6 inches and is coarsely bound in muslin, flowered cottons, or leather. At least some of the books were printed on imported Italian papers, as decipherable watermarks indicate, from types that can be traced to the Boston Type and Stereotype Foundry specimen book.[11] They reflect a kind of crude practicality, a frontier craftsmanship that made no attempt to resemble the fine art of printing.

In 1844, when production at the press slowed and Martínez was absorbed in the demands of his duties as a priest and educator, he agreed to loan the Ramage press to the Mexican government. It went back to Santa Fe along with Baca, the printer, to produce two short-lived newspapers in 1845, *La Verdad* and

El Payo del Nuevo Mexico, and, after the American takeover, the newly established *Laws of the Territory of New Mexico* (1846), printed in both English and Spanish, and popularly known as the *Kearny Code*.

Though the much traveled press was back in Taos by 1857, Padre Martínez never regained his publishing vigor. By the time *Historia Consisa del Cura de Taos Antonio José Martínez* appeared in 1861, the press had already changed hands. This Padre Martínez biography is thought to have been written by Vicente Ferrer Romero, who, along with José Manuel Medina, had taken over operation of the Taos press.[12] Padre Martínez died in 1867.

John Menaul, ca. 1876.

The Laguna Mission Press

JUST ONE YEAR LATER Presbyterian missioner John Menaul and his new bride Harriet McMechan set out for a post in West Africa, where he would have his first experience with the printing process, an experience that would forever shape his missionary work.

A native of Ireland, Menaul studied medicine at the University of Pennsylvania and theology at Princeton Seminary before assuming his role with the Presbyterian Foreign Missions. Though he accepted the Africa assignment with enthusiasm, the region's hot, humid climate and primitive conditions took a devastating toll during his two-year stay, claiming the life of his wife and leaving his own health badly compromised. He returned to this country with his two young daughters in 1870 and quickly opted for the dry Southwest heat. In the year following his return, he accepted a missionary position in Arizona Territory and began work with Navajo Indians at Fort Defiance. There he met and married fellow missioner Charity Ann Gaston.[13]

He was well equipped for the work. He taught school, administered to medical needs, and even instructed his students in the use of a loom and spinning wheel, the latter skills he acquired in his youth in Ireland.[14] Despite all he had to offer, Menaul was plagued by what he considered his failings. In his first year at Fort Defiance, he wrote Dr. John C. Lowrie, secretary of the Presbyterian Foreign Missions Board, "I have felt very much dissatisfied with myself

Laguna Pueblo, ca. 1883. Photograph by Ben Wittick.

ever since I came here. I cannot feel that I am the right man in the right place, and yet it seems a providential impossibility for me to go elsewhere."[15]

Language was his biggest stumbling block. In the same letter, dated December 12, 1871, Menaul complained that he was unable to understand the Navajo tongue and thus had no means of working for the Indians.

In considering a new post, he repeatedly emphasized his mechanical know-how and recently acquired skills as a pressman. "I might fill a useful post at some of our printing stations," he wrote Lowrie in 1873. "I printed the *Shorter Catch* in Benga, at Gaboon and had never before seen a type set or press worked."[16]

In 1875, after years of discontent, Menaul left Fort Defiance, citing unsavory Indian agents and the tension of joint church-government administration of agency affairs as reasons for his departure. That summer he responded favorably to a request from the Presbyterian Foreign Missions Board to establish a permanent mission at Laguna Pueblo, where he would at last have a chance to put his printing skills to work and would make his mark as New Mexico's premier linguist printer.

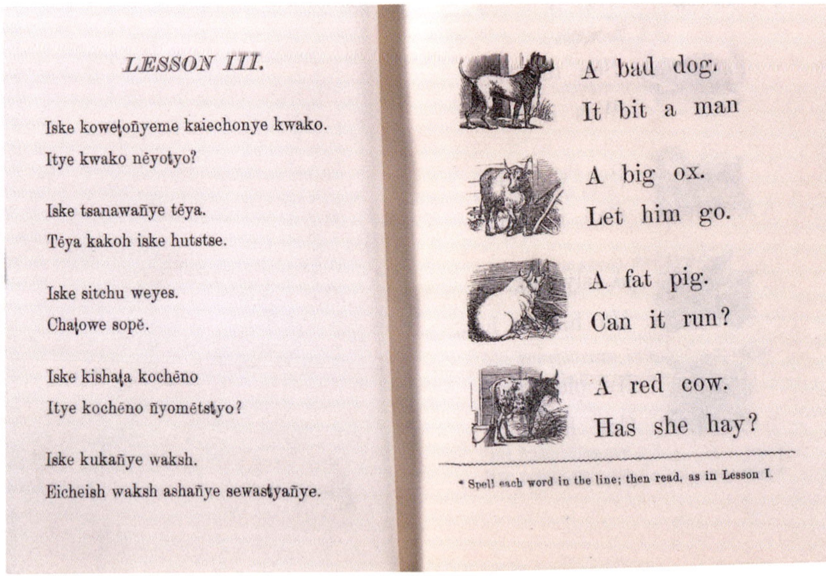

LESSON III.

Iske kowełoñyeme kaiechonye kwako.
Itye kwako nĕyotyo?

Iske tsanawañye tēya.
Tēya kakoh iske hutstse.

Iske sitchu weyes.
Chałowe sopĕ.

Iske kishała kochĕno
Itye kochĕno ñyomētstyo?

Iske kukañye waksh.
Eicheish waksh ashañye sewastyañye.

A bad dog.
It bit a man

A big ox.
Let him go.

A fat pig.
Can it run?

A red cow.
Has she hay?

* Spell each word in the line; then read, as in Lesson I.

THE LAGUNA MISSION PRESS
Lessons in English and Keres, *Laguna Indian Translation of McGufeyf's [sic] New First Eclectic Reader*, printed by Menaul in 1881–82.

The Keres-speaking Lagunas were known for their hospitable nature. Located between Albuquerque and Grants along a well-traveled route to the west, the pueblo became a way station during the nineteenth century when Anglo farmers and ranchers moved nearer to Laguna lands. Even during the Spanish Colonial period, Laguna was a safe haven for refugees from pueblos in turmoil and continued to accept new residents, both Navajo and Pueblo, well into the 1800s.

Passing through the region in 1870, Charity Ann Gaston was no exception to Laguna hospitality. Mistakenly thought to be a missionary to the pueblo, she was greeted by members of an official delegation who pleaded with her to remain.[17] Six years later, along with her husband, she was once again cordially received.

Realizing that a common language was the key to his success in working with the Indians and the printing press an invaluable tool in the process,

Menaul quickly set out to accomplish his goals. Before the end of 1876 he had established a day school and put out a request for a press, which arrived the following summer, thanks to an eastern donor Menaul refers to only as "W. Semple."[18]

The Keres tongue presented more of a challenge. In his *Third Annual Report of the Laguna Mission*, produced in 1879, Menaul lamented that he was limited in his printing production because of his inability to understand the language. "Our great trouble is that we have no means of getting at it," he said. "We have no means of analysing the words or finding out how they are formed, or by what laws sentences are formed; and we have no one knowing enough of the language to help us."[19]

Despite the difficulties, Menaul proceeded to print three Bible selections between 1877 and 1879—*Psalm XXIII* and *Exodus, Chapter XX*, in the Laguna language, as well as *Psalm XXIII* in both English and the Laguna language. Translations may have been the work of his Sabbath School students, as Menaul indicated that the group of thirty had been busy studying and creating other bilingual material. Eventually he developed a working knowledge of Keres and became fluent in Spanish, which was understood by many Lagunas.

Unlike Padre Martínez, Menaul was a capable printer, with mechanical know-how and enthusiasm for the process. His reports to the Home Board tallied thousands of impressions which he was involved in creating. When the Semple press broke down during the summer of 1878, he replaced it with a Washington hand press.[20] With the new equipment and an increased supply of type, Menaul promised even greater production. He reported doing 3,500 pages of printing for the Day and Sabbath Schools in the months after its arrival, a fair output on a hand press. In 1879 he produced a small pamphlet titled *The Catechism for Young Children*, as well as the twenty-page *Third Annual Report of the Laguna Mission*. Between 1880 and 1881 he printed three other reports, including two under the heading of "La Resolana," and a Spanish language newspaper, *La Solana*, for the children of his Sabbath School.

His best-known work, a Laguna Indian translation of one of the most popular school books of the day, appeared in 1882. With the help of a volunteer interpreter and translator, he created a bilingual version of *McGuffey's New First Eclectic Reader*. The book was a monumental task in Menaul's ongoing effort

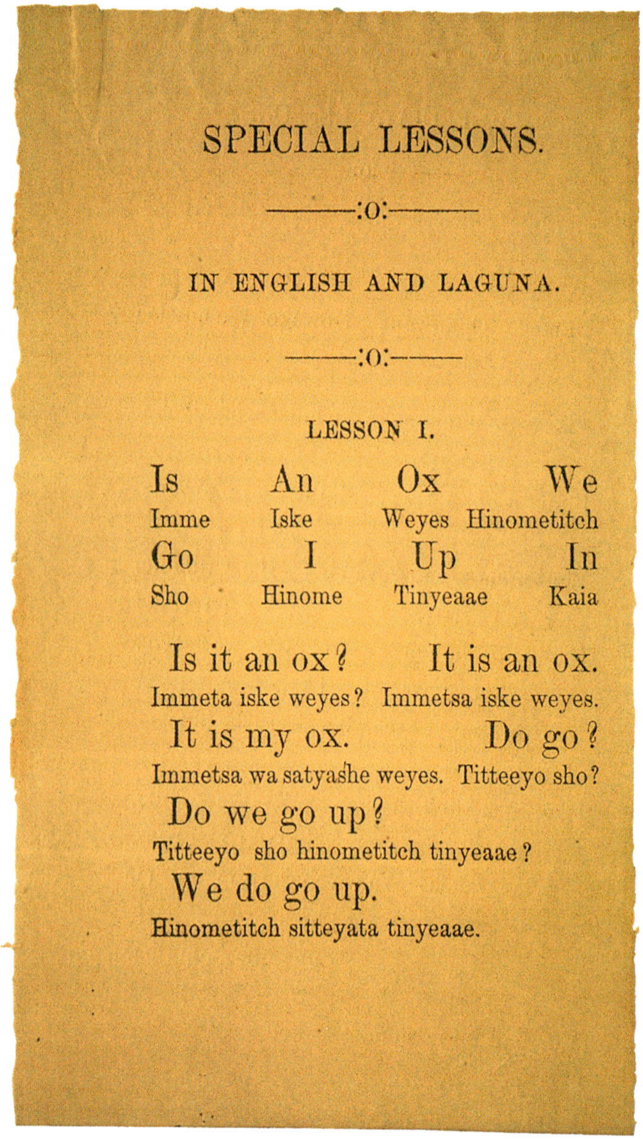

SPECIAL LESSONS.

———:o:———

IN ENGLISH AND LAGUNA.

———:o:———

LESSON I.

Is	An	Ox	We
Imme	Iske	Weyes	Hinometitch
Go	I	Up	In
Sho	Hinome	Tinyeaae	Kaia

Is it an ox? It is an ox.
Immeta iske weyes? Immetsa iske weyes.
It is my ox. Do go?
Immetsa wa satyashe weyes. Titteeyo sho?
Do we go up?
Titteeyo sho hinometitch tinyeaae?
We do go up.
Hinometitch sitteyata tinyeaae.

THE LAGUNA MISSION PRESS
Bilingual *Special Lessons* printed by Menaul sometime after 1882.

to develop a written Keres language. In the introduction to the primer he cites some of the challenges he faced — a wide variety of whispers and clicks used in spoken Keres defied the limited phonetical range of the alphabet, while words and ideas expressed in *McGuffey's Reader* had no equivalent in the Laguna culture. His greatest difficulty, he said, was the "unsettled" state of the language based on an absence of previous writings.

In producing the book, Menaul hand set and printed the Laguna translation on sheets that would be interleaved with the original *McGuffey's* text. The finished work was sent off to a bookbinder in Albuquerque along with copies of the reader and explicit instructions on how to take the bound volumes apart and reassemble them with the additional pages. Printing the book took better than a year. It was done, Menaul said, in between his medical duties and his work in the Sabbath School.[21]

For the next eight years, he continued producing works in English and Laguna — a *First Reader*, *Special Lessons*, and two additional selections from the Bible. In the face of a growing antimissionary sentiment,[22] he left Laguna in 1889 and went to Albuquerque, where he became pastor of the newly formed Spanish Presbyterian Church. There he continued to print thousands of Spanish language religious tracts, several hymnals, and beginning in 1902 a Synod periodical called *La Aurora*.

Menaul's printing work came to an end in 1904 when he presented his equipment to the industrial training program at Albuquerque's Menaul School, named for his brother James, a founder of the city's First Presbyterian Church. Two years later, a fire at the school destroyed it all.

CLARK'S STUDIO
Mariachi de Santa Fé, sheet music for the song of the Santa Fe Fiesta, cover design and woodcut illustration by Willard Clark, ca. 1939.

Chapter 2

Artists, Writers, and the Private Press Golden Era

1920—1940

In the years following World War I, New Mexico attracted a growing tide of artists and writers who would lend their talents to the private press effort. War weary and disillusioned by an increasingly industrialized society, they came from the East seeking unique qualities offered by the Land of Enchantment—an inspirational landscape, crystal clear light, a healthy climate, and the romance of centuries-old Hispanic and Indian traditions.

"Soon I had found my own adobe," wrote poet Witter Bynner shortly after settling in Santa Fe in 1922, "one of the oldest, with a broadbeamed roof to shed homely dirt on me in windy weather and primitive rain in wet. I was above the troubled world. I was washed clean of the war. I was given communion each night when sunset would elevate the host on the Sangre de Cristo mountains. I had found something not to be found elsewhere in These States, a town too much itself to be feverishly imitating its neighbors."[1]

It was a migration that began in the waning years of the nineteenth century and swelled as improved roads and railways eased the journey. First came the artists. A lifelong interest in Indians brought founding father of the Taos art colony Joseph Henry Sharp in 1893. In turn, his glowing reports drew fellow artists Ernest L. Blumenschein, Bert G. Phillips, and Irving Couse. Together with Oscar F. Berninghaus and W. Herbert (Buck) Dunton the six formed the Taos Society of Artists in 1915.[2] Santa Fe was not far behind. In 1904 painter/photographer Carlos Vierra was the first of many artists who sought the curative properties of the dry Southwest climate and ended up making the city their permanent home.[3]

The glories of New Mexico sunshine, fresh mountain air, and healing mineral waters had been noted by travelers for centuries. Not even under the Sicilian skies, Josiah Gregg assured his readers in 1844, could a "purer or more wholesome atmosphere be found."[4] By the early twentieth century the favorable climate was responsible for drawing health-seekers from throughout the country. New Mexico became a major center for the care of consumption sufferers, among them Alice Corbin, one of Santa Fe's first literary colonists.

A Chicago poet, Corbin moved here with her husband, artist William Penhallow Henderson, and daughter Alice to take advantage of Sunmount Sanitorium care. As an editor of *Poetry: A Magazine of Modern Verse*, she introduced New Mexico to a wide circle of her literary associates, including Carl Sandburg, Vachel Lindsay, and Witter Bynner. Along with others, in 1933 she helped form a cooperative publishing venture "to help good writing grow from native American soil."[5] Their Writers' Editions, printed by Walter Goodwin's Rydal Press, represent some of the finest small press work of the era.

The year 1917 saw the arrival of one of the Taos art community's most avid supporters—Mabel Dodge Sterne (later Luhan). A wealthy New York socialite, Luhan was well known for her Greenwich Village salons, where she gathered free-thinking artists and writers. In Taos throughout the 1920s and 1930s, she hosted the famous—D. H. Lawrence, Willa Cather, and Mary Austin, among hundreds of notables—while expressing her enthusiasm for her newfound home in articles she wrote for national magazines and newspapers. As a patroness of promising young talent, she took poet and writer Walter Willard (Spud) Johnson under her wing, gave him a job as her personal secretary, and in 1927 provided the first home for his Laughing Horse Press at her Los Gallos estate.[6]

As news of the expanding arts communities traveled via word of mouth and exposure of work produced here, another generation of artists began to arrive. New Mexico encouraged the migration, providing exhibit and studio space in the newly remodeled Palace of the Governors[7] and in Santa Fe's new Fine Arts Museum, dedicated in 1917. Among this new wave of arrivals were two who would help propel the private press movement into a new era of artistry. Gustave Baumann and Willard Clark used their talents as woodcut artists to capture the spirit of the region in fine-lined imagery that appeared in books they handcrafted throughout the period.

The exceptional quality of work produced by small printing houses during the 1920s and 1930s was not exclusive to New Mexico. Throughout the country fine printers like Carl Purlington Rollins, Ralph Fletcher Seymour, Will Ransom, John Henry Nash, and Edwin and Robert Grabhorn set a new standard of excellence in book production.

Despite the Great Depression that ravaged much of the country during the 1930s, New Mexico's independent publishers continued to benefit from the combination of literary and visual talents that converged here in the early part of the century. They set their own high standards, producing some of the state's best-known literary treasures.

The Press of Gustave Baumann

BY THE TIME he arrived in New Mexico, Gustave Baumann was already widely admired for his woodblock prints. Born in Germany in 1881, he worked in Chicago in catalog and advertising illustration, but carving and printing color prints was clearly his craft and his calling. For Baumann, being a fine craftsman and an artist—sketching, carving, and printing—were seamless elements in the whole of his creativity.

He studied for a year at the Arts and Crafts School in Munich in 1909, mastering Old World woodblock techniques. A lean, fairly tall man, Baumann looked the part of a German woodcarver—with gold-rimmed spectacles, pipe, cap, and work apron. After his studies abroad, he returned to Chicago and joined the Palette & Chisel Club, formed by fellow artisans whose day jobs were also in advertising art.[8] Carving and printing from basswood blocks relieved the tedium of the commercial graphics grind. Patient, diligent, and highly skilled, Baumann was carving out his future.

Gustave Baumann in 1913, at his Washington press in Brown County, Indiana.

Seeking the serenity and lack of distractions useful for this painstaking endeavor, he set up a workshop in rustic Brown County,

July

Fish still a-bitin'-*some;* but 'most
Too hot fer anything but layin'
Jest do-less like, and watchin' clost
The treetops and the squirrels playin'-
Their tail-tips switched 'bove knot and limb,
But keepin' most in sequestration-
Leavin' a big part to the im-
Magination.

THE PRESS OF GUSTAVE BAUMANN
All the Year Round, 1912, woodcut illustration by Gustave Baumann.

Indiana, in 1909. There he met James Whitcomb Riley, the Hoosier folk poet. Baumann produced twelve woodcuts in color and even hand cut the text for Riley's book *All the Year Round*, published in 1912. Before his days east of the Mississippi were done and while his reputation for superb printmaking continued to grow, he also made the woodcut illustrations for *Pirates! or, the Cruise of the Black Revenge* (1916), a bawdy tale of the Spanish Main set in thirteen acts. In Brown County he introduced his distinctive "hand and heart" printer's mark.

Walter Ufer, a Chicago art pal and Taos colony pioneer, pestered Baumann to come to Taos. After seven years in Brown County and confessing wanderlust, he would give Provincetown, Manhattan, and rural western New York short tries before he finally got on the train to New Mexico in 1918. At dawn on the second day out of Chicago, he first glimpsed the landscape that would bring forth his most astonishing color prints, as well as an award-winning book. Fifty years later he would recall, "There is no mountain so tall as when you see it from level prairie ground: there it is, bathed in inscrutable blue. . . . Passengers glue their noses to the windows."[9]

As he headed north to Taos on the "Chile Line" narrow-gauge railroad, subjects for his sketchbook and brush popped up everywhere. Spanish villages that seemed to rise out of the earth, activities of the Pueblo Indians, and surprising colors in strong light and shadow caught his eye and moved his hands creatively over the next several decades. Always he had in mind making high-quality copies that could be sold more than once.

Although inspiring surroundings and a conducive pace of life were at hand in Taos, Baumann didn't take to it, saying later with characteristic tact that such a "concentration of so many high-powered artists brings its problems."[10] At summer's end and short on cash, he went to Santa Fe, expecting to leave for the East after a show of his work at the Fine Arts Museum.

But in Santa Fe things changed immediately. Paul Walter, the museum's curator, gave the thirty-seven-year-old bachelor a workspace in the museum basement and arranged for a $500 bank loan. With a more diversified work environment and a less fractious social scene than Taos, Santa Fe also provided a measure of the tranquil, solitary hours essential to Baumann's exacting work. He began making woodcuts immediately from his sketches and watercolor gouaches. For blocks to become art, though, required "sharp tools, a complete disregard for time, and considerable patience," yet Baumann was also mindful that time "was the final arbiter" of the value and recognition of one's efforts.[11] After a year in town, he sent for his printing equipment, including the Washington style hand press he had bought in 1917.

Baumann's press was a Reliance Midget, made by the Paul Schniedewend Company of Chicago, a favorite of woodblock printers for its strong, even pressure. He used this press for the rest of his long working life in Santa Fe.[12] In addition to the thousands of impressions made for some two hundred editions of his luminous woodblock prints, he would produce two books with that press. In so doing, he bridged the realms of art, literature, craftsmanship, and book publishing in New Mexico.

The first book was *Chips an' Shavings,* "among which a Hoosier carpenter and his friend the barber discourse on hair-register and other intricacies of the color woodcut, with three woodcuts in the early Indiana manner and a few studio secrets."[13] Baumann had cut the blocks during his Brown County days more than a decade earlier. The text is an appropriately folksy dialogue that reveals some of the secrets of successful color woodcut printing. The book was published in 1929 with a "Velarde Press of Santa Fe" imprint, in an edition of one hundred copies.

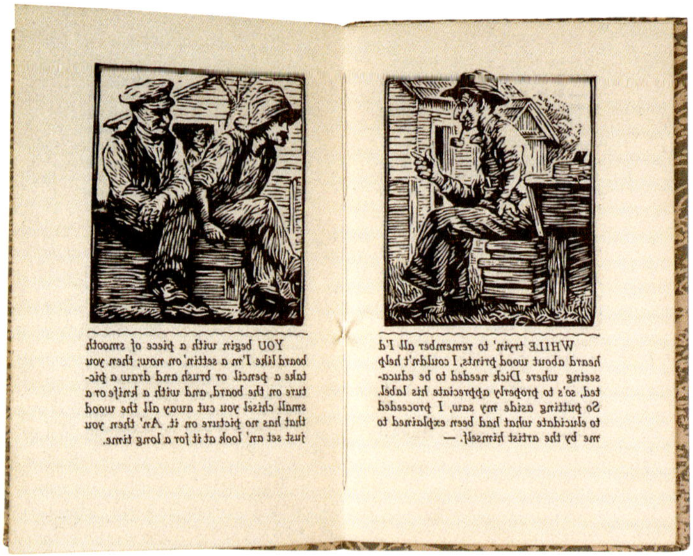

THE PRESS OF GUSTAVE BAUMANN
Chips an' Shavings, produced by Baumann in 1929.

Like several Santa Fe artists and craftspeople of the time, Baumann designed his own house, artfully carving its posts and lintels. That same year, 1923, at a San Felipe Pueblo Christmas ceremony he met Jane Deveraux Henderson, a young opera contralto and actress. They married in 1925 and became a popular Santa Fe couple for the rest of his ninety years.

To free himself from social and domestic distractions, he built a workshop detached from the house. There he toiled diligently, often beginning in early morning and pausing only for lunch or afternoon tea. He carved blocks, ground dry pigments to mix inks from his own secret recipes, then printed, recut imperfect blocks, and printed again until the result met his exacting standards. Counter to the usual printmaking custom, Baumann never brought in an assistant, student, or apprentice. He did not permit even close friends into his well-organized and-equipped studio. Hours there were his alone.[14]

Inspiration for his second complete book, *Frijoles Canyon Pictographs*, emerged from his fascination with the painted images left by ancient Puebloans on cliff walls and caves of the Pajarito Plateau some forty miles northwest of

WRITERS' EDITIONS, INC. ANNOUNCES

A BOOK FOR THOSE INTERESTED
IN THE ART OF THE PRIMITIVE SOUTHWEST

FRIJOLES CANYON PICTOGRAPHS
BY GUSTAVE BAUMANN

FOREWORD BY
ALFRED VINCENT KIDDER

THE PRESS OF GUSTAVE BAUMANN
Frijoles Canyon Pictographs announcement, 1939.

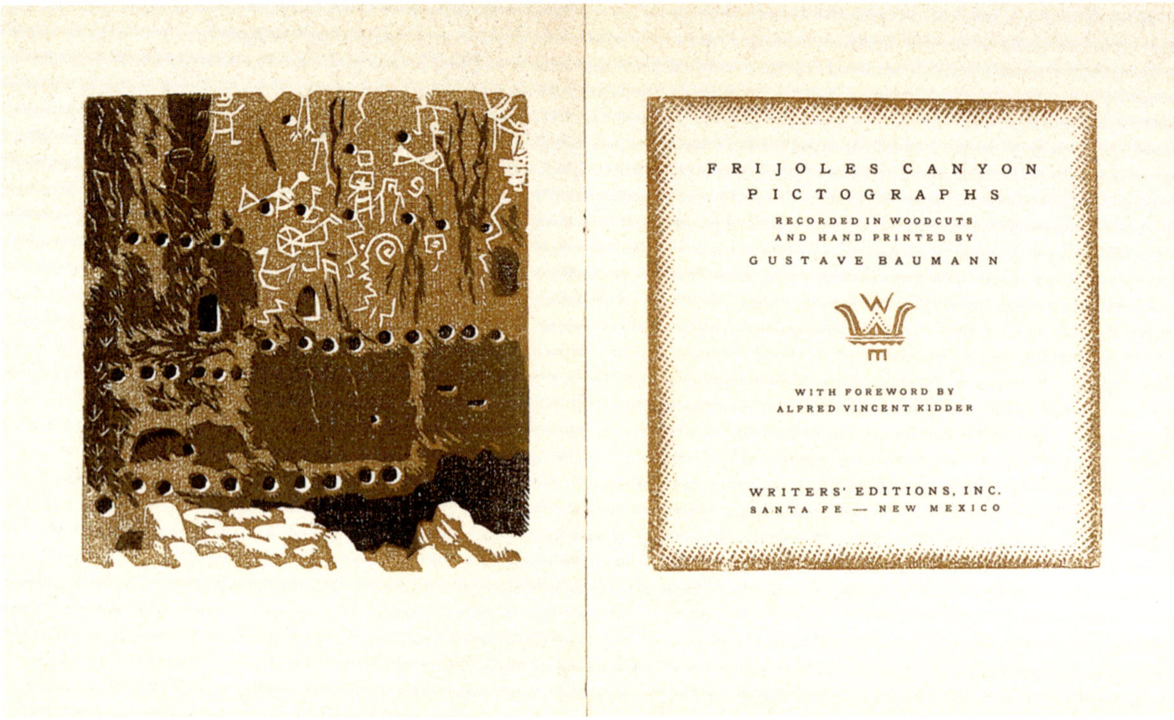

FRIJOLES CANYON
PICTOGRAPHS
RECORDED IN WOODCUTS
AND HAND PRINTED BY
GUSTAVE BAUMANN

WITH FOREWORD BY
ALFRED VINCENT KIDDER

WRITERS' EDITIONS, INC.
SANTA FE — NEW MEXICO

The Press of Gustave Baumann
Frijoles Canyon Pictographs, title page, 1939.

Santa Fe. He became concerned that through vandalism, theft, and natural erosion, this breathtaking legacy might well be lost.[15]

Baumann wrote and illustrated the entire book, printing twenty-six woodcuts of the pictographs and the canyon on high-quality paper. Folding out the center pages reveals a 28-inch panorama of *The Deer Hunt* pictograph, printed from blocks that Baumann carved during his first year in New Mexico. Close-up images of animals, spirits, and symbols from the cliff walls were printed in sand-colored ink. Endpapers show an impressive panorama of the canyon from an elevated view. Even the cover's array of pictograph images, printed on cloth, were produced by Baumann's meticulous hand.

By the late 1930s, book arts in Santa Fe had taken shape as a gathering of talented, versatile collaborators. Willard Clark set the type and printed the text for Baumann's pictographs book. Hazel Dreis bound the 480 copies in handmade cases. *Frijoles Canyon Pictographs* came out in 1939 as one of the last books published by Writers' Editions, a unique cooperative of New Mexico writers, poets, and printers. Baumann's last book effort, it was honored as one of the "Fifty Books of the Year" by the American Institute of Graphic Arts.

Baumann continued to play an active role in the art and graphics scene in Santa Fe well into the 1960s, making meticulous, complex, and beautiful color woodcut prints unsurpassed in color-relief printmaking.

Clark's Studio

SANTA FE OF 1928 looked pleasantly familiar to nineteen-year-old Willard Clark as he stopped off in New Mexico's dusty capital while on a rail trip to California to persue a commercial art career. It was supposed to be a short pause to meet a family friend, but he "forgot all about California" when he saw Santa Fe.[16] What began as a momentary layover turned into a lifetime connection with the City Different during which Clark created an illustrative and typographic style that became a part of Santa Fe's identity.

Clark had grown up in Argentina, where his father was a General Motors import executive. He studied art throughout his youth in Buenos Aires and part time at Grand Central School of Art in New York. Santa Fe with its surrounding mountains reminded him of a village in the foothills of the Andes. He spoke the common language here. "The people were my kind of people. They were Spanish. It was my kind of place."[17]

Self-confident, determined, gentlemanly, and broadly skilled, Clark quickly made Santa Fe his home — painting signs, making tinwork, decorating cupboards. He opened an art gallery, probably the town's first, in two tiny rooms under the staircase at old Sena Plaza in the heart of town. Although the gallery didn't last long, Clark made choices over the next few months that would set his course for years to come and put him at the center of printing and graphic arts in Santa Fe throughout the 1930s. His work arose as the central force in establishing much of Santa Fe's image to the rest of the world — all through his charming and simple printed designs.

Willard Clark in his Clark's Studio shop, ca. 1938.

Santa Fe did not have a full-service print shop at the time. Seeing a need that made economic sense, Clark would become the city's job printer — but by no means an ordinary printer. His artistic sense would inform nearly all his work. Less than a year after he arrived he opened El Estudio Press next to Roberta Robey's small but worldly Villagrá Book Shop, also in Sena Plaza. To get things going, he bought a hand-operated table model 8 × 12 Chandler & Price platen press,[18] studied its workings, and taught himself how to print.[19] Right from the start Clark appreciated job printing as a vehicle for artistic expression. Fortunately, so did a lot of his clients. For example, Clark's simple, amusing design for the "Do Not Disturb!" door hangers for La Fonda were so appealing to tourists that they were often taken as souvenirs, which resulted in frequent reprints and helped spread Santa Fe's particular mystique.

Decorated stationery, letterheads, business cards, labels, forms, restaurant menus, import catalogs — Clark printed nearly every job that came through the door. As his reputation and the appeal of his work got around, customers expected him to do design elements for their jobs, often on the "I need this tomorrow" basis. However, the closest engraving shop was in Denver,

The Villagra Book Shop

July · 1933

SENA PLAZA SANTA FE, NEW MEXICO
PHONE 666

Clark's Studio
Villagrá Book Shop promotional pamphlet, 1933.

CLARK'S STUDIO
Sprouts cover label, Willard Clark woodcut, 1930.

and it took a week to ten days to get the metal cuts back. So Clark did them himself, carving basswood blocks or making boxwood engravings for the images.[20] By working quickly and skillfully in his evening hours, he could complete work overnight: "I could get a job, do the drawing, make the block, and get it on the press the next morning."[21]

For headings and titles, Clark chose Neuland, a bold, distinctive, yet hand-wrought looking typestyle designed by Rudolf Koch. It seemed to fit perfectly with Santa Fe's ambience in the 1930s. Neuland met easily with Clark's chiseled lines depicting stylized scenes of humble churches, soft-edged adobe houses, burros laden with firewood, hombres in sombreros, shawl-clad women, bright-eyed birds, and billowing cottonwoods. Balance, restraint, a quiet but winsome charm, and perfect touches of southwestern color characterized the graphic output from Clark's press.

In February 1930 he published *Sprouts* by Richard Miller, the first of three books of poetry. It was a small hand-set book with eleven of his own woodcuts. The Villagrá Book Shop asked him to print a series of small booklets to promote titles available at the store, for which he made original woodcuts of appealing Santa Fe scenes for the covers. Clark would design and print *A Single Glow* by Axton Clark for Villagrá in 1933, and later *The Legend of Enchanted Mesa, and Other Southwest Poems*, a private project for poet/author Ozelia Rach-Wolski.

Bertha Berchtold, the local woman whom Clark married in 1930, became the indispensable business and sales department for the print shop. A growing family and enterprise called for better quarters. The following year, working on a shoestring, he designed and deftly hand built his adobe house on today's Sosaya Lane in the old Acequia Madre neighborhood then favored by artists and craftsmen. "There was no architect or contractor, just a stupid young man who needed a house badly for the family," Clark reflected later with typical humility.[22] Halfway through the project, he realized how convenient it would be to have his shop (renamed Clark's Studio) right there, so he added a second story for the family home. On kitchen cabinets, walls, and elsewhere were examples of Clark's handiwork and that of his friends — such as a light sconce the resourceful Spud Johnson had fashioned from a cigarette tin.

A strong ethic of collaboration and sharing of abilities prevailed among literary and crafts people in Depression-era Santa Fe. Gustave Baumann brought in woodcuts for his Christmas cards. He appreciated the speed and quality of Clark's printing. Usually secretive about his techniques, Baumann loosened up a little over time so that Clark could master the grinding, mixing, and application of homemade color inks. Fellow printer and colorful humorist Spud Johnson came in one day and picked out three of Clark's woodcuts for his *Laughing Horse* magazine.

Clark had a hand in designing and printing a couple of ambitious but short-lived publications, including the lively *Santa Fe Plaza, A Weekly News Magazine of Old Santa Fe.* Its masthead was a perfect Clark expression of the charm of the old town. Johnson, poet Alice Corbin, novelist Oliver LaFarge, and the editor of the *New Mexican,* Santa Fe's daily newspaper, contributed to this effort, which championed the "survival of the village under the press of Cosmopolis."[23]

Over several years he designed and printed exquisite booklets for McCrossen Hand-Woven Textiles, using as many as six colors for an illustration. The cover of *Karajo, An American Romance in Cloth*, produced for McCrossen, is a fine composition from three woodblocks with hand-carved lettering. He also produced richly illustrated catalogs of imported goods for the Old Mexico Shop and did menus for La Fonda and the Fred Harvey hotels strung along the main line of the Atcheson, Topeka and Santa Fe Railroad.

The route of the legendary Santa Fe Super Chief roared by some twenty miles south of town, but in 1937 railroad executives ran a special excursion of industry bigwigs and journalists to Santa Fe and asked Clark to print a small souvenir book for the guests. *From To-Day to Yesterday: The Super Chief in Old Santa Fe* was printed in black, brown, and dark orange ink on fine paper. A splendid and collectable example of Clark's design perfection, it mirrors the romantic essence of the City Different in that era.

When Walter Goodwin moved his Rydal Press from the village of Tesuque to nearby Canyon Road in 1937, Goodwin and Clark joined in a unique alliance. An announcement, printed in Clark's Neuland and Rydal's signature Perpetua type, stated that "Orders placed in either shop will be handled to the

THE SANTA FE PLAZA

AUGUST 1 - 1937 — A WEEKLY NEWS MAGAZINE OF OLD SANTA FE — VOL 1 • NO 1

— PRICE TEN CENTS —

NATIVE MARKET

- AN OLD PLAZA -

SPANISH INDIAN CRAFT CENTER OPEN AUG 7 IN ANCIENT ANALCO

Senores y Senoras y Senoritas, chicos y ninos, caballeros y paisanos, ladies and gentlemen, the Santa Fe Native Market, Clarkson and Curtin Props. bazaar of Spanish, Mexican and Indian crafts and products of the country, center of Fiesta and Mecca of tourists, situate on the Calle de Colegio in the historic precincts of four-century-old Analco in Old Santa Fe—will open to the public and the world August 7.

Thanks to the vision and enterprise of Major R. Hunter Clarkson, Miss Leonora Curtin and associates, the gente and friends, a hustling crew of artisans and the co-operative folk of this Villa.

It is a meeting place and place for sale and exchange of wares, handicrafts and other products of the Spanish-American and Indian communities of the Santa Fe region. Here the craftsmen and producers display and sell in familiar and traditional environment; the native atmosphere is preserved here among the people of Santa Fe and the hill country and their visitors make Fiesta.

The Market consists of:

Thirty booths and small handicraft shops for low rent; the Market works with all agencies to help the people make and sell better things.

El Teatro Analco, community theater for native plays and pastorals.

El Cantina Analco, cafe and canteen in the native fashion.

El Cantinita, smaller quainter, more native.

Baile de los Paisanos, miniature bandstand or pagoda and dance floor for folk dances.

Display rooms, work rooms, shops, for making of things in tin and wood and textiles and what not.

Molina de las Tortillas, the tortilla mill where this famous native delicacy is turned out in quantity.

The Native Market, established by Miss Leonora Curtin, Major R. Hunter Clarkson and associates, will be open daily form 11 A.M. to midnight, with dances every night except Sunday, special and varying entertainment in the way of folk songs and dances and native amusements.

Spanish Night in the Native Market is a new and charming feature of the Santa Fe Fiesta.

Things to notice at the Native Market;

The adobe bancos or benches; the very old quaint wooden fireplaces; the wide portales or porches, thick ancient walls, old wooden vigas, or beams, adobe floors, the painted wall decorations, the Mexican kitchen, the zaguan or entry-way, the massive and venerable wooden doors with their old iron hinges, at the main entrance. Many door-and window-frames are of great age. This district was known to the early Spaniards as the Barrio Analco, meaning the Place Beyond the River, where were the little houses of the Mexican Indian servants of the conquistadores.

There is ample parking space for cars, wagons, burros.

The Native Market personnel in part:—

Manuel Lujan, general manager;

Indian craftsmen, Maria and Julian of San Ildefonso; Cata and group from San Juan, Margarita Tafoya of Santa Clara.

Indian silver work in charge of Frank Patania.

Weavers—E. D. Trujillo, Jose Ramon Ortega of Chimayo, the latter in charge of weaving of neckties; Alfredo Catanach, Valentin Rivera, Max Ortiz.

(Continued to page 8)

A THEME SONG FOR THE ANCIENT VILLA

I love Kansas and Oklahoma,
I love Texas and Arizona,
But most of all, I'm ready to go
All the way with New Mexico!

How can anyone ever be
A part of our ancient ancestry,
Without long days in our sun-drenched soil!
With treasures more rare than gold or oil!

This is the secret we hold to keep;
The lonely herder who follows the sheep
Shares the secret with us who know
The lure of Nuevo Mexico!

———Alice Corbin

VAMOS WITH THE VAQUEROS TO THE EIGHTH ANNUAL SANTA FE HORSE SHOW ON SUNDAY

With half a hundred cowboys roping and riding, stake and bending races and other western events, a Trail class, the eighth annual Santa Fe horse show, August 1 in the afternoon at the municipal stadium, north end of town, also includes as a climax a short steeple chase, eight jumps, with tight corners, but plenty of action all visible from the stands. Few small western towns stage a horse show; Santa Fe, with an unusual number of riders presents a unique combination of east with west in this equestrian exhibition, distinctly a Home Town Show, and not too fashionable. It is put on by the Santa Fe Horse Association, whose members are not horses but which aims to encourage all horse activities in the Ancient, and foster an annually increasing crop of skilled riders. Director, T. B. Catron; judges, Lieut. Col. Harry Chamberlain, Lyle Brush, Brush ranch; Mrs. Catron. Ringmaster and grounds, Major Grove Cullum; assistants Capt. Gene B. Baca and Capt. Owen Wood. Executive committee, Catron, Jesus Baca, Jim Clarkson, Major Cullum, Malcom Bigelow.

No seats facing the Sun!

Prospects on the eve of the show were for a full list of entries featuring the children's and cowhand classes; a big sale of tickets boxes taken by local tycoons including the Ex-Secy. of War Pat Hurley; governor, mayor, W.P.A. officials, adjuntant general and other dignitaries invited guests, many entries from out of town.

BROTHER OF JACQUES CARTIER AN ANCESTOR OF JACQUES

Jacques Cartier, famous French explorer, was an ancestor-in law of Jacques Cartier, New York and Santa Fe dancer. "He was a bachelor, but I am a direct descendant of his brother Pierre," said Jacques this week. "The eyes of the original Jacques were brown and mine are blue, but with a goatee I look startlingly like him." Jacques knows because he once did Cartier in a dance number. "But the audience got it too quick, somehow or other, and always laughed" said the dancer. "It didn't go over so good, probably because they thought it was coincidence and not genealogy." The Gaspe peninsula and the granite point where the Allen Fiskes built their home and hibernated for a winter, along with the Jacques Cartier cliffs, is all familiar country to the dancer, who has often vacationed there, eating strawberries and raspberries. "The country is beautiful beyond compare" said the descendant of its French discoverer of 1534.

1

Clark's Studio

The Santa Fe Plaza, August 1, 1937, printed at Clark's Studio.

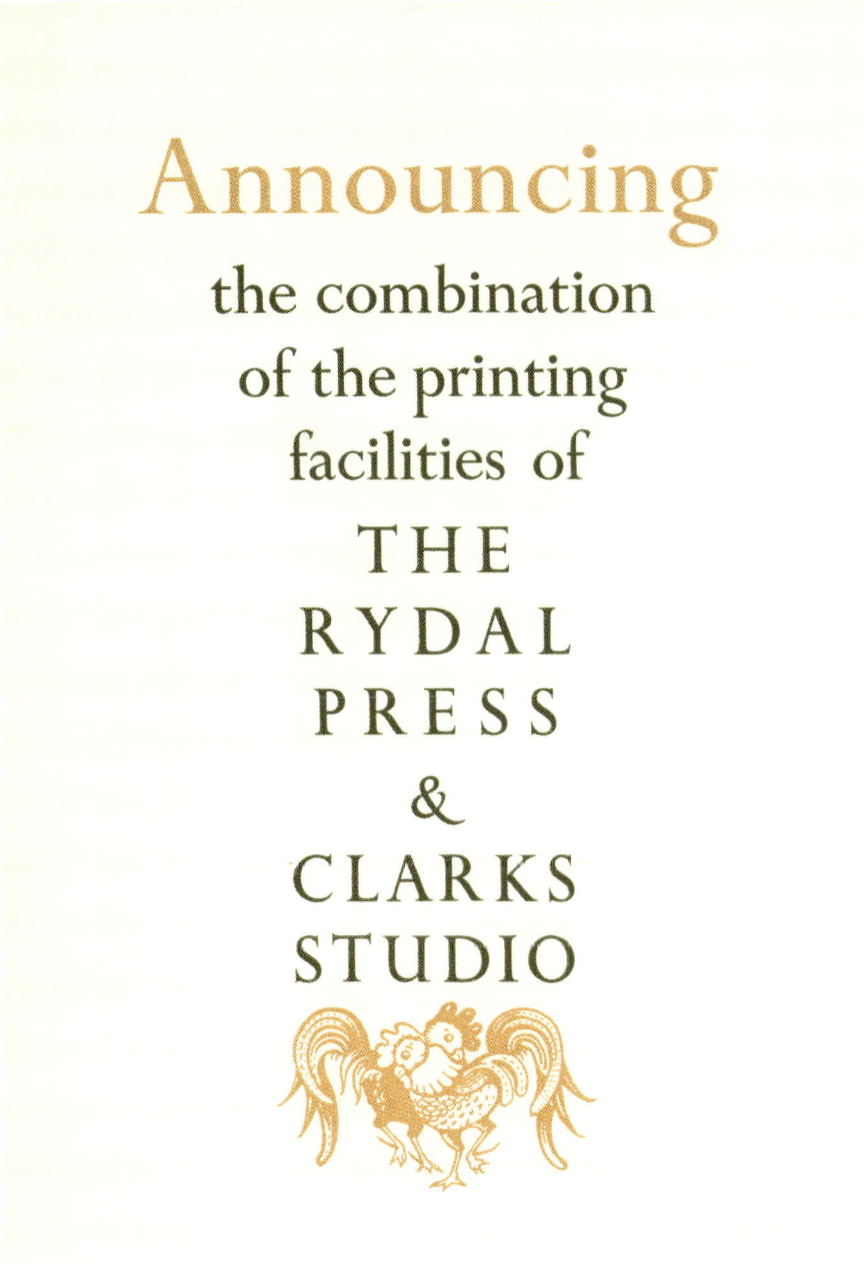

Announcing
the combination
of the printing
facilities of
THE
RYDAL
PRESS
&
CLARKS
STUDIO

CLARK'S STUDIO
Rydal Press and Clark's Studio announcement, 1937.

CLARK'S STUDIO
Annunciata and the Shepherds, with Willard Clark woodcut illustrations,1938.

best advantage for the customer," with services for designing and printing, reproduction of intaglio and color plates, hand engraving in wood, copper, and steel, and bookbinding.[24]

Clark added more printing equipment as orders burgeoned through the Depression years. When David Allen came down from Rydal to work for him in the late 1930s, eight presses crowded Clark's Studio. Equipment had grown to include Miehle Vertical and Kluge automatic presses (great for high-volume orders), a second Chandler & Price, a Colt's Armory press, a Vandercook proof press, and a Model X Linotype machine for rapid typesetting. Allen found Clark to be a patient teacher, "careful about telling me what I had done wrong and how to do it right. . . . His work just flowed."[25] Allen worked on at least two significant projects at Clark's Studio. The first was a series of booklets about Navajo blankets for the Laboratory of Anthropology written by Dr. Harry P. Mera.[26] Clark, Gustave Baumann, and Allen combined their energies in printing Baumann's ambitious *Frijoles Canyon Pictographs*.

Clark's Studio was at its busiest when Goodwin recommended Willard to legendary book designers Bruce and Helen Gentry as the perfect choice to make wood engravings for *Annunciata and the Shepherds* by Janette Sebring Lowrey. Set in San Antonio, Texas, it is a delightful Christmas story woven into a *Las Posadas* procession. Clark crafted eight color illustrations for this book, published in 1938 under the Gentrys' own imprint, Gentry Press of New York.

While Clark's illustrations may appear innocent, they reflect the work of a superb graphic designer with a sophisticated sense of balance and proportion in both type and pictorial elements, and complete command of a strong and charming style. One's eye travels easily around his prints, noticing hints of mirth (a spider dangling from a tree, a neat bow on a burro's tail, a bottle of *vino* in the pocket of a local strolling home after a night on the town). Like the man himself, Clark's work was at once sensible, innovative, and humane.

By the early 1940s other print shops and an engraver had opened for business in Santa Fe, and war clouds loomed on the horizon. Although Clark's

Studio was still doing well, Willard decided to pull the plug in 1942. He sold his equipment and signed on as a tool and die maker with the secret Manhattan Project in Los Alamos. He would work at the National Laboratory, commuting from Sosaya Lane, until retirement three decades later. But the creative output of Willard Clark, the printer and printmaker, was to have a warmly received rebirth in the 1980s (see Chapter Five).

Ranchos Press

LIKE GUSTAVE BAUMANN and Willard Clark, Ralph Pearson was a skilled printmaker. A Midwesterner by birth, he trained at the Art Institute of Chicago and developed a reputation as a master of modernist etchings before making his way to New Mexico around 1919. Inspired by Walter Ufer and other Chicago artist friends who had preceded him to the area, he brought his wife Margaret Hale[27] and daughter Pavli to settle in the foothills of the

Ralph Pearson, Margaret Hale, and daughter Pavli at their Ranchos de Taos home, ca. 1920.

Taos mountains. In the village of Ranchos de Taos he launched an unlikely combination business venture—hogs and greeting cards—that would evolve into the Ranchos Press.

Making a living as an artist on the heels of World War I was a challenge, one that Pearson offset with a pig farming business. In a letter to a client he emphasized that "raising hogs is only a means on this ranch, and is not being done for the sake of the piggies."[28] His work, he declared, was the only thing that mattered. And his work was producing etchings, some in the form of personalized greeting cards and bookplates, which he marketed throughout the country. "I am etching again with a big new press, and a huge new studio, just finished, and every convenience at hand," he told his Aunt Emma Pearson in 1920, "and I must not take time for letters at present. For there has been a big revival of interest in my work and orders are going out all over the country."[29]

The following year the American Bookplate Society published a limited-edition portfolio of twelve of his plates.[30] Exceptional in quality, Pearson's etched bookplates were said to be prepared with the same integrity as his large work and had already won him the society's awards. His line of Southwest greeting cards, popularized by a growing interest in New Mexico tourism, featured images of Southwest landscapes, Indian pueblos, adobe missions, and plant life of the area.

By 1921 the booming little business had reached capacity with forty different vendors selling the cards in cities throughout the country.[31] Although Pearson's wife handled much of the correspondence and sales, help was welcomed when Joseph O'Kane Foster showed up that same year. Foster brought a literary element to the growing concern. In Chicago he had been a Hearst newspaper reporter and had aspirations of one day becoming a novelist. In New Mexico he took Pearson's greeting card business in hand, dubbing it Vancil Foster Greeting Cards (a reference to his mother's maiden name), and breathed new life into the cottage industry.

He introduced hand-colored cards with clever verses. For this work the company relied on young educated women from the East, tempting them with promises of adventure and a healthy climate. A 1922 Vancil Foster correspondence claimed that such New Mexico opportunities were enough to repay prospective employees for the cost of their railroad fare. In exchange for the

RANCHOS PRESS

Hand-colored Vancil Foster greeting card, ca. 1925.

RANCHOS PRESS

Joseph O'Kane Foster letterhead, ca. 1925.

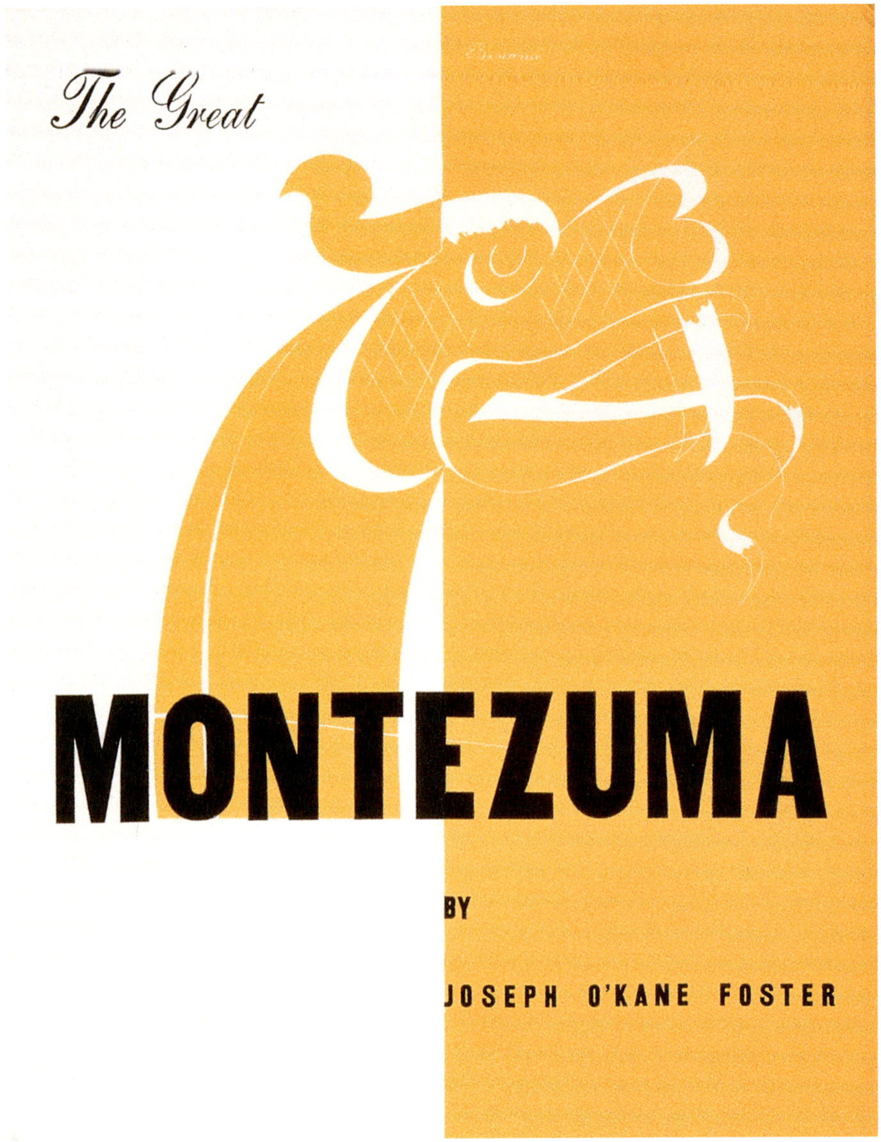

Ranchos Press

The Great Montezuma, designed by surrealist painter Thomas Benrimo for the Ranchos Press, 1940.

work they were promised "a roof, of canvas or mud, three square meals a day, washing and a horse to ride or team to drive."[32]

About twenty women were hired to do the job of hand coloring, among them Emily Hahn, who later became a well-known *New Yorker* writer and author of a long list of books, including *Mabel: A Biography of Mabel Dodge Luhan* (1977). For a short time after her graduation from the University of Wisconsin in 1926, Hahn lived in Taos in a tiny, wood-heated adobe house and rode a horse named Tom.[33] She worked for Vancil Foster Greeting Cards until her mother paid a surprise visit to convince her that graduate studies might hold a more promising future than the work of a Ranchos Press hand colorist.

Not long after Foster came on board, Pearson and Hale went separate ways. The restless artist went on to California in 1923, leaving Hale and her new business partner to manage Vancil Foster Greeting Cards. Together the two spent the next five years expanding the enterprise, adding the designs of Taos artists Ila McAfee, Manville Chapman, and Barbara Latham Cook, and supplementing Pearson's original intaglio presses with letterpress printing equipment.[34]

Though the business flourished, Foster never lost sight of his dream to become a novelist. Shortly after marrying Margaret Hale in 1928 he closed Vancil Foster and took his new family to live in Europe. There he indulged his longtime interest in the history of Spain's conquest of the New World, studying manuscript collections in Spain, France, and Italy.[35] Four years later he returned to Taos and began to write the only book he would produce on the Vancil Foster presses—his magnum opus titled *The Great Montezuma*. Written as a classic poem, the book recounts the destruction of the Aztec culture and its emperor Montezuma by conquistador Hernán Cortes.

Foster revived the greeting card company's old platen presses for the work, hand set all of the type, printed a phenomenal 1,250 copies, and even hand bound the edition, which appeared in 1940 under a brand new Ranchos Press imprint.[36] The somewhat controversial book design was done by his new neighbor, a surrealist painter named Thomas Benrimo.

Benrimo had settled in Ranchos de Taos in 1939 after a varied career in art, which included set painting for New York theatrical events and teaching at Pratt Institute, in addition to his own work.[37] Perhaps inspired by the stage, he used a rainbow of colored papers as a backdrop for the text. Colors, he noted in the book's colophon, are capable of "releasing sensations that have a definite mood value." And so he used his palette in an attempt to enhance the reader's experience, to heighten the tempo of the text. Some took objection to the design element. One critic called the use of color "dazzling" and complained that it sometimes obscured the type.

After completion of *The Great Montezuma*, Foster put the printing equipment in storage and went on to pursue his literary aspirations. He produced three fairly successful novels between 1942 and 1954, including *In the Night Did I Sing*, *A Cow Is Too Much Trouble in Los Angeles*, and *Street of Barefoot Lovers*. His *D. H. Lawrence in Taos* was published by the University of New Mexico Press in 1972. Though the Ranchos Press never produced another book, the greeting card company survived. Renamed Taos Cards by new owners Rick and Lynn Yaple, it was moved to Albuquerque in 1966. Original Vancil Foster designs are still among the company's offerings.[38]

The Laughing Horse Press

WHILE ARTISTS WERE BUSY capturing the flavor of New Mexico in colorful imagery, Walter Willard Johnson was providing a forum for the region's literary voices in the pages of his Laughing Horse Press publications. Johnson, affectionately known as "Spud," came to New Mexico about the same time Joseph O'Kane Foster showed up from Chicago. He was one of the earliest members of the Santa Fe and Taos literary colonies, the first to become a private press printer and publisher. In time he would become legendary. Following his arrival in Santa Fe in 1922, he spent nearly two decades producing a nationally recognized literary journal, along with whimsical broadsides and pamphlets that won him a place in the collective memory of his readership. It was all part of a grand plan laid out long before Johnson could be claimed by New Mexico.

Spud Johnson was born in Illinois in 1897 and raised in Greeley, Colorado, where in 1916 he enrolled in what was then Colorado State Teachers College. As the founder and editor of his high school newspaper and the owner of a small hobby press, the young journalist gravitated toward both manual and literary courses.[39]

His first days at the college began with a bookbinding class, marked by the smell of glue boiling in an iron pot and the sound of a guillotine cutter slicing through stacks of paper. The combination of technical and academic studies was designed to satisfy the teenage Johnson's newly proclaimed interest in books—"how to write them and how to make them."[40] Inspired by a book on the Roycrofters, a handicraft community set up by Elbert Hubbard in East Aurora, New York, in 1895, Johnson mapped out a future for himself complete with a whitewashed cottage, work as a craftsman, and dedication to some not-yet-determined ideal, all of which would have to wait.

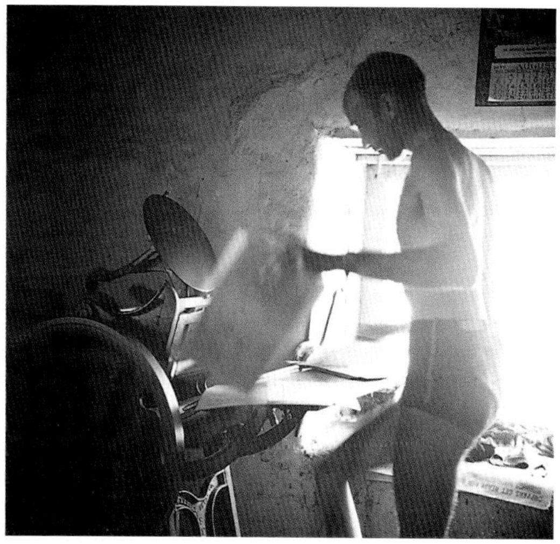

Spud Johnson clad in swimming trunks, Laughing Horse Press, ca. 1930.

In the meantime, Johnson worked as a cub reporter for the Greeley newspaper and wrote humorous sketches for the college monthly magazine before transferring to the University of Colorado in Boulder and eventually going on to Berkeley. There, at the University of California, his literary career began to take shape. He met and studied with Witter Bynner,[41] whose associations with prominent Bay Area writers drew him into the wider realm of avant-garde arts and letters and whose friendship would later bring him to New Mexico. Together with fellow students James Van Rensselaer, Jr., and Roy Chanslor he launched the *Laughing Horse*, a pamphlet designed as "a thorough and unrestrained horselaugh to the entire academic setup to which they felt so scornfully superior."[42] Fed up with conventional campus newspapers and journals, the trio debuted their pamphlet on April 10, 1922. The issue, financed with Johnson's $50 loan, met with roaring success. The entire edition of 500 copies sold out and paved the way for a second and third issue.

By the time the fourth edition appeared, Johnson was in New Mexico, the guest of Bynner, who had recently settled in Santa Fe. Here in the Southwest he gathered literary contributions that would propel the journal to overnight notoriety. *Laughing Horse* number four appeared in the fall of 1922 with a scandalous D. H. Lawrence review and excerpts from an Upton Sinclair exposé of the University of California. Sinclair's document, included in his 1923 book titled *The Goose-Step: A Study of American Education*, accused the university of corruption and oppression and brought the wrath of the institution down on the young publishers. Chanslor, the only one of the three officially enrolled at the university, was expelled and charged with printing obscene material, a charge that was later dropped when the case went to court.[43]

Despite university suppression, the little pamphlet flourished with the publicity and appeared three more times to a greatly enlarged subscription list before Johnson inherited it and "restabled the *Horse*" in New Mexico. Here he converted the magazine into a "journal of, by and for New Mexicans"[44] with a distinguished list of contributors that included both local and nationally recognized writers and artists — Mary Austin, Alice Corbin, William Penhallow Henderson, Haniel Long, Alfred Knopf, Andrew Dasburg, Frank Waters, Gustave Baumann, Will Shuster, Sherwood Anderson, and Carl Sandburg, among others. A progressive publication with a national readership, *Laughing Horse* celebrated New Mexico's cultural diversity in prose, poetry, and artwork.

In 1927, after a short stint as a *New Yorker* staff writer, Johnson made his home in Taos and moved closer to the plan of his youth. He acquired a hand- and foot-operated press on which he would craft his publications and earn the self-proclaimed title "pamphleteer of no mean wit and experience." Though a whitewashed cottage was a remote possibility in northern New Mexico, Johnson installed his little Kelsey Star platen press in what he describes picturesquely as a "country hut in the curve of the Rio del Pueblo, a mile outside of the town of Taos."[45] The hut was a cabin belonging to Mabel Dodge Luhan, founding member of the Taos literary colony and Johnson's new employer. As he had done for Witter Bynner in Santa Fe, Johnson helped with Luhan's typing and performed secretarial duties.

The undetermined ideal he long ago vowed to uphold would evolve in the pages of his publications. He spoke out against censorship, championed Indian rights, and defended the environment, earning a reputation as a "gentle crusader" and "the aesthetic and intellectual conscience of Taos."[46]

Though never to be celebrated as fine printing, Johnson's Laughing Horse Press work projected an irresistible folk charm. His publications were

THE LAUGHING HORSE PRESS
Laughing Horse literary magazine, (left to right) issues no. 15, 1928; no. 8, 1923; no. 17, 1930.

done on a rainbow of colored newsprint and punctuated with linoleum and woodblock illustrations, sometimes spontaneously carved from unconventional materials like old fruit crates. Printing conditions were less than ideal. In an apology that ran in his first *Laughing Horse* production, Johnson stated, "If certain pages are very pale grey in effect and others very dark with viscous black ink, that is partly because some of the printing was done at night and looked quite well by candle light, partly because the paper seems to be a species of blotter, partly because there is no automatic ink-feed on the Laughing Horse Press, partly because this is the printer's first job and partly because . . . ." And then, in true Johnson style, he goes on to dismiss the preciousness often associated with letterpress printing, saying, " if it were perfect, it might just as well be machine-made, whereas we are sure that the 'artist's' hand is evident on every page — in the shape, if in no other way, of inky finger prints."[47]

The Kelsey press moved from Johnson's bedroom to his kitchen and finally to his own print shop, where the roof was always in danger of caving in. Nevertheless, he produced eight intermittent issues of *Laughing Horse* on the press through 1939. In between he did job printing for his friends, published pamphlet poetry, and in 1938 introduced a lively little Taos newspaper called

Spud Johnson and his mobile bookshop, Taos, ca. 1940.

the *Horse Fly*, billed as the "Smallest and Most Inadequate Newspaper Ever Published." The editorial policy, a curious mix of fact and fiction, was defended in Johnson's tongue-in-cheek "Philosophical Apology," which appeared in the January 28, 1939, edition: "a small town weekly can often give as accurate an account of Life in the Village, by printing fictitious news, as it can by limiting its reports to actual happenings: in fact, can frequently produce an even more authentic effect by such a dodge, since most of the facts and particularly the implications of the genuine article can never be published, anyway. . . ."

Flavored with Johnson's wry humor, the one-sheet periodical took a stand on local issues, promoted arts events, and kept track of the comings and goings of *Taoseños*. It died one year after it was introduced, succumbing to Johnson's lumbago and the economic crunch that too often undermines private publishing ventures.

Like the *Horse Fly*, Johnson's pamphlets are a whimsical mix of truth and storytelling. *Buck Dunton and Desperado* (1929) is Johnson's larger-than-life version of the Taos painter's encounter with a highwayman, while *The Ballad of Santa Fee Sal*, done around the same time, presents the "sad song" of a woman who came here seeking refuge from city life only to find that development had followed her.

For Johnson printing was never a livelihood but a labor of love. He supplemented Laughing Horse Press publications with work at the *Santa Fe New Mexican* in 1930 and at the *Taos Valley News* as editor from 1933 to 1935. For a short period of time, he managed the Villagrá Book Shop, a hub of Santa Fe literary activity, and even created his own mobile bookshop, which he fashioned from a secondhand tea cart and stationed on the Taos Plaza. Throughout the years he continued as a freelance writer, producing poetry that appeared in national publications and in 1935 was collected in a volume entitled *Horizontal Yellow*. Until his death in 1968 he contributed a column to the Taos newspaper. Perhaps not the most famous member of the Santa Fe and Taos writers' colonies,

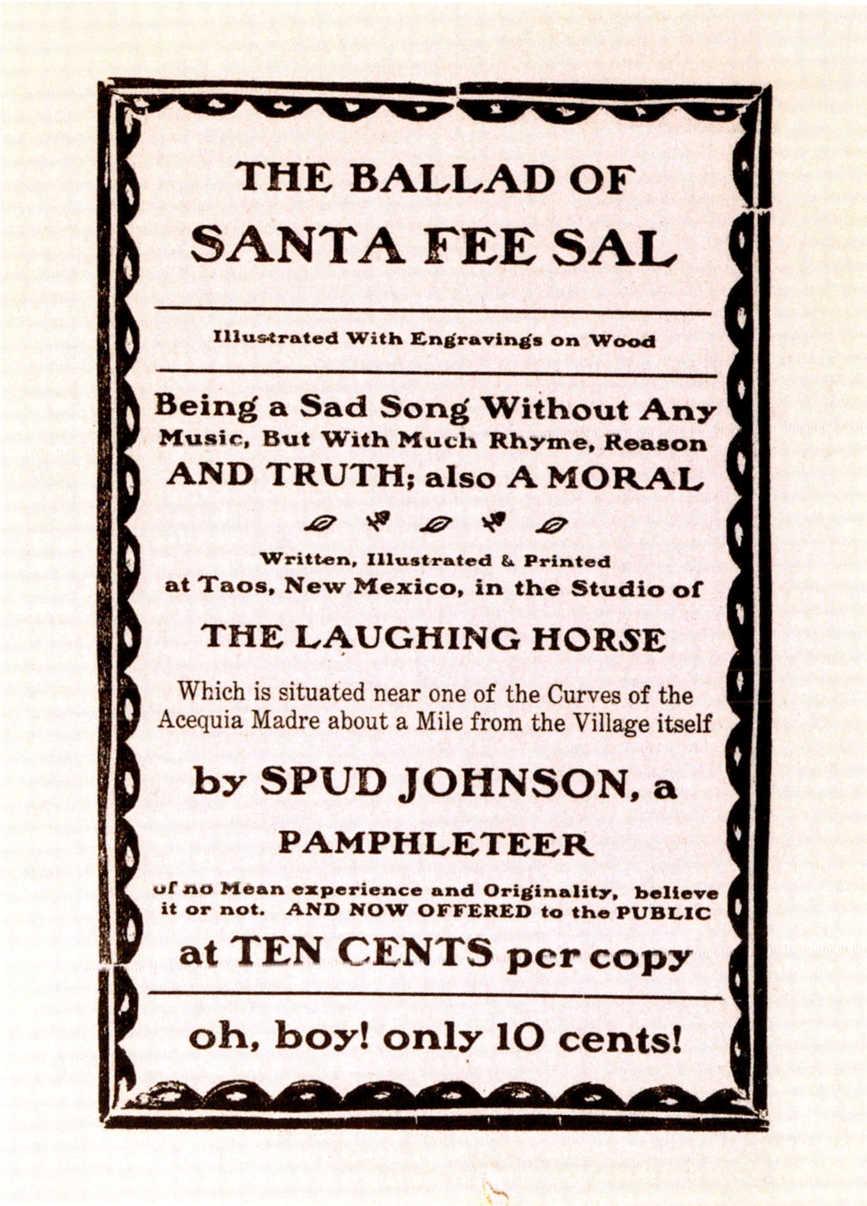

THE BALLAD OF
SANTA FEE SAL

Illustrated With Engravings on Wood

Being a Sad Song Without Any Music, But With Much Rhyme, Reason AND TRUTH; also A MORAL

Written, Illustrated & Printed at Taos, New Mexico, in the Studio of

THE LAUGHING HORSE

Which is situated near one of the Curves of the Acequia Madre about a Mile from the Village itself

by SPUD JOHNSON, a PAMPHLETEER

of no Mean experience and Originality, believe it or not. AND NOW OFFERED to the PUBLIC

at TEN CENTS per copy

oh, boy! only 10 cents!

THE LAUGHING HORSE PRESS

The Ballad of Santa Fee Sal, illustrated pamphlet poem by Spud Johnson, ca. 1930.

Johnson remains one of the most beloved, and his Laughing Horse publications a colorful moment in New Mexico literary history.

The Rydal Press

WHILE SPUD JOHNSON had a lighthearted approach to publishing and a utilitarian hand at the composing stick and press, Walter Lippincott Goodwin, Jr., brought an entirely different sensibility and talent to the art and craft of printing in the region. His vision of typographic excellence and refinement made for books of subdued elegance and impeccable taste. His Rydal Press will always be linked to the first and most productive publishing cooperative in the Southwest.

Goodwin arrived in Santa Fe in 1933 with an exceptional printing and publishing pedigree. Scion of a Philadelphia Main Line family, he had been production manager and book designer at the venerable J. B. Lippincott publishing house for six years. The Rydal Press began as Goodwin's off-hours private press project about 1930. The Rydal name came from the family's estate and the town of Rydal, Pennsylvania.

Walter Goodwin, ca. 1935. Photograph by Brett Weston.

Having a little press at home and a few fonts of handset type was not unusual then among publishing professionals devoted to the art of the book. Goodwin had some New York friends who wanted to do limited-edition books, so Arrow Editions became a Rydal imprint. Curiously, the first Arrow book was a version of Marx and Engels' 1848 *Communist Manifesto* (bound in black with striking red lettering), but other titles would be mainly verse. One was *Tom*, a "poetic paraphrase of *Uncle Tom's Cabin* in the form of a ballet scenario" by e. e. cummings.[48] Always at Rydal there was the ideal to see into print worthy contributions that would not have passed the bottom-line litmus test of the major publishers.

Meanwhile in Santa Fe, Haniel Long, Alice Corbin, Peggy Pond Church, and Raymond Otis, all writers and poets, were working up a well-conceived plan for a cooperative "to publish good books that otherwise might not see the light of day"—including their own and works of merit by other writers living in the Southwest.[49] The Depression had discouraged big New York publishing houses from taking chances on quality books of limited appeal. Also, there was a new movement in the country: Regionalism, in both arts and letters, was beginning to have its time in the sun. Writers' Editions was an early child of both trends.[50] Members financed their own projects and sometimes other members' works. An editorial committee examined the literary standards of writers asking to join. Books would be offered in quality editions at affordable prices. Members pooled their address lists to assure vigorous advance sales. Affable Ray Otis, fourth member of the founding group, brought an indispensable business sense into the picture. All they needed was someone who understood book production, design, and quality printing.

Alice Corbin and husband artist William Penhallow Henderson, 1932. Photograph by Will Connell.

Alice Corbin and Haniel Long knew and admired Goodwin's work and convinced him to move Rydal to New Mexico. Goodwin immediately gave notice to Lippincott, and a few months later he and his printing equipment were on their way West.

The Rydal Press found its first New Mexico home in the old frame dining hall of a defunct health sanitarium in the village of Tesuque just north of Santa Fe. Goodwin installed a Kelly Model B cylinder press, cases of hand-set type, and would add a Smythe sewing machine for assembling folded signatures of printed paper in preparation for binding. It was the intention of both the Rydal Press and Writers' Editions "to make books which were not to fall in the de luxe price class yet had sufficient care in their making to give them a pleasing and permanent dress."[51] Both would succeed admirably in this endeavor for at least the next seven years. Although Rydal served Writers' Editions as a production facility, the press also published books under its own name, did jobs for other publishers, and printed several Arrow Editions that were still in progress.

The first three Writers' Editions books, all poetry, appeared in quick order before the end of 1933. The eighty-four pages of *The Sun Turns West* by

Alice Corbin were hand set, printed in an edition of 500 and bound at The Rydal Press. Haniel Long's *Atlantides* and Peggy Pond Church's *Foretaste* were printed in editions of 250 copies each.

After a short time, it became clear that hand-set text type consumed too much time for such ambitious endeavors. Consequently, Goodwin purchased a Monotype composing machine, a somewhat exotic but superior choice for fine typography. His designer's eye led him to secure fonts of Perpetua, a handsome and very readable type designed by Eric Gill in England. The Rydal Press became the first in the United States to employ this exceptional face for machine composition. The use of Perpetua became a Rydal hallmark.

The "Little Saint," the Rydal Press printer's mark, ca. 1935.

In 1934 Rydal acquired a 10 × 12 Colt's Armory platen press, favored by many fine printers. It had belonged to San Francisco's sibling book designers Bruce and Helen Gentry. Bruce Gentry moved to Santa Fe that same year to join the Rydal staff as designer/craftsman and stayed for three very productive years. Well-known illustrator and type designer Warren Chappell created the Rydal Press printer's mark, a "little saint" holding a pair of old fashioned printer's inking balls.[52]

Haniel Long's *Interlinear to Cabeza de Vaca: His Relation of the Journey from Florida to the Pacific, 1528–1536*, is an especially enduring Writers' Editions book, designed by Bruce Gentry and printed by Rydal in 1936. After being shipwrecked somewhere on the Gulf Coast, Lieutenant Núñez Cabeza de Vaca and two companions wandered west and south for eight years, often barefoot and naked. When at last they reached Mexico City, Núñez wrote a circumspect letter to his king, humbly describing his experiences. But it is not too difficult to read between his lines, which Long did brilliantly. "Núñez finds out that people are his brothers and sisters and feels a genuine concern for them," reflecting a sense of humanity rarely expressed at that time. "I believe this to be the account he wished to send to the King," Long explained. "I preserve the course of his narrative [but] I allow him to speak as though unafraid of his king and his times."[53]

Interlinear had at least three Rydal printings and 1,015 copies in its first year. A small (forty-eight pages, 4½ × 7 inches) but truly important book, it has been returned to print frequently but not always under the same title.

"Without the harmonious setting provided by Walter Goodwin, without the mechanics of financing and distribution developed by the cooperative efforts of Writers' Editions, this jewel might never have attracted its subsequent wide audience," Peggy Church wrote of *Interlinear* years later.[54]

On the other hand, *El Gringo, or New Mexico and Her People* (1938) ran to 350 pages. This ambitious reprint of Territorial Attorney W. W. H. Davis's account of the people of New Mexico is a comprehensive description of mid-eighteenth-century everyday life in the Southwest, where Spanish and American cultures met and mingled for the first time. While Davis viewed local habits through the lens of condescending Victorian morality, he caught every little detail, giving the book its lasting value. Rydal quality shows here, too, with the use of fine papers and carefully positioned initial letters.

True to its lodestar of publishing regional authors and subjects, Writers' Editions produced Spud Johnson's *Horizontal Yellow* in 1935.

By the summer of 1937 work at the Rydal Press had outgrown the old dining hall. Goodwin moved his operation to larger adobe quarters at 998 Canyon Road, a location nearer to commercial clients as well as several local writers and craftspeople, including Willard Clark. At the same time, Goodwin acquired most of the letterpress shop of the *New Mexican*, which permitted expansion of Rydal's printing services.

Membership in Writers' Editions had grown to double digits by 1938, but the Rydal Press also was building its own considerable list. *When I Am Dead*, by Santa Fe's literary doyenne Mary Austin, came out in 1935—the year after she died. Rydal published anthropologist Sylvanus G. Morley, as well as notable regional and national writers Paul Horgan, Fray Angélico Chávez, Eugene Manlove Rhodes, and Frieda Lawrence. "Rydal Press has endeavored to make this section of the country conscious of the development in better made books, as well as to help in making the country as a whole interested in the Southwest," Goodwin wrote in 1938 after Rydal had printed some thirty titles.[55]

Haniel Long's *Malinche (Doña Marina)*, a story of the consort of Mexico's conqueror Hernán Cortez printed by Rydal in 1939, was the last Writers' Editions book.[56] The enterprise ended as the decade of the 1930s came to a close. Seventeen Writers' Editions titles made it into print and, due to their consistently high quality, also into fine printing immortality. Preparation for war and

THE RYDAL PRESS

of Santa Fe New Mexico

A BRIEF ACCOUNT OF ITS HISTORY AND ITS PURPOSE

THE ROYAL CITY OF THE HOLY FAITH OF SAINT FRANCIS OF ASSISI WAS THE FULL TITLE GIVEN TO THE LITTLE TOWN OF SANTA FE, NEW MEXICO, by the Spanish. Today it is merely called Santa Fe, which means "Holy Faith," and the rest of the ponderous appellation has gone the way of so many of the more laborious and lengthy methods and practices in this streamlined era. However, the country in which it lies has not changed so much in spite of the three cultural influences to which it has been subjected; Indian first, then Spanish, and finally the American pioneer. For all this, Santa Fe still remains a town of mud houses (with some of hollow tile), the prevailing spoken language is over fifty per cent Spanish, voting ballots are printed in the two languages, and politically and physically the town is more like a foreign country than almost any other part of the United States.

It may have seemed out of the ordinary to some to have picked this particular locality for the establishment of a press of any kind, especially one primarily for the printing of books, so often associated with the large commercial publishing of the East, and particularly one which has as one of its aims the development of the mechanized side of bookmaking.

From its original inception The Rydal Press has been partly experimental. Its birth is not recorded in any registry, but it grew from a small

THE RYDAL PRESS

Account of the Rydal Press featured in *The Colophon: The Annual of Bookmaking*, 1938.

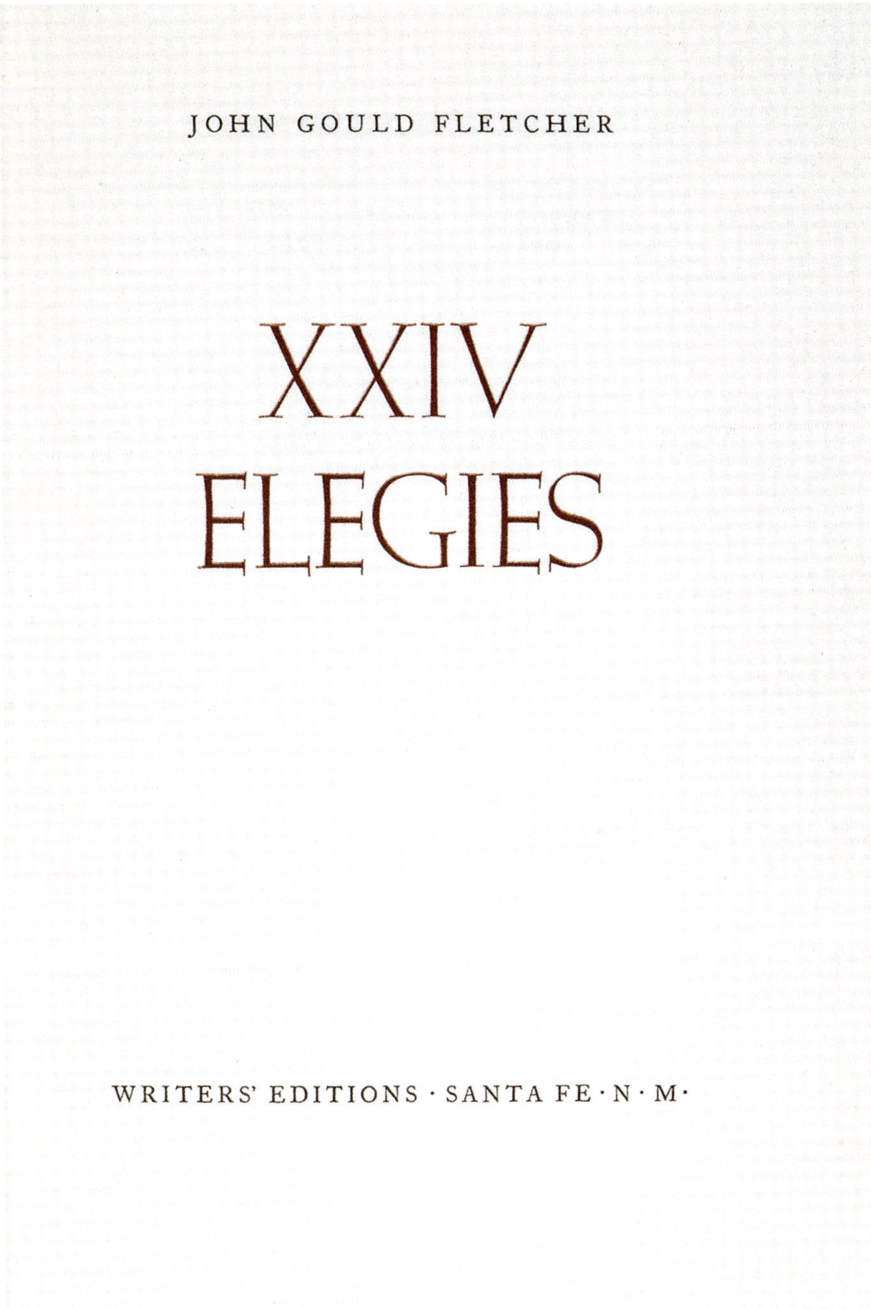
JOHN GOULD FLETCHER

XXIV ELEGIES

WRITERS' EDITIONS · SANTA FE · N · M ·

THE RYDAL PRESS

XXIV Elegies title page, Rydal printing, 1935.

the ensuing dispersal of writers are often the reasons given for the demise of Writers' Editions, but Peggy Pond Church wrote that the untimely death of Ray Otis in 1938 took a very essential wind out of its sails.[57]

John Gould Fletcher's *XXIV Elegies* (1935) and Baumann's *Frijoles Canyon Pictographs* (1939) were selected by the American Institute of Graphic Arts (AIGA) for the esteemed "Fifty Books of the Year" list. Peggy Church's *Familiar Journey* (1936) also received recognition by AIGA for excellence of format.

Photography became Walter Goodwin's passion as the decade ended. By late 1941 he had sold Rydal Press to Gordon Stevenson and Dale Bullock, a newspaperman from Raton. Goodwin left New Mexico in 1946, but would return years later to run a quarter horse ranch in Pojoaque, north of Santa Fe. Bullock became sole owner of the Rydal Press and would publish about eighty more books. As the decades passed, the operation on Canyon Road became more active as a commercial job printing firm and passed out of Bullock's hands in 1976. It would remain for Clark Kimball to bring the respected Rydal name back for a second run at private publishing in the 1980s.

The Seton Village Press

AT THE INVITATION of renowned naturalist Ernest Thompson Seton, Maurice and Marceil Taylor launched their private press efforts in New Mexico in 1938.[58] A prolific author and illustrator, Seton was well known for his dramatic wilderness tales for young people. Like other artists and writers who made their way here in the 1920s and 1930s, he was inspired by the untamed beauty of the New Mexico landscape and the romance of the Indian culture. With a plan to create an outdoor educational center, he purchased a 2,500-acre tract of land near Santa Fe and settled there in 1930.

The Taylors were the young idealistic proprietors of a private press based in Cedar Rapids, Iowa, when their path crossed that of Seton and his wife Julia in October 1937. As an outlet for Maurice's philosophical interest and Marceil's artistic talents, the two published *Quest: A Journal of Adventure in Philosophy and Art*, originally titled *Experiences in Understanding*. The quarterly magazine, done under the Taylors' Parnassian Press imprint, carried the work of young writers from throughout the country together with text and illustrations generated by the publishers.

The fortuitous meeting of the two couples followed a Seton lecture at Coe College in Cedar Rapids. Mutual interests ignited a conversation brimming with ideas and ending with talk of the Taylors moving their Parnassian Press to New Mexico, where the educational center had been operating for the past seven years as the Seton Institute. The Taylors accepted the invitation and within months moved their printing equipment to Seton Village.

Ernest Thompson Seton lecturing at the College of Indian Wisdom, Seton Village, 1938.

Situated in the piñon- and juniper-studded hills a few miles southeast of Santa Fe, the village was part of the land the Setons had purchased in 1930. Carved out of the DeVargas Land Grant, the acreage offered sweeping views of four mountain ranges and an abundance of plant and animal life. It was an ideal setting for the institute that promoted outdoor education as a means of spiritual rejuvenation. Seton's Woodcraft League,[59] an international youth movement somewhat akin to the Boy Scouts of America, was headquartered at the village along with the College of Indian Wisdom,[60] a summer camp where students learned arts and crafts, as well as Indian and nature lore. Both youth programs greatly molded the face of the village and the atmosphere of the Taylors' new home.

Brightly painted animal totems and buildings decorated with Indian symbols lit up the muted landscape. There was a craft shop, museum, dining hall, a small zoo or wildlife refuge, and an entire "Indian Village" designed to accommodate summer campers. Based on Seton's own interpretation of traditional Indian dwellings, the village included tipis, hogans, and wickiups.

Another group of structures, with names like Zoo Lodge, Dobie House, and the Submarine, served as a retreat for artists and writers. From a hillside overlooking it all, the Setons presided from their thirty-room adobe "castle."[61] It was a setting that would inspire a major change in the Taylors' publishing agenda. In Iowa they had put the Parnassian Press to rest. Here in New Mexico they would introduce Seton Village imprints, distinctively flavored by the Southwest.

Maurice Taylor outside the Seton Village Press, 1939.

Marceil Taylor, 1940.

In January of 1938, a steamer trunk weighted with three hundred pounds of foundry type arrived at the village, along with the Taylors' platen press. Maurice and Marceil came via bus, a journey that allowed Maurice to put the finishing touches on an essay he had planned for the first Seton Village Press publication.[62] One month later a hand-set eleventh issue of the Taylors' quarterly *Quest* came off the Chandler & Price press. An intricate linoleum block print of a tree spread across the cover, an homage to the new surroundings.

Only one other *Quest* was issued in 1938 before the Taylors stopped publication of the journal altogether. According to a prospectus in the twelfth issue, the publishers had shifted their attention to hand techniques involved in the bookmaking process. Perhaps influenced by the predominance of handicrafts at Seton Village, Maurice wrote, "The creative motive of each author will be shared by the craftsmen of the book . . . so that wordcraft and bookcraft will become continuous phrases of expression."[63]

Over the next four years the Taylors would make good on their plan, producing twenty-four distinctively handcrafted editions, most of them printed from hand-set type. The books draw from the Setons' prolific writings, highlight New Mexico folk and Indian cultures, and recall Maurice's avid interest in the work of young poets and authors. Three titles appeared in 1938, before the Taylors barely had time to settle into Seton Village. The first was *The Buffalo Wind*, an autobiographical booklet written by Seton in the style of an Indian orator. A gem of the hand bookmaking process, *The Buffalo Wind* was printed from newly purchased Lydian type[64] on handmade papers, highlighted with hand-colored decorative initials printed from linoleum blocks, and hand bound in buffalo hide. Two hundred copies were created to commemorate the author's seventy-eighth birthday.

Julia Seton's *The Indian Costume Book* appeared almost simultaneously. Bound by Marceil in plywood covers, the book reflected the Taylors' determination to use what they considered to be the "right" materials despite the required labor. They sanded and varnished a thousand pieces of wood for the edition and then, with the aid of a bookbinder's press, embossed front covers

THE SETON VILLAGE PRESS
Printed map of Seton Village, ca. 1938.

with an eagle feather design. With sixty-eight illustrations, *The Indian Costume Book* offers a detailed description of traditional tribal clothing along with instructions for re-creating some of the items. One hundred special copies of the 500-volume edition were hand colored.

Though relative newcomers to the area, the Taylors quickly developed an appreciation for the folklore of New Mexico. Traditional music, stories, recipes, and proverbs all became subject matter of some of the most engaging work produced at the Seton Village Press in 1941. *Children Sing in New Mexico*, designed and printed by Maurice for a Clarendon, Texas, publisher, presents twenty-four pages of folk tunes, such as a song about Juan Tomás Canales, "The Tamale Man." The music was provided by J. S. Mackay, the text in English and Spanish by Roy A. Keech,[65] and the illustrations by well-known Texas artist H. D. Bugbee. Musical scores that run throughout the book were reproduced from pen-and-ink drawings painstakingly created by Marceil Taylor.

Two companion volumes — *The Folklore of New Mexico* by Aurora Lucero-White and *Shadows of the Past* by Cleofas Jaramillo — shed light on northern New Mexico Spanish-inherited customs. The Lucero-White book is a rich collection of ballads, fairy tales, proverbs, and conundrums, all presented in Spanish and illustrated with linoleum block prints. *Shadows of the Past* is a memoir filled with homespun stories and family history. *El Palacio* magazine praised the two books when they appeared in October 1941, saying, "It is a subject for rejoicing when such excellent material is published by members of the old families of this region who have unique access to the old traditions."

Perhaps the most eye-catching Taylor production focusing on New Mexico traditions is *Pagans Praying* by Roy A. Keech (1940). The book offers a glimpse of Pueblo Indian dances through the eyes of the author and the illustrations of Taos Pueblo artist Pop Chalee.[66] As was customary at the Seton Press, the Taylors printed an energetic 1,150 copies of the publication. A special edition of 150 books featured four hand-painted full-page illustrations, with brushwork done by Marceil and the Taos artist. Though distinctively designed and printed by the Seton Village Press, the book was financed and distributed under the Clarendon Press imprint.

Somewhat less elaborate in production, the Seton Village Press poetry books, representing about a third of the press's output, expressed Maurice's

The Seton Village Press
Linoleum block illustration from *The Folklore of New Mexico*, produced at the Seton Village Press in 1941.

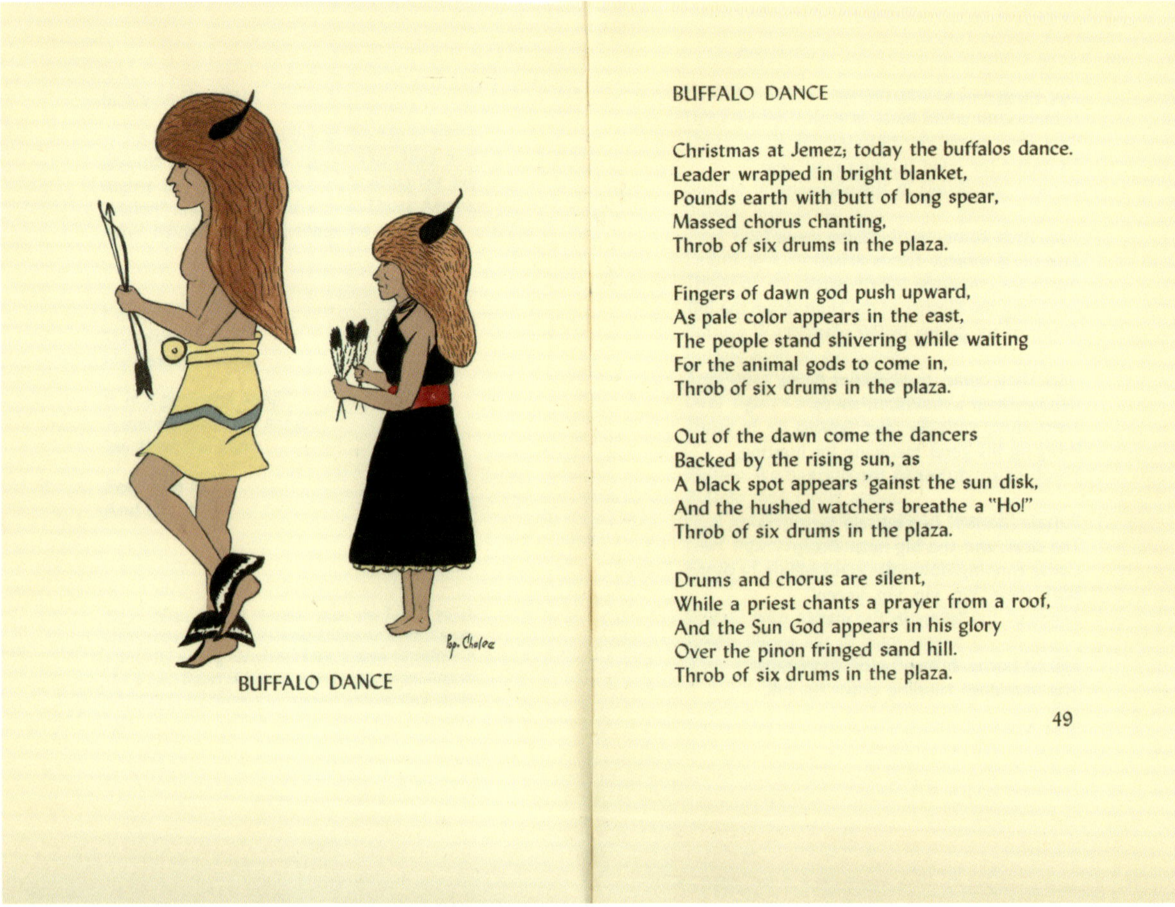

BUFFALO DANCE

BUFFALO DANCE

Christmas at Jemez; today the buffalos dance.
Leader wrapped in bright blanket,
Pounds earth with butt of long spear,
Massed chorus chanting,
Throb of six drums in the plaza.

Fingers of dawn god push upward,
As pale color appears in the east,
The people stand shivering while waiting
For the animal gods to come in,
Throb of six drums in the plaza.

Out of the dawn come the dancers
Backed by the rising sun, as
A black spot appears 'gainst the sun disk,
And the hushed watchers breathe a "Ho!"
Throb of six drums in the plaza.

Drums and chorus are silent,
While a priest chants a prayer from a roof,
And the Sun God appears in his glory
Over the pinon fringed sand hill.
Throb of six drums in the plaza.

49

THE SETON VILLAGE PRESS

Pagans Praying, hand-colored illustration and printing by the Seton Village Press, 1940.

fondness for literary works in small, handsome volumes. *From My Medicine Sac* by Clark Brown was completed in 1939 along with *Pine and Bamboo*, a collection of work by a young poet named Gene McKenzie. Roy A. Keech's *Poems of New Mexico*, which Taylor described as "a polyphonic guidebook to Santa Fe and the Southwest,"[67] appeared a year later.

Additional books of verse brought the Taylors together with Alan Swallow, who was to become the West's best-known poetry publisher. The collaborative efforts were launched in 1942 when Swallow was a young faculty member at Western State College of Colorado in Gunnison. Together they produced three titles before the escalating war interrupted all further literary plans. Swallow was inducted into the armed forces, and the Taylors, destined for military-related service, reluctantly prepared to close the Seton Village Press. Years later, Maurice Taylor still recalled the period with a note of sadness: "In the later days of 1942 when we knew that the Seton Village Press had to be closed soon, the long hours of manual occupation, sitting at the typecase, were a form of malingering consolation," he wrote.[68]

The last imprint issued from the Taylors' press was *The Preacher of Cedar Mountain*, in 1943, authored appropriately by Ernest Thompson Seton. By the time the commercially bound books arrived, Maurice and Marceil were well on their way to California. They never returned to live at the village, nor to their private press work. Although some printing was done there during the 1960s, the Taylor imprint was never revived. Seton died in 1946 and with him the dream of a Seton Village spiritual center

LABORATORY OF ANTHROPOLOGY
Merle Armitage cover for *Style Trends of Pueblo Pottery*, published by the Laboratory of Anthropology, 1946.

Chapter 3

The War Years and Beyond

1941–1955

THOSE PRIVATE PUBLISHERS who managed to struggle through the Depression could hardly escape the hardships of World War II that shadowed the 1940s. In the first two years of the decade, hundreds of New Mexico businesses closed, among them four of the six small publishing houses that had shown such promise in the previous years. Like legions of Americans, Willard Clark and Maurice and Marceil Taylor went off to join the civilian labor pool mobilized in the war effort. Joseph O'Kane Foster of the Ranchos Press and Laughing Horse proprietor Spud Johnson turned to more reliable work to weather economic challenges. Others brave enough to launch private press efforts in this precarious climate — Hazel Dreis, Edward McLean, and Alan Swallow — had left New Mexico before 1945.

It was a rough time for the entire printing industry. Despite an unprecedented demand for books throughout the war years, production was crippled by paper rationing and other restrictions that affected both the quality and flow of supplies.[1] Metal type was difficult to get, skilled labor hard to find. With the help of federally funded arts programs, however, one of the era's most successful private publishing ventures emerged alongside a growing interest in southwestern anthropology.

Beginning in the late nineteenth century, New Mexico attracted a steady stream of scholars who studied the ancient and contemporary Indian cultures in the areas surrounding Santa Fe and Taos, best known among them were Frank Cushing, a National Museum curatorial assistant whose research at Zuni

Pueblo began in 1879,[2] and Adolph Bandelier, who launched his New Mexico investigations in 1880 under the auspices of the newly formed Archaeological Institute of America.[3]

Along with the fieldwork came a number of Santa Fe–based professional organizations—in 1898 the Archaeological Society of New Mexico, in 1907 the School of American Research,[4] and in 1909 the School of American Archaeology, directed by Edgar L. Hewett and housed in a newly remodeled Palace of the Governors museum. Throughout the early 1900s these organizations were closely allied with the arts and formed a cultural hub for local society.

Although it opened later, in 1931, Santa Fe's Laboratory of Anthropology was an important part of this network. An independently established research facility and museum, the laboratory became a showcase for Native American studies, a depository for Indian craft collections, and eventually the purveyor of some of the finest publications of the period.

Another bright spot of the era came in the abbreviated appearance of New Mexico's first fine book bindery. For a period of about four years beginning in 1939, the workshop of Hazel Dreis produced beautifully handcrafted bindings for private press books, as well as a few titles under her own Hazel Dreis Editions imprint.

In the aftermath of the war New Mexico struggled to regain its footing. Tourism, strangled by fuel shortages, was revived, and the state's cultural attractions became major travel destinations. A vigorous growth in Santa Fe's population during the 1930s continued in the postwar years, resulting in a greater number of artists and craftspeople working in the city and a wider spectrum of art forms.[5] A burgeoning number of women artists included Dorothy Stewart, whose Pictograph Press veered from traditional Southwest themes to introduce colorful books extracted from the works of Shakespeare.

Innovations in printing technology, retarded by the war, resumed with the introduction of sophisticated, high-speed machinery. By 1950 web-fed offset presses were capable of finely registered multicolor printing, and photo composition was just around the corner—advances unnoticed by private press printers who favored hand techniques.

Despite postwar progress, New Mexico's private press movement hung by a thread well into the 1960s. All but one of the small publishing houses established between 1940 and 1955 had disappeared by the end of the era, leaving a small but handsomely crafted collection of books as testimony to their efforts.

Laboratory of Anthropology

AT FIRST GLANCE, a center for Native American research may seem an odd place to find artful book production, but a closer look reveals a strong connection between the arts and Santa Fe's Laboratory of Anthropology that goes back to its opening in 1931. Initially funded by John D. Rockefeller, the research center and museum were quartered in a new building designed by architect John Gaw Meem, whose Pueblo Revival style became synonymous with Santa Fe. It housed the collections of the Indian Arts Fund, established by a group of local artists and writers whose concern for the preservation of indigenous crafts brought them together in 1925 to start acquiring examples of the work. Further ties with the Santa Fe arts colony were forged through the laboratory's participation in projects funded by Franklin D. Roosevelt's New Deal legislation, which brought both economc relief and cultural preservation to New Mexico.

From 1935 through 1947, the newly created institution would reflect the fruits of these associations, publishing books and portfolios that struck a balance between art and scholarship. This was not a private press in the strictest sense. No printing equipment was acquired to do the job. No personal opinion was put forth. Instead, the privately funded publications expressed the vision of an entire organization. The laboratory hoped to profit from book production but made no effort to alter its focus for the sake of mass appeal.

To do the work, the laboratory assembled a highly skilled production team, eventually including the talents of the most innovative typographic designer in the country, highly creative illustrators, and a selection of well-established fine printers.

Publications first became a focus in 1935 when the laboratory's Board of Trustees established a revolving fund to support publishing activities along with a Popular Publications Committee headed by novelist Oliver LaFarge.[6]

Louie Ewing, ca. 1936.
Photograph by Edward Weston.

To supplement a dwindling Rockefeller endowment and to meet a growing demand for Southwest information, the laboratory issued a series of pamphlets on Navajo blankets, Pueblo pottery, and archaeological research, along with more in-depth studies under what was called the *Memoir* series. The initial publications were straightforward, typographically plain, and lacking in the eye-catching design quality of later laboratory books.

The first laboratory-sponsored New Deal project was a portfolio of Navajo weavings artfully executed in linoleum block prints by Ruth Connely. Funded by the Public Works of Art Project,[7] *Twelve Examples of Navajo Weaving* was drawn partially from the laboratory's textile collection with an aim towards encouraging a revival of older Navajo designs. The edition of 100 copies was distributed by the Santa Fe Indian School in 1935.

While the ensuing war years brought a slowdown in Laboratory of Anthropology publication efforts, they ushered in a long-term collaboration with a promising young artist named Louie Ewing. Ewing had grown up on an Idaho farm and studied art for a short time in California before coming to Santa Fe in 1935. Along with his mentor and teacher Stanley Breneiser, he had come to accept a teaching position at Eidolon, a newly established arts and crafts school located on Canyon Road.[8] When the project failed and teaching jobs ran out, Ewing turned to the Works Progress Administration's (WPA) Federal Art Project, which had arrived in New Mexico the year after he did.[9]

With federal assistance he began to explore new developments in the very old process of silkscreen printing. He recalled his pioneering efforts in a 1964 interview: "I remember our first print. I think it took us about three days to produce it because we made our squeegees to move the paint across the screen out of an auto tire because there wasn't a squeegee invented then. And then we used a window cleaning thing and that didn't work because the oil melted the rubber."[10]

To the silkscreen technique he brought his finely tuned drawing skills, an eye for the subtleties of light and color, and a persistence that transformed him into a master silkscreen printer in the years that followed. His newly acquired skill led him to the Laboratory of Anthropology in 1940 for the beginning of a long and productive association. He launched work on a WPA project, silkscreen reproductions again featuring Navajo blankets from the laboratory collection. The fifteen multicolor prints created from Ewing's original paintings became a portfolio along with text by curator Kenneth Chapman. The edition, which Ewing said took about a year to complete, comprised 200 copies.[11]

Merle Armitage, ca. 1940.

In 1942, as the Navajo blanket portfolio was being distributed, Ewing went to work on another laboratory project, this time without the assistance of the WPA. The *Masterpiece* series, both an inducement for membership and a showcase for the museum's collections, was published over a six-year period. Ewing created drawings of select museum items and made silkscreen reproductions of the work in editions of 500. Each $10\frac{1}{2} \times 13\frac{1}{2}$-inch image was enclosed in a printed folder and accompanied by descriptive text.

The first *Masterpieces of Primitive American Art* appeared from 1942 through 1943, followed by a second and third series with the same title and then *Modern Masterpieces of American Indian Art.* A 1947 series was made up of reprints from the previous collections. Each series included six prints. For a mere $30 a year laboratory members received one of Ewing's exquisitely executed prints every two months.

Sometime after 1944, the *Masterpiece* folders took on a bold new appearance, credited to Merle Armitage, one of the leading forces in modern American book design. Armitage was well known in California, where he had produced operas, founded the Los Angeles Grand Opera Association, and in 1932 embarked on a career as a book designer, shaking the foundations of the world of graphic arts with his nontraditional approach.

"I became, in certain circles, the destroyer of book tradition, the bad boy of typography, the usurper of the placid pools of bookmaking," Armitage wrote in 1963. "But through the years some of my most criticized inventions have been quietly adopted, i.e., use of the endsheets, double-page title pages, large readable type, generous margins, etc."[12]

For a short period after the war Armitage lived in Santa Fe and, as a member of the Laboratory of Anthropology, offered his services free of

Laboratory of Anthropology

"Chihuahua Polychrome Olla," from *Masterpieces of Primitive American Art*, second series, produced by the Laboratory of Anthropology in 1944.

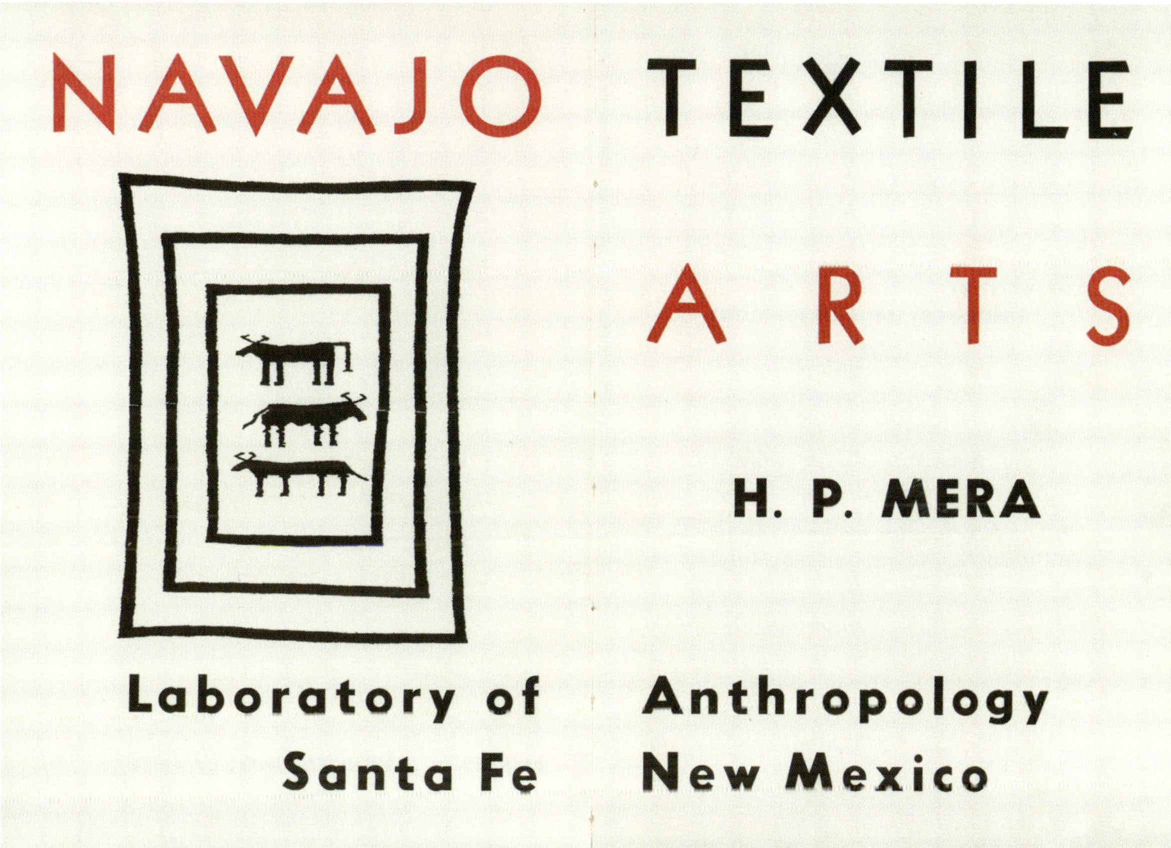

LABORATORY OF ANTHROPOLOGY

Navajo Textile Arts, a 1947 Laboratory of Anthropology publication.

LABORATORY OF ANTHROPOLOGY
Linoleum block print from *Twelve Examples of Navajo Weaving*, a portfolio produced in cooperation with the Laboratory of Anthropology, 1935.

charge.[13] Thus came forth the laboratory's most outstanding publishing effort.

With the encouragement of Willard Hougland, assistant to the director of the laboratory, and Trustees President James Webb Young, an experienced letterpress printer, Armitage created a whole new demand for laboratory publications. He designed new covers for old material that previously "had the appeal of a pamphlet produced by the Government Printing Office." In reference to work he did on one of the *Memoir* series, Armitage wrote, "I took some of the Indian symbols from the text, gave them a suitable handling, made new covers, and the edition sold out in eighteen months. A great lesson in the power of design."[14]

In 1946 he designed the laboratory's *First Penthouse Dwellers of America*, a book by Ruth Underhill. "The best thing I can say about this one," Armitage wrote, "is that the Hopi chief, Temechi, gave copies to his grandchildren as a book that seemed to catch the spirit of the Indian and his urban houses."[15] He did at least seven additional laboratory book projects, including *Saints and Saint Makers* (1946) by E. Boyd, the first major publication on the art of *santo* making, and in 1947 both H. P. Mera's *Navajo Textile Arts* and Leonora Curtin's *Healing Herbs of the Upper Rio Grande* with illustrations by California artist P. G. Napolitano.

He used printers known for their fine press work, among them Lynton Kistler, a second generation Los Angeles printer, and Santa Fe's Rydal Press. Kistler, who had worked with Armitage since the early 1930s, was best known for the lithographic printing he did for well-known artists.

Sales of the books once again reflected the results of improved design and printing quality. In two months the laboratory sold nearly 600 copies of the E. Boyd book. The publishing fund became so healthy that it was used to supplement the laboratory's payroll in 1946.[16] But publications alone could not carry the institution, which had struggled to make ends meet since Rockefeller support fell short of expectations. For its own survival, the Laboratory of Anthropology became part of the Museum of New Mexico in 1947. That same year Armitage moved on to New York, where he was hired to revamp *Look* magazine as its chief designer. Thus the unique circumstances that had produced the laboratory's distinctive publications were forever altered.

Hazel Dreis Editions and Libros Escogidos

BOOKBINDER HAZEL DREIS and her protégé Edward McLean had already come and gone from Santa Fe by the time the Laboratory of Anthropology publishing program reached its peak. Inspired by views of the Sangre de Cristo Mountains and the appeal of a "quiet life," Dreis moved her successful California bindery to Santa Fe in 1939, where it became the first of its kind. She acquired ten acres of land in old Agua Fria Village and took on the task of remodeling a two-hundred-year-old adobe hacienda.[17] There she ambitiously planned to set up an art center alongside her home and workshop.

Although the art center dream never materialized, until 1942 the successful workshop was responsible for many hand-bound, locally produced editions, including Gustave Baumann's award-winning *Frijoles Canyon Pictographs* (1939). Drawing upon the creative Santa Fe climate, Dreis and McLean also introduced their own imprints, collaborating with artists and writers to publish limited-edition books. Hazel Dreis Editions and McLean's Libros Escogidos appeared sporadically through the 1950s, beginning with Dane Rudhyar's *White Thunder* (1938), a Dreis production. Their publications were flavored with the history and culture of the Southwest.

The daughter of a Midwest newspaper publisher, Dreis grew up in a print shop, where she played with type rather than dolls and learned to operate a press.[18] As an adult she naturally gravitated to newspaper work and went to San Francisco, where she became a reporter.

Shortly after World War I her growing interest in bookbinding took her to England to study with British master Lawrence de Coverly. Accounts differ on how long she spent there, but by the early 1930s she brought her newly acquired skills back to San

Hazel Dreis, ca. 1930.

Edward McLean, bookbinder, ca. 1940. Photograph by Myron Tanenbaum, Sr.

Francisco and set up an experimental craft community, fashioned, Dreis said, after the medieval guild system. The group of bookbinding apprentices lived and worked together and even camped and hiked en masse. "We feel that we must keep together, as separation from our interests would be detrimental to our aims," she stressed.[19]

Together the group worked on binding entire editions, including some for San Francisco's famed Grabhorn Press. Walt Whitman's *Leaves of Grass*, produced by the Grabhorns for Random House in 1930, was hand sewn on leather thongs and laced into veneer mahogany boards. It was reputed to be the largest handbound edition ever done in this country and brought Dreis national recognition when it was named one of the year's fifty best books by the American Institute of Graphic Arts.[20] An oversize quarter leather case binding was done for the Grabhorn's *Taos Pueblo*, a collaboration between photographer Ansel Adams and Mary Austin that appeared in 1930.

The Dreis studio, which had moved to Arroyo Grande in southern California, was a hub of book activity by the time Edward McLean made his way there in 1934. A native of Colorado, McLean developed an early interest in dance and went to New York where he worked with the Ted Shawn and the Ruth St Denis Company, known as the Denishawn Dancers.[21] He toured with the group during the 1920s. At the time, Ruth St Denis was hailed by critics as a major force in popularizing modern dance.

By 1930 McLean and his sister Jane had formed their own troupe, Petit Ballet Intime, and were appearing throughout the country, sometimes startling their audiences with their daring performances. A February 20, 1931, headline in Denver's *Rocky Mountain News* claimed "Youth's Nude Dance Shocks Audience of Society Folk." According to the article, McLean, clad only in "grease paint and subtle lightings," demonstrated a contemporary style of expressionist dance.

All of that came to a halt in 1934 when McLean fell from a scaffolding in the Hollywood Bowl, where the troupe was preparing for a performance.[22]

Hazel Dreis Editions and Libros Escogidos
Hazel Dreis's special binding for *The Habit of Empire* (1938), by Paul Horgan;
McLean's colcha stich binding for *The Culture of a Contemporary Rural Community, El Cerrito* (1942), by Irving Rusinow.

Already acquainted with Dreis and her work, he placed himself under her tutelage and launched a new career. His was a seven-year apprenticeship, beginning in California and continuing in the Santa Fe bindery.

In the newly established Agua Fria Village studio, Dreis and McLean focused their creative efforts on the rich culture of the Southwest. McLean developed skills as a design binder, producing one-of-a-kind volumes with cover materials that reflected the book's theme—colcha stitch patterns and tinwork for a book on rural New Mexico villages, rawhide for the story of life on the Argentine pampas, and snakeskin for works on the German invasion of France.

His first Libros Escogidos release, titled *15 New Mexico Santos*, came in 1941. It featured the serigraph imagery of Louie Ewing, whose skill and reputation as an illustrator had spread following his Laboratory of Anthropology work. The

HAZEL DREIS EDITIONS AND LIBROS ESCOGIDOS

"San Férnandes," from *15 New Mexico Santos*, a 1941 Libros Escogidos edition.

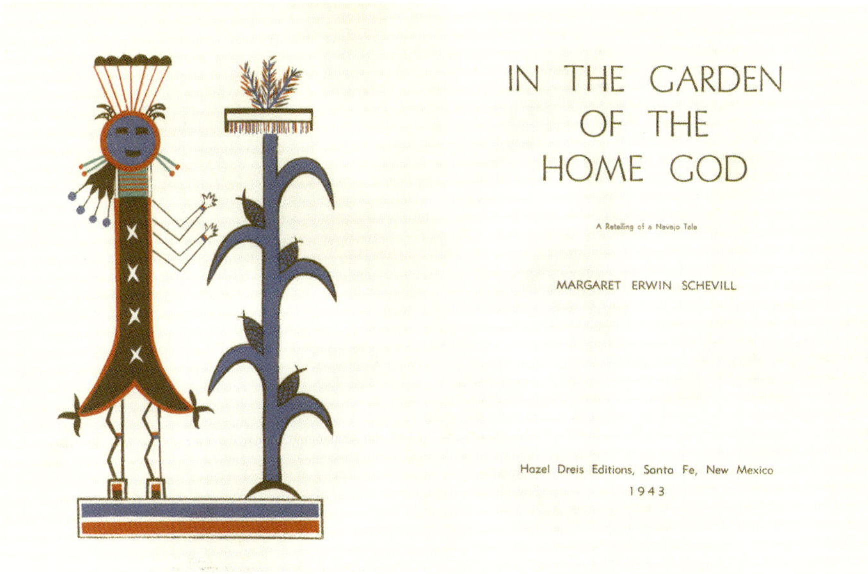

HAZEL DREIS EDITIONS AND LIBROS ESCOGIDOS
In the Garden of the Home God, title page with Louie Ewing frontispiece, from the 1943 Hazel Dreis edition.

fifteen prints created for the book capture the weathered colors and subtle wood textures of fine old *bultos* and *retablos* selected for the book from private collections. The text is by James MacMillan, one of the collectors.

Neither Dreis nor McLean involved themselves directly in the printing of their privately produced books. Instead, they brought together author and illustrator, selected a fine printer, oversaw the design of the piece, and, more often than not, hand bound the books. *15 New Mexico Santos* was printed in an edition of 200 at the Rydal Press. Binding of the large quarto-size book (12¼ × 9¼ inches) was done by Dreis in blue French wrappers and accompanying slipcase.

Louie Ewing serigraphs again appear in the second Hazel Dreis Edition. *In the Garden of the Home God* (1943) is a retelling of a Navajo tale by Margaret Schevill, a painter whose enthusiasm for the Southwest led her to study and write about Indian mythology. The delicate Ewing images were adapted from

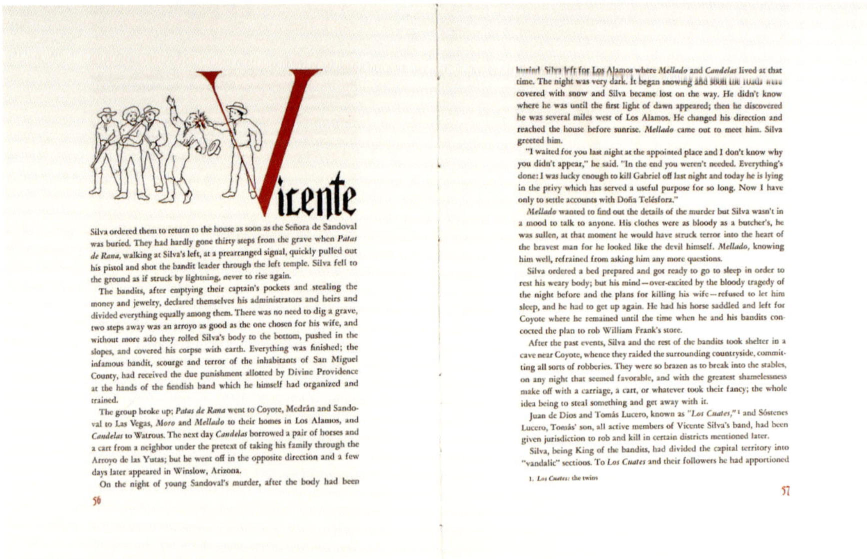

Vicente

Silva ordered them to return to the house as soon as the Señora de Sandoval was buried. They had hardly gone thirty steps from the grave when *Patas de Rana,* walking at Silva's left, at a prearranged signal, quickly pulled out his pistol and shot the bandit leader through the left temple. Silva fell to the ground as if struck by lightning, never to rise again.

The bandits, after emptying their captain's pockets and stealing the money and jewelry, declared themselves his administrators and heirs and divided everything equally among them. There was no need to dig a grave, two steps away was an arroyo as good as the one chosen for his wife, and without more ado they rolled Silva's body to the bottom, pushed in the slopes, and covered his corpse with earth. Everything was finished; the infamous bandit, scourge and terror of the inhabitants of San Miguel County, had received the due punishment allotted by Divine Providence at the hands of the fiendish band which he himself had organized and trained.

The group broke up; *Patas de Rana* went to Coyote, Medrán and Sandoval to Las Vegas, *Moro* and *Mellado* to their homes in Los Alamos, and *Candelas* to Watrous. The next day *Candelas* borrowed a pair of horses and a cart from a neighbor under the pretext of taking his family through the Arroyo de las Yutas; but he went off in the opposite direction and a few days later appeared in Winslow, Arizona.

On the night of young Sandoval's murder, after the body had been

56

buried, Silva left for Los Alamos where *Mellado* and *Candelas* lived at that time. The night was very dark. It began snowing and soon the roads were covered with snow and Silva became lost on the way. He didn't know where he was until the first light of dawn appeared; then he discovered he was several miles west of Los Alamos. He changed his direction and reached the house before sunrise. *Mellado* came out to meet him. Silva greeted him.

"I waited for you last night at the appointed place and I don't know why you didn't appear," he said. "In the end you weren't needed. Everything's done: I was lucky enough to kill Gabriel off last night and today he is lying in the privy which has served a useful purpose for so long. Now I have only to settle accounts with Doña Telésfora."

Mellado wanted to find out the details of the murder but Silva wasn't in a mood to talk to anyone. His clothes were as bloody as a butcher's, he was sullen, at that moment he would have struck terror into the heart of the bravest man for he looked like the devil himself. *Mellado,* knowing him well, refrained from asking him any more questions.

Silva ordered a bed prepared and got ready to go to sleep in order to rest his weary body; but his mind—over-excited by the bloody tragedy of the night before and the plans for killing his wife—refused to let him sleep, and he had to get up again. He had his horse saddled and left for Coyote where he remained until the time when he and his bandits concocted the plan to rob William Frank's store.

After the past events, Silva and the rest of the bandits took shelter in a cave near Coyote, whence they raided the surrounding countryside, committing all sorts of robberies. They were so brazen as to break into the stables, on any night that seemed favorable, and with the greatest shamelessness make off with a carriage, a cart, or whatever took their fancy; the whole idea being to steal something and get away with it.

Juan de Dios and Tomás Lucero, known as *"Los Cuates,"*[1] and Sóstenes Lucero, Tomás' son, all active members of Vicente Silva's band, had been given jurisdiction to rob and kill in certain districts mentioned later.

Silva, being King of the bandits, had divided the capital territory into "vandalic" sections. To *Los Cuates* and their followers he had apportioned

1. *Los Cuates:* the twins

57

HAZEL DREIS EDITIONS AND LIBROS ESCOGIDOS

Text page from *Vicente Silva and His 40 Bandits*, a 1947 Libros Escogidos publication.

Navajo sandpaintings. Schevill credited Lorenzo Hubbell, a personal friend and Navajo trader, for assisting her in collecting material for the story. The book was printed at Fred Harvey's Santa Fe Press, a commercial printing establishment that did its own publishing as well.

By 1942 McLean had gone to Washington, DC, for steady work that would carry him through the war years, initially in the rare book room of the Library of Congress and later in the bindery at the Folger Shakespeare Library.[23] Dreis followed and also assumed a position at the Folger. Despite a shift in geography, both Libros Escogidos and Hazel Dreis Editions issued new titles in 1947, recalling Southwest interests.

McLean's *Vicente Silva and His 40 Bandits*, the story of a ruthless New Mexico outlaw, bore a Washington imprint. Written in the nineteenth century by newspaper reporter Manuel C. de Baca, the Libros Escogidos version is translated by Lane Kauffman with illustrations and calligraphy by Fanita Lanier. The large edition of 500 was printed by a firm in Brattleboro, Vermont, while Dreis and McLean collaborated on the binding.

Beautiful on the Earth, the third and last Hazel Dreis Edition, was produced that same year. This collection of Navajo myths is another work of Margaret Schevill, accompanied by Ewing illustrations. Although Dreis oversaw the printing at the Merrymount Press in Boston,[24] the book's imprint cites Santa Fe as the place of publication.

With the war years behind her, Dreis returned to California in 1948.[25] There in her Monterey Peninsula studio she continued to work on fine bindings and took on an occasional student but never produced another Hazel Dreis imprint. She died in 1964.

McLean made his way back to his home state of Colorado in 1953, opened his own bookbinding school, worked for the Denver Public and University of Denver libraries,[26] and issued one last Libros Escogidos title in 1958. The 1774 correspondence of John Rowzee Peyton, the son of a wealthy Virginia planter, makes up the text of McLean's *3 Letters from St. Louis*. The letters relate a fantastic adventure of shipwreck, capture by the Spanish, a grueling overland march, imprisonment in Santa Fe, and eventual escape. A first-class production, this Libros Escogidos edition of 350 copies was printed in Holland by the centuries-old firm of Joh. Enschedé en Zonen and bound by Dreis.

In the late 1960s McLean accepted a position restoring rare volumes at Duke University, North Carolina, but spent his final years in Colorado, where he died in 1982.[27]

Sage Books

OUT OF THE WAR-RIDDEN 1940S emerged another young literary enthusiast who would become an icon of independent publishing in the West. Although he is best known for his work in Denver, for a short period of time between 1940 and 1942 Alan Swallow produced his first trade book and what he considered his finest printing on a little Kelsey hobby press in a garage in Albuquerque.

His love affair with books developed at an early age. In his teen years he devoured the Haldeman-Julius classics between customers at his filling station job in Gardner, Montana.[28] The Little Blue Books, inexpensively priced and

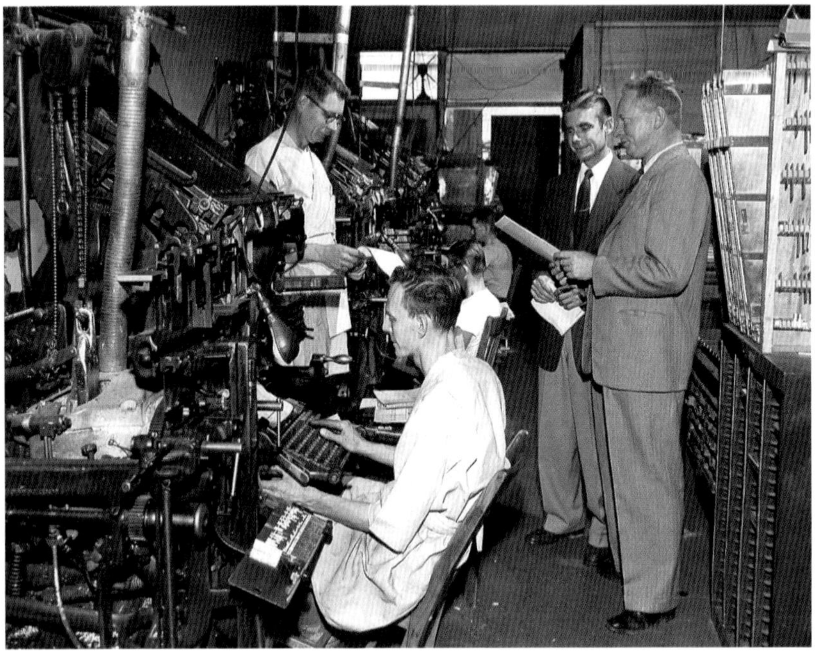

Alan Swallow (far right) in the back shop, University of Denver Press, ca. 1952.

of good quality, made a lasting impression on the young Swallow, whose later acclaim as a publisher grew out of his dedication to introducing fine new writers at the risk of financial loss.

In high school and college he took up the study of literature, worked for campus publications, and wrote poetry which was accepted by small journals. His literary enthusiasm went beyond writing and into the realm of book production. As a sophomore at the University of Wyoming he was mimeographing his own magazine called *Sage*.[29] In 1940, in his final days as a graduate student at Louisiana State University, he borrowed $100 from his father, purchased a secondhand 5 × 8 Kelsey table model press and taught himself the process of letterpress printing while producing a book of student work.[30] Twenty years later, when he was mailing out as many as 70,000 books a year from his garage workshop in Denver, he was still designing, in part printing, and packaging his Swallow titles.[31]

With his LSU doctoral degree in hand, in the summer of 1940 Swallow accepted a teaching position at the University of New Mexico and moved to Albuquerque along with the little Kelsey press. He had already decided to begin printing books in earnest. Shortly before arriving in the Southwest he had consulted with a typographic designer friend, purchased all new metal type fonts, and hand set text for a book of poems by Lincoln Fitzell titled *In Plato's Garden*.[32] He completed the work in Albuquerque that fall and commissioned Santa Fe's Hazel Dreis to do the hand binding. Later in his career, with many more publications under his belt, Swallow still considered the Fitzell book his best printing effort.[33]

While teaching at the university that year, he met Horace Critchlow, a graduate student who shared his interest in independent publishing and who provided the resources to acquire larger, more efficiently operating presses. The two formed a partnership under the imprint of Swallow & Critchlow and moved their equipment into a rented garage.

To support their own work they offered job printing services under what they called Big Mountain Press. Sage Books was the name they reserved for a series of publications of regional interest done in 1941 and 1942. Among these, two of the most noteworthy are *3 Spanish American Poets*, a translation of the works of Carlos Pellicer, Pablo Neruda, and Mario de Andrade; and *Rocky Mountain Stories*, edited by Ray B. West, Jr. The book of Western tales lists seven contributors, including such notables as Paul Horgan and Wallace Stegner.

In keeping with Swallow's aim to produce an economical product, the two Sage Books are not lavish productions. Unaccompanied by illustration or ornaments, the typography is straightforward, the letterpress printing clean and crisp. By staying with simple design and printing the work themselves, the two were able to turn out affordable books. *3 Spanish American Poets*, a paperback, sold for fifty cents, a reasonable price even in 1942.

The partnership, however, was short-lived, interrupted when Critchlow was drafted into the army in 1942. Swallow let the larger equipment go, kept his original type and Kelsey press, and moved on to Gunnison, Colorado, that year.[34] There he issued several volumes of poetry, some printed in New Mexico at Maurice and Marceil Taylor's Seton Village Press, before his own induction into the army. Eventually he settled in Denver, where he taught at the University

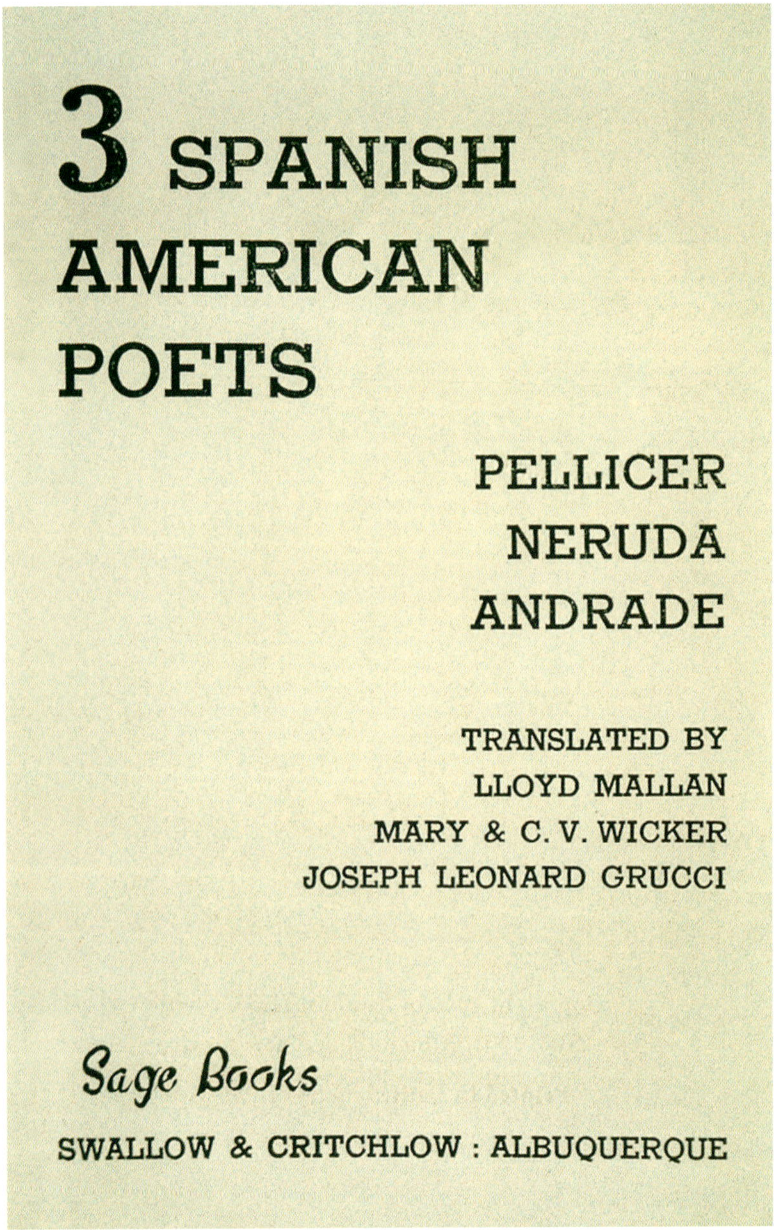

3 SPANISH
AMERICAN
POETS

PELLICER
NERUDA
ANDRADE

TRANSLATED BY
LLOYD MALLAN
MARY & C. V. WICKER
JOSEPH LEONARD GRUCCI

Sage Books

SWALLOW & CRITCHLOW : ALBUQUERQUE

SAGE BOOKS
3 Spanish American Poets, title page printed by Swallow and Critchlow in 1942.

of Denver, helped to found the university's press, and served as its director from 1946 to 1950 while continuing his own work.

Before long the volume of his own business merited full-time attention, and he left the university to focus his efforts on the Swallow Press. Books of poetry, literary criticism, and Western Americana were the mainstay of the little publishing house, which put out more than four hundred titles before Swallow's career ended. He was widely recognized for his courage and integrity as a publisher and for his unflagging devotion to excellence in literature. Trusting his own vision, he took chances on overlooked writers, among them Frank Waters. Swallow issued *The Man Who Killed the Deer* in 1942 when larger publishing firms ignored the work.[35] Later the book became a huge success, was printed and reprinted in several editions, and used in course work at colleges and universities.

Swallow died at the typewriter in 1966, leaving an inspirational legacy for independent publishers to follow.

Motive Book Shop

TAOS PUBLISHER JUDSON CREWS shared Alan Swallow's passion for poetry, though his own shoestring operation never rivaled Swallow's commercial success. The two crossed paths on more than one occasion. Swallow was one of the poets Crews represented in his first literary magazine, *Vers Libre*, published in the late 1930s in Waco, Texas, on what Crews called a "cheap, dumb, rattletrap duplicator." In 1942 he took the opportunity to borrow Swallow's little Kelsey press, an alternative to the cantankerous mimeograph machine he had grown accustomed to using.[36] Later Swallow helped nudge Crews into becoming a printing publisher when he encouraged him to produce *No Is the Night* (1949).

Although Swallow had rejected the manuscript, a collection of Crews's poetry, he urged him to edit the piece and publish it himself. An apprentice printer at the Taos newspaper, Crews used his fledgling skills to do just that. "I produced *No Is the Night*, the whole damn thing, single-handed — except for manufacturing the paper and the ink," he said. "It taxed my shaky skills to the

Judson Crews working on the press at the Taos newspaper *El Crepúsculo*, ca. 1950.

limit, though for the first effort it was not half bad."[37] Thus he embarked on nearly two decades of publishing in Taos.

The literary path that brought Crews to northern New Mexico began in Texas, where he started writing poetry in elementary school and then moved on to writing a Wild West novel, which he said failed to impress his teachers. In high school he continued writing poetry, combining his literary skills with activity as a tackle on the football team, and after graduation in 1936 launched *Vers Libre*. Free verse was an unpopular form at the time, according to Crews. Nevertheless, he produced an issue of the magazine every few months for the next two years.

At Baylor University in 1938 he abandoned *Vers Libre* and started a new magazine and press called *Motive*, along with a mail-order book business of the same name. He gravitated to a circle of young bohemian poets and established himself as the campus literary figure, widely publishing his work and consistently capturing university prizes.

In 1942, having completed his undergraduate studies, he left Waco to join the army, taking Motive Book Shop and its stock of avant-garde literature

VERS LIBRE

The Magazine of a New Horizon

VOL. II, NO. 4 • JAN. - FEB. - MAR. • PRICE 25c

MOTIVE BOOK SHOP

Vers Libre cover, Motive Book Shop, 1936.

Patrocinio
BARELA
Taos Wood Carver

Compiled and Published by
Mildred Tolbert
Wendell B. Anderson
Judson Crews
Taos, New Mexico, 1955

MOTIVE BOOK SHOP
Title page, *Patrocinio Barela: Taos Wood Carver*, printed by Judson Crews in 1955.

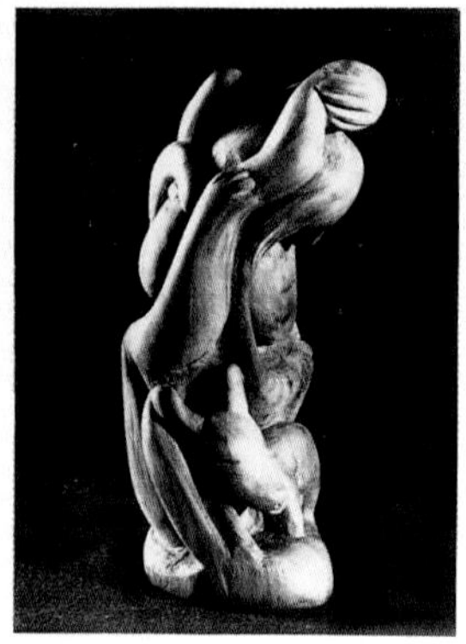

MOTIVE BOOK SHOP
Mildred Tolbert photograph from *Patrocinio Barela: Taos Wood Carver.*

on the road. He sold his duffle bag full of books by correspondence and introduced the works of a new generation of writers — Henry Miller, Gertrude Stein, Anaïs Nin, Kenneth Patchen — to many he met in his travels.[38]

Later he would have the opportunity to become personally acquainted with some of his literary heroes. Between 1945 and 1946 he was in and out of northern California's Big Sur, meeting Henry Miller along with many poets and artists who had settled there. He made a lasting impression on the author, who remembered Crews with a "shaggy beard and manner of speech of a latter-day prophet. He lived almost exclusively on peanut butter and wild mustard greens and neither smoked or drank," Miller wrote in his 1957 account *Big Sur and the Oranges of Hieronymus Bosch.*

Although these were restless years in which Crews traveled back and forth from Texas to California, he continued to write, producing the manuscript for a new novel, which he optimistically sent off to Miller for review. When the work received scathing criticism,[39] a discouraged Crews left all behind and set out for Taos, where he planned to study art but never strayed far from independent publishing.

There he met and married photographer Mildred Tolbert, got his feet wet as an apprentice printer, and spent nearly twenty years doing double time, working at the Taos *Star* and later at *El Crepúsculo* while moonlighting his own books, magazines, and pamphlets out of the newspaper plants. Crews used his meager journeyman salary to finance the publications which he said, "cost considerably less to produce than a cheap fifth of scotch."[40]

After he printed *No Is the Night* in 1949 under his Motive Book Shop imprint, he launched a series of literary magazines with such offbeat titles as *Suck-egg Mule* and *The Deer and the Dachshund.* Unlike mainstream magazines they featured unknown but promising talent. *Suck-egg Mule* appeared from 1951 to 1952, according to Crews, never living up to its name. "I managed to print two issues of it at *El Crepúsculo* in the first year I worked there, 1950–51. It included mostly good people. Poetry."[41] Later he reduced the magazine format and, with his newly developed pasteup skills, added artwork.

For *The Deer and the Dachshund* he went back to the mimeograph machine, which he dubbed the "mule" of small literary publications. It came out from 1951 to 1954 for the purpose of mail order exchange rather than local distribution.

One of his most lavish productions, a jumbo portfolio titled *Taos: a de luxe magazine of the arts*, came out in 1951. It was entirely a community effort—from the poetry of Spud Johnson and Crews to the prose of Mabel Dodge Luhan and Frank Waters, and the artwork of Thomas Benrimo, Dorothy Brett, and Victor Higgins. Crews credits the entire staff of *El Crepúsculo*, where he printed 125 copies of the thirty-six-page folio with the help of family and friends. Though the deluxe package was reasonably priced at $3, Crews said he could not recall ever selling a single copy. It was good but local, he offered as an explanation. Thirty years later collectors were paying as much as $50 for the rare item.[42]

Despite the lackluster success rate of his magazines, he persisted through the 1950s. In 1957 he issued *Poetry Taos*, number one, which included a Robert Creeley short story and Max Finstein's first published poem. It was another major fiasco, according to Crews, who never produced a second issue. *The Naked Ear* was his last Taos magazine. He did twelve numbers between 1956 and 1959.

Among the impressive list of contributors were Charles Bukowski, Diane di Prima, Alfred Morang, and Langston Hughes.

His real success story came in 1955 in the form of a joint venture, a collaborative publishing effort that involved his wife Mildred Tolbert and longtime friend and poet Wendell Anderson. The book *Patrocinio Barela: Taos Wood Carver*[43] was a labor of love published by the trio. It featured twenty-four black-and-white Tolbert photographs of Barela and his carvings, along with the artist's own revealing commentary recorded by Anderson and set into verse form by Crews. In addition, the book included a reprint of an earlier interview with Barela by Kit Egri titled "I Lead a Heavy Life."

In regard to his own role in the publication, Crews said, "This volume required an entire year of my life, and every cent Mildred and myself could alot to it, to produce 250 copies, which I priced at the absurd price of $2.50 a copy. I was concerned to try to recover the cost of the materials that had gone into the actual production. I feared it would not sell—any more than *Taos* Portfolio had."[44] Despite his fears, the entire edition sold within a year. It was republished in 1962 and 1976 by Taos Recordings and Publications.

Crews continued printing until the mid-1960s when he went back to Texas. "Leaving Taos in 1966 was the end of a chapter in my life—or perchance of several volumes," he said.[45] Some years later he resumed producing photocopied poetry pamphlets but nothing to equal the enthusiasm of his Taos Motive work.

Pictograph Press

ALTHOUGH DOROTHY STEWART settled in Santa Fe in the mid-1920s, it was 1948 before she acquired a printing press and began introducing brilliantly colored illustrated books. She was one of the first women here to take on the challenge of private press work.

An artist with a particular zest for life, she loved animals, music, theater, and most of all the people and places of Mexico. One of her earliest book efforts was inspired by that country's architecture. *Hornacinas, Niches and Corners of Mexico City* is a documentation of small alcoves strategically placed to identify houses and entire neighborhoods before Mexico City adopted a numbering system. Works of art, the *niches* provide a setting for sculptural figures of saints. Following several years of research, Stewart wrote text and created scores of charcoal sketches of these architectural features, which were reproduced for the book by master lithographer Isidoro Bayardi. *Hornacinas* was published in 1933 in Mexico by Editorial Cultura and dedicated to Mexican street crowds.

Dorothy Stewart at the Pictograph Press, ca. 1950.

The daughter of a wealthy Philadelphia couple, Stewart received a privileged education, her artistic talents nurtured from a young age. She studied at the Pennsylvania Academy of the Fine Arts, pursuing interests in pantomime, stage design, and fresco painting, which later took her to Italy and Greece. In France she was a student at the American School of Fine Arts in Fontainebleau.[46]

Her first visit to Santa Fe was in 1921. "We came via Mesa Verde National Park, Gallup, and Albuquerque by automobile, which was a roundabout but interesting way of reaching Santa Fe where I had been invited to speak to a meeting of the League of Women Voters," recalled Stewart's sister Margretta Dietrich.[47] The two were instantly smitten by the city's quaintly rural atmosphere and its ancient adobe structures with lush inner gardens. Dietrich particularly remembered their first meal in Santa Fe at the Blue Parrot. Housed in a historic building at the corner of Palace Avenue and Burro Alley, the eatery included multiple patios that accommodated grazing sheep as well as diners. So enchanted were the sisters that they returned the following spring and eventually settled in Santa Fe, making their home in a nineteenth-century adobe hacienda on Canyon Road.

Though the sisters were often at the center of Santa Fe's social activity, hosting a whirlwind of gala dinners and parties, Stewart still found time to develop her artwork. She created linoleum block illustrations for a 1930 Laughing Horse Press pamphlet titled *Adobe Notes*. Printed by Spud Johnson, the lighthearted manual focused on traditional Southwest building techniques. In 1936, as a WPA artist, she painted murals at the entrance of Albuquerque's Little Theater, depicting a clash between Christians and Moors portrayed in New Mexico folk plays. With few exceptions, her prolific prints and paintings were simply signed with the initials D. N. S.

With a penchant for all things mechanical, she transformed her automobiles into extraordinary vehicles. Her first car, Dietrich recalled, combined a new Ford Model T frame with a Packard body salvaged from a junkyard. She followed this up with a Baby Austin, creating a kind of covered wagon look by replacing the car's conventional roof with hoops and sheeting.[48] A free spirit, Stewart endlessly traveled New Mexico's primitive roadways in her homemade vehicles, looking for ancient petroglyph sites.[49] She drew copies of the rock art and later transferred the imagery into linoleum block illustrations for her books.

After Dietrich purchased a second nineteenth-century residence adjacent to her Canyon Road home, Stewart set up a studio just east of the building, which later became known as *El Zaguán*. The studio doubled as the Galeria Mexico where the artist hosted concerts, lectures, shadow puppet plays, and exhibitions representing her wide range of interests. Jean Buchanan, a longtime Stewart friend and neighbor, recalled that the events were well attended with as many as fifty people crowded into the studio. "Dorothy would send me up the road where they sold tamales and have me bring them back for the programs," she said. "The concerts were a great treat, since there was not much entertainment in Santa Fe at the time."[50]

Stewart's Pictograph Press was launched sometime around 1948 when she acquired type and printing equipment from a defunct Spanish language newspaper in Española, New Mexico, and moved it into her Canyon Road studio.[51] Buchanan remembered that the metal type arrived in a complete jumble and that the two spent hours sorting the pieces.

Shortly after putting her hand-fed platen press into action Stewart focused on subject matter near and dear to her own heart—the plays of William Shakespeare. In 1949 she completed a book of excerpts from *Hamlet* in a long horizontal format, a sort of paper stage upon which linoleum block-printed characters perform. Printed in an array of somber tones, as many as eight per page, *Hamlet, Prince of Denmark* packs about one-tenth of Shakespeare's drama into thirty-four pages, weaving together a selection of favored scenes. Though the abridged plot may be incomprehensible to those unfamiliar with the play, the book, done under Stewart's original San Vicente imprint, was heralded as a work of art. The 100 copies sold readily to collectors.

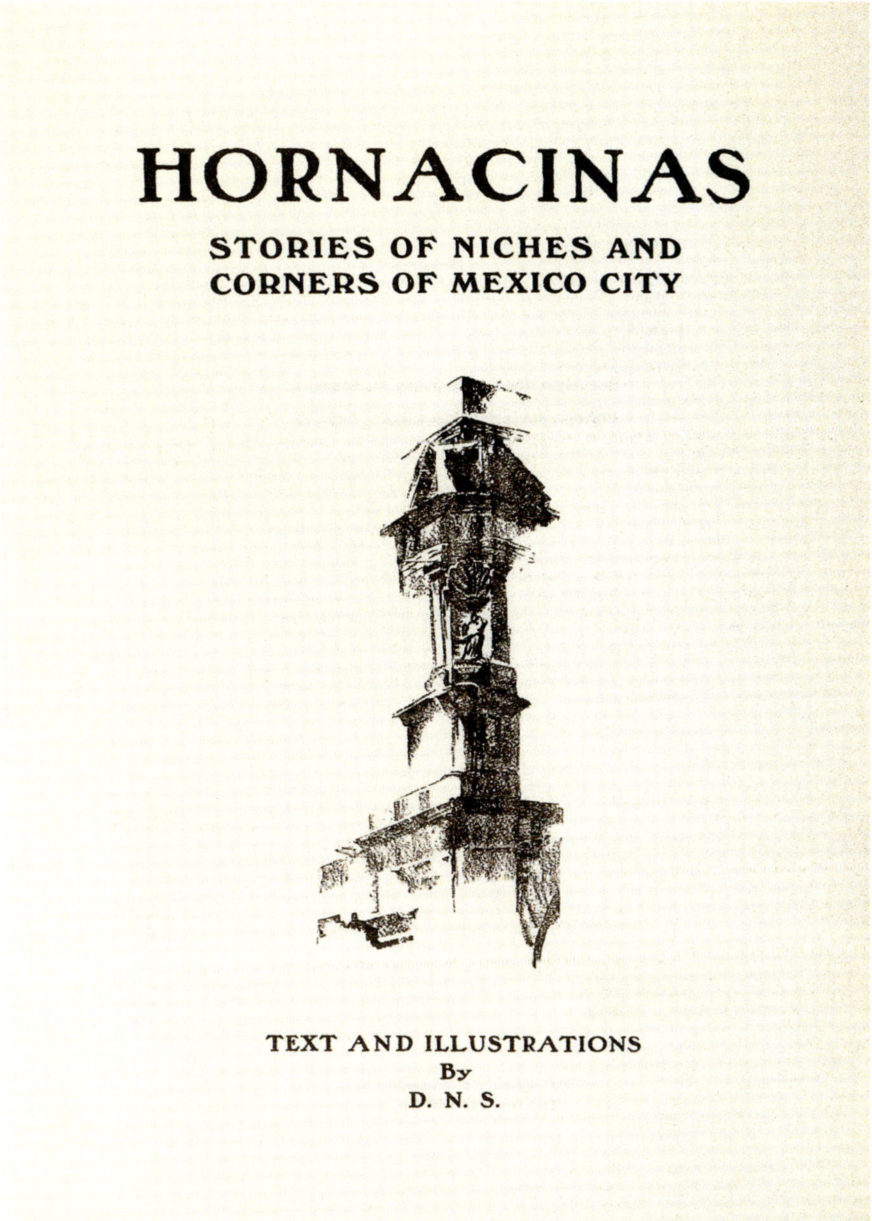

HORNACINAS

STORIES OF NICHES AND
CORNERS OF MEXICO CITY

TEXT AND ILLUSTRATIONS
By
D. N. S.

Pictograph Press

Title page, *Hornacinas: Niches and Corners of Mexico City,* produced by Dorothy Stewart in 1933.

Pictograph Press

Linoleum print from the 1953 Pictograph Press edition of *A Midsummer Night's Dream.*

PICTOGRAPH PRESS
Title page from *Hamlet*, illustrated and printed by Dorothy Stewart in 1949.

Three years later she started work on an abbreviated presentation of *A Midsummer Night's Dream*. As she had done for *Hamlet*, Stewart energetically cut scores of linoleum blocks, depicting an elaborately costumed cast of Shakespearean characters—printed in a riot of color. This time the text lines also appeared in various shades of pink, blue, red, and green, matching the color of the character to which the speech was attributed. Stewart printed the thirty-seven-page book on Japanese papers, as she had done with *Hamlet*. With the help of her friends she bound the 117 copies in paper covers and encased them in white corrugated cardboard slipcases. It was released in 1953 under her new Pictograph Press imprint.

Along with her Shakespeare works, in 1950 Stewart published a *Handbook of Indian Dances*. The booklet makes use of her linoleum block illustrations and as many as thirty colors to portray seven ceremonial Indian dances. A facsimile was put out by the Museum of New Mexico in 1952 when the original edition had sold out. Her avid interest in Southwest Indian rock carvings influenced the 1950 production of *San Cristobal Petroglyphs*, a collaboration with longtime friend Agnes Sims. The portfolio of seventeen linoleum block prints and six

PICTOGRAPH PRESS
San Cristobal Petroglyphs, printed by Dorothy Stewart in 1950.

text pages (12 × 9 inches) is printed in two colors, a tame presentation in contrast to most Pictograph Press work.

Stewart's books succeeded on the basis of her charming linoleum block prints and not because of her eye as a typographer. She used old metal fonts that came with the Española equipment along with a collection of worn and broken type discarded by commercial Santa Fe print shops. Unusual scripts and curlicue copperplate gothics became her trademark. In a tribute to the artist, Gustave Baumann discreetly referred to Stewart's disregard for typographical rules as an ability to "revel in the most difficult combination of type and illustration."[52] Nevertheless, her work shines with a kind of folk art appeal.

Likely, Stewart's Pictograph Press would have gone on producing imaginative and colorful works had it not been for her untimely death in Mexico in 1955.

RINI TEMPLETON
Rini Templeton illustration from *Homage to Neruda*, 1973.

Chapter 4

Vigor and Variety: A Small Press Revival

1960–1975

In the 1960s and 1970s, the New Mexico private press movement gained new momentum. More small publishing houses came and went during the two decades than in any other period, a vigor reflected throughout the entire printing industry. Advances in technology that brought high-speed offset presses and photocomposition rendered letterpress equipment obsolete. The hand-operated machinery, long favored by craft-conscious private printers, became available at little or no cost. Printing enthusiasts wasted little time in hauling it off and putting it to use in shops that sprang from garages, living rooms, and basements.

Amateur printing associations established in England and the United States during the 1940s and 1950s sparked further interest in the craft and raised standards of workmanship among small press users. John Ryder's enthusiastic manual *Printing for Pleasure* appeared around the same time. Issued in England in 1955 and widely circulated in this country, the book guided novices through the letterpress process and inspired a new generation of printers.

In New Mexico, where a growing population created a flow of fresh ideas and new approaches to art, this resurgence of printing interest led to a healthy and diverse private press climate. There were publishers of history, poetry, cookbooks, political material, and even a press dedicated to the fabrication of presses. They came and went, some producing no more than a single title.

Attracted by Santa Fe's growing reputation as an arts colony, in 1965 Jon and Louise Webb moved their successful Loujon Press here from New Orleans.

It was an unfortunate move in which their Chandler & Price platen press, precariously held together with coat hangers and rope, suffered further damage and remained out of commission for a month.[1] They stayed only long enough to learn that the city offered few production advantages. Essential supplies, like paper and Linotype, were unavailable locally and had to be brought from Albuquerque, sixty miles away. Though Santa Fe printers had grown accustomed to such logistical problems and still today rely on a flow of materials from sources outside the city, the Webbs found the inconveniences reason enough to repack hundreds of pounds of equipment.

Four months after their arrival they moved on to Tucson, Arizona.[2] There they continued to produce the well-regarded literary magazine *Outsider*, along with the work of Henry Miller and Charles Bukowski, for which they had become known. Miller's *Insomnia or the Devil at Large*, the last Loujon Press book, lists Albuquerque as the publishing site and may indicate a more successful return to New Mexico around 1970 when the book appeared.

In El Rito, New Mexico, the short-lived printing effort of Wilder Bentley resulted in one notable book of poetry titled *Adrift in Valueland*. The son of Wilder Bentley, "the Elder," one of San Francisco's most influential hand press printers,[3] the younger Bentley made his home in the northern New Mexico village for a short period during the late 1960s and early 1970s. A self-proclaimed "poet, artist and convicted vagrant," Bentley set up his printing operation in a crumbling adobe storage shed, lit only by the light of a single window.[4] With a treadle-operated platen press and borrowed type, in 1970 he produced a 10-copy edition of the book he wrote to guide readers out of a materialistic culture. A skillful craftsman, Bentley embellished *Adrift in Valueland* with a linoleum block print and hand-illuminated initial letters, then bound the quarter leather copies, using the face of an old banjo to create printed cover labels.[5]

Other private publishers with more staying power—Jack Rittenhouse at the Stagecoach Press and Lightning Tree proprietors Jene and Jetta Lyon—upheld a tradition of finely printed regional material. Rittenhouse focused on the history of the Southwest, while the Lyons branched out to include books of local poetry, cookery, and folk material. The two became the most successful small publishing houses of the period, with Lightning Tree continuing on through the 1980s.

While New Mexico's privately printed works maintained a strong regional focus throughout the period, local topics slowly began to give way to a broader spectrum of subject matter, as evidenced in the work of Taos activist Rini Templeton. Her powerful black-and-white imagery depicting antiwar demonstrators, striking laborers, and Hispano activists articulated the sixties' political turbulence.

Though the period produced few extraordinary examples of the book craft, it brought an infusion of energy that would propel the private press movement into a wide-open range of literary and artistic expression.

The Stagecoach Press

SUCCESS OF THE STAGECOACH PRESS was no accident. Proprietor Jack D. Rittenhouse discovered the world of books very early, inhabiting the children's section of the Terre Haute, Indiana, public library from the hour it opened until closing time. In short order, he was working for the library, retrieving books from delinquent patrons. "Books became as natural a part of my life as breathing," he once remarked.[6]

During the Depression, Rittenhouse landed a "job" at the *Terre Haute Journal-Gazette*—no pay but free use of the newsroom typewriter. He began writing book reviews and lived on the money he received by selling his review copies at half price to the local library. He rode freight trains to New York City in 1935, found work as a mail room sorter at Alfred A. Knopf, a major publisher, and haunted the stalls on "Booksellers Row." A talented copywriter, Rittenhouse later worked for several print advertising firms, but books and how they were written, made, and sold were currents that would resurface and define his role in the world.

Jack Rittenhouse at the Stagecoach Press in Houston, 1958.

Young Rittenhouse and his wife Charlotte were living in Los Angeles in the mid-1940s when inspiration came for a book that is a genuine American classic. "After World War II, when men were coming back from overseas, Jack decided they would need a guidebook to help them find their way to California," Charlotte recalled.[7] From Los Angeles to Chicago and back, he plied U.S. 66 in a tiny American Bantam car, taking notes on every town, tourist court, gas station, and garage he encountered. Hoping to make the journey as driver-friendly as possible, he included the mileage to each entry and wrote descriptions of the historic and geologic features all along the way. Jack Rittenhouse's *A Guide Book to Highway 66* (1946) was the first complete guidebook to a transcontinental highway ever published—quite literally the mother of all highway guidebooks. He designed and published the book himself, in an edition of 3,000 copies priced at just one dollar, and sold them at several of the travel-oriented businesses described in the guidebook.

Energized by his success producing a book by himself, he researched and wrote *American Horse-Drawn Vehicles* (1948) and started gathering old letterpress printing equipment. He was invited to join the Zamorano Club, a group of rare book enthusiasts, where he was further encouraged by "the manners, the enthusiasm and intellectual sparkle" of club members.[8] He acquired a 3 × 5 Kelsey hobby press and then a 1872 Gally Universal press. Foot powered, this fine 7 × 11 platen press was capable of producing better letterpress impressions than any other press of its kind.[9] The Stagecoach Press name appeared first in 1949 on a sampling of seventeen letterpress typefaces Rittenhouse collected.

The first hardbound books from the Stagecoach Press were published after a move to Houston, where Rittenhouse continued in the advertising business and also wrote historical articles for trade magazines that would eventually number in the hundreds. *The Man Who Owned Too Much: Maxwell's Land Grant*, slipcased and printed in an edition of 450 copies in 1958, introduced the tone and style that were to become hallmarks of Stagecoach Press editions.[10] Meanwhile, he acquired a Mergenthaler Linotype machine[11] for efficient setting of lines of letterpress text type.

After driving through New Mexico several times, absorbing the state's Wild West landscapes and intricate history, the Rittenhouses finally made the move to Santa Fe in 1962. Here the Stagecoach Press would come into full

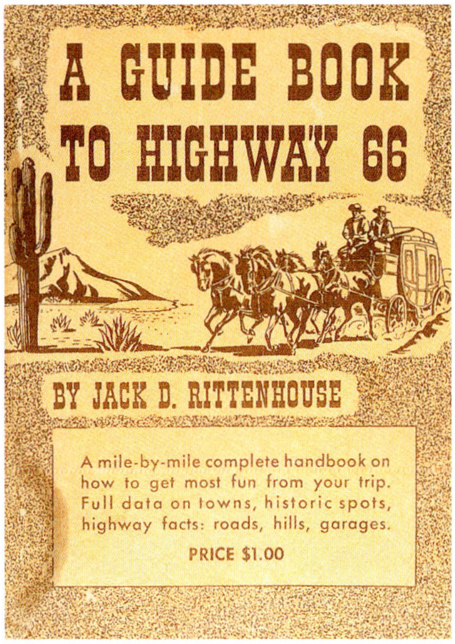

STAGECOACH PRESS
A Guide Book to Highway 66, produced by Jack Rittenhouse in 1946.

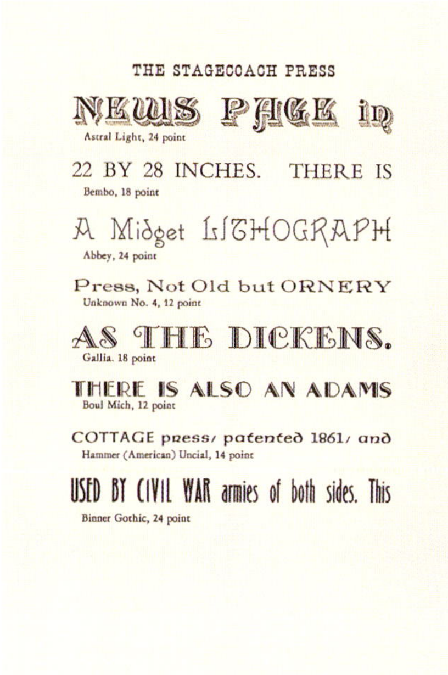

A sampling of Stagecoach Press vintage types, 1960.

flower as a quality private press specializing in books about the West. The Gally press, Linotype, racks of California job cases full of classic hand-set type, guillotine paper cutter, and a splendid Vandercook proof press[12]—ideal for printing the series of books he had in mind—were set up in a small block building just off Cerrillos Road, once a part of Route 66 itself. Stagecoach was now a full-time operation. Soon after the move to Santa Fe, Rittenhouse met Richard Polese, a young college student eager to find a summer job where he could learn the craft of printing from the ground up. A year later, with Polese on board full time, running the presses, sorting type, and operating the Linotype, the Stagecoach Press quickly established itself as a consistent producer of hand-printed books, publishing four to six new Southwestern Americana titles a year for the next five years.

Rittenhouses's surefire formula assured a solid market for nearly every Stagecoach Press title produced in Santa Fe. Most books printed on the

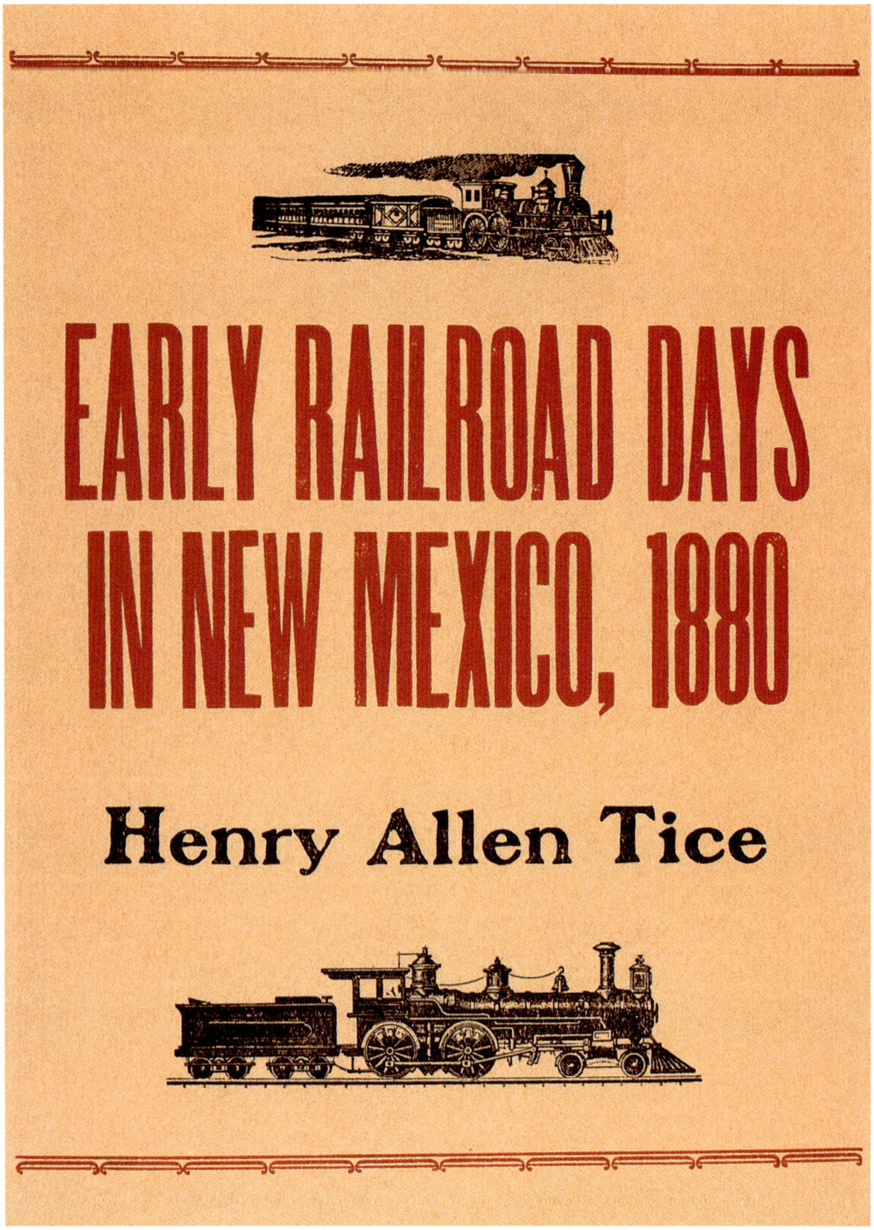

Stagecoach Press

Cover, *Early Railroad Days in New Mexico*, Stagecoach Press, 1965.

Vandercook were in a 5 × 7-inch page format, printed four pages up, cloth bound, and run in limited editions of 500 to 750 copies, priced from $4.50 to $6.50. At least half of the press run was pre-sold to subscribers — enthusiasts of authentic Western Americana, university libraries, and collectors of books as visually pleasing and tactile objects.

Rittenhouse's designs were always tasteful and appropriate to the subject, with occasional clever graphic flourishes on the title pages. For example, the author's name and publisher imprint for *Early Railroad Days in New Mexico* (1965) is in P. T. Barnum display type, rising as smoke from a nineteenth-century locomotive. Texts were usually set in legible and refined Linotype Caledonia, with chapter titles and initial capitals chosen from Rittenhouse's collection of some 150 type fonts. Books were enlivened with old engravings, dingbats, and sometimes original art, such as the José Cisneros drawings in *Baca's Battle* (1962). Quality papers that were readily available were chosen for text. Printing was usually done in black plus a second color.

Many Stagecoach Press books were firsthand accounts of the southwestern frontier — drawn from trail journeys, military outposts, mining camps, and railroading — but several were written or compiled expressly for Stagecoach. *Fallen Guidon: The Forgotten Saga of Jo Shelby's Confederate Command*, an account of a Civil War brigade that never surrendered but instead marched south to offer its services to Emperor Maximilian, came out in 1962. W. Dick Grisso of Oklahoma City compiled *From Where the Sun Now Stands: Addresses by a Posse of Famous Western Speakers* (1963), and Jack Schaefer, author of the classic Western novel *Shane* (1949), penned the history of *The Great Endurance Horse Race* (1963), a six-hundred-mile dash from Evanston, Wyoming, to Denver in the early twentieth century. Rittenhouse researched and wrote *Cabezon: A New Mexico Ghost Town* (1965), the story of one of the state's oldest and most colorful but least-known outposts.

Collectors came to expect quality and refinement in each new Stagecoach Press book. Working with considerable foresight, passion, and discipline, Rittenhouse usually had several projects in planning, writing, or printing stages. All the while, he was gaining widespread and well-deserved recognition as the final authority on books about the Southwest. He wrote and produced *New Mexico Book News* from 1964 until 1967. The first president of the Santa Fe

Corral of Westerners, he was later elected president of the Historical Society of New Mexico. With an unassuming manner, distinct authority, soft wit, and pipe in mouth or hand, Rittenhouse shared generously what he knew and often what he possessed. No appointment was necessary to drop in and chat with him about books, history, or printing.

Certainly the most curious Stagecoach Press book was *Fort Union in Miniature* (1963), by historian Robert M. Utley, "the smallest book in the West."[13] With pages less than an inch square, it was hand set in tiny 6-point type and printed and bound entirely by very steady hands. It was hand sewn with marbled endpapers and thin leather cover. A limited edition of 99 copies was bound in Pueblo deerskin. Another unique Stagecoach Press offering was *Disturnell's Treaty Map* (1965), a full-size reproduction of the map attached to the 1848 Treaty of Guadalupe Hidalgo that defined the U.S. border with Mexico. Rittenhouse wrote and printed the accompanying text about the controversial map's role in the treaty, and had the folded map and text casebound to appear as a cloth hardcover book.

Rittenhouse signed on as director of the Museum of New Mexico Press in 1967 and moved the Stagecoach Press to a shop next to his home. Within months, he was offered a more lucrative job selecting manuscripts about the American West and overseeing production and advertising at the University of New Mexico Press in Albuquerque. The position required him to shut down the Stagecoach Press. Rittenhouse did not surrender his other interests, however. He compiled award-winning bibliographies and, after retiring from UNM Press, went into buying and selling rare books full time and found great satisfaction in assembling special book collections for libraries.[14]

"Central to everything was a passionate interest in the literature of the West," Rittenhouse wrote to his friend Dwight Myers. "I wanted to write it, read it, print it, sell it, collect it, evangelize upon it, talk about it, teach about it, study about it, and travel to all the places mentioned in it."[15]

With extraordinary breadth of knowledge and a persistent passion to learn and share more, Rittenhouse was regarded as the dean of southwestern bookmen well before he died in 1991. Lawrence Clark Powell voiced the sentiments of dozens of collector/scholars when he wrote that of the thousands of books he owned those of the Stagecoach Press were the ones most treasured,

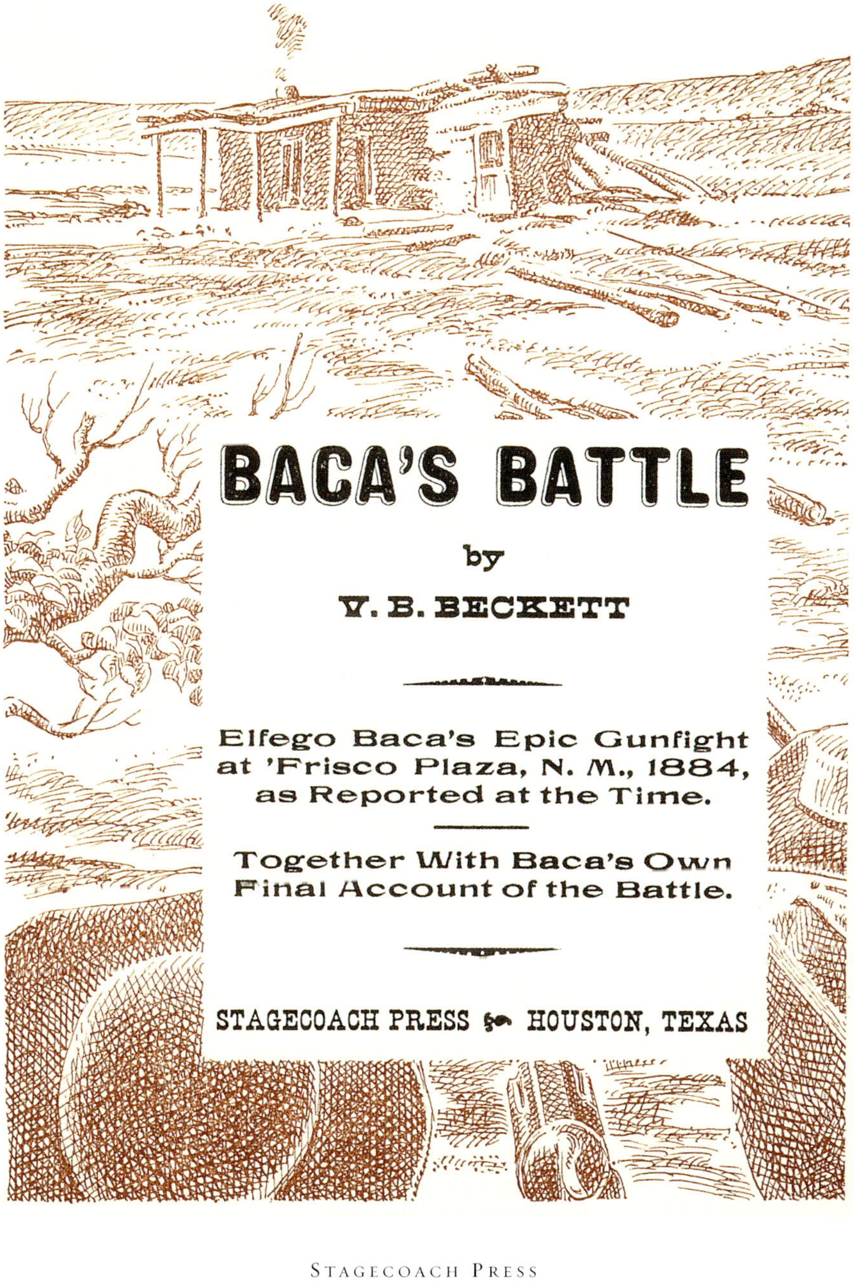
BACA'S BATTLE

by

V. B. BECKETT

Elfego Baca's Epic Gunfight at 'Frisco Plaza, N. M., 1884, as Reported at the Time.

Together With Baca's Own Final Account of the Battle.

STAGECOACH PRESS HOUSTON, TEXAS

STAGECOACH PRESS

Baca's Battle, title page with José Cisneros illustration, Stagecoach Press, 1962.

"because they are the products of one man's vision and desire and craftsmanship, the products of personal toil and pleasure, manufactured in the true sense of that word: *by hand*."[16]

The Lightning Tree

LIKE JACK RITTENHOUSE, Jene Lyon made his way to Santa Fe after gathering considerable talents related to printing and books elsewhere. Jene and his wife, author Jetta Carleton Lyon, arrived at a time when living costs were low and you could do just about anything your heart desired — provided you did most of it by hand. The Lightning Tree was a well-planned and nurtured "affair of the heart," producing more than fifty quality titles, from cookbooks and poetry to environmental guides and a landmark collection on the book lore of the West.[17]

"I came to book publishing in something of a nineteenth-century way — through the back shop," Lyon reflected in 1984.[18] At his working-class high school in Kansas City, the boys got a lot of shop — in his case, print shop. But Jene's quick talents with the Linotype and job presses led to other opportunities. On the GI Bill, he enrolled at the University of New Mexico in 1946, edited the literary magazine and yearbook, and found work with a great mentor at UNM's printing plant. He later studied book design at Columbia University and got a plum job with Grove Press in New York. Jetta Carleton, groomed at *The New Yorker*, gained some literary fame with her best-selling 1963 novel *Moonflower Vine*. Their marriage was a happily symbiotic one. Later, at Lightning Tree, Jene was publisher, printer, business and marketing manager, designer, and typesetter. Jetta was the whole editorial department and was known to come up with a cold martini or hot tea, whichever would save the day.

Jene and Jetta Lyon at the Lightning Tree shop, 1986. Photograph by Vickie Lewis.

Sale of film rights to Jetta's novel in the late 1960s allowed them to buy fifty-six pristine but hilly acres in the Cerros Negros southeast of Santa Fe. A tall, very old bifurcated ponderosa pine stood on the land. Years earlier it had been struck by lightning, leaving wide yellow scars spiraling down both trunks. As they explored the expanse of wilderness around them, Jene and Jetta occasionally got lost. "The tree gave us our bearings," Jetta wrote. And it gave their home and venture a name: The Lightning Tree. Across the arroyo Jene built their adobe home by hand and then the large detached print shop they called the barn.[19]

Jene Lyon's engagement with private printing began in 1968, when he paid $350 for the workings of the little printing shop assembled by the legendary Spud Johnson. Included were woodcuts and tools used by D. H. Lawrence and Spud's 7 × 9 Kelsey treadle press. The press sat out under a pine tree for better than a year while Lyon finished the shop building. His first hand-printed book was *Growing Herbs as Natural Insect Repellants*, twelve pages plus packets of seeds.

The Lightning Tree began as a serious book publishing venture in 1972, "beholden to none and responsible to all."[20] Hot type for the first Lightning Tree books was set at a Roswell shop, but things changed quickly. Jene Lyon located a Model B Kelly cylinder press, capable of printing 16-page signatures. It came down from Colorado on a flatbed truck "loaded with missiles headed for White Sands," which lumbered up the winding dirt road to the shop, felling small trees along the way.[21] In 1973, Jene bought a Model 31 Linotype machine from the *Las Vegas (NM) Optic* on the cheap. Most newspapers at this time had converted to cold type composition "and were dying for someone—anyone—to get the old machines out of their shop." By a stroke of luck, Jene met Linotype wizard Hugh Nesbit, "a gentleman of sagacity and much patience," who soon "subdued the monster, overhauled its intestines, corrected its diet and pacified its behavior."[22]

The Lyons' first titles appeared in 1983: a cookbook, a book of poetry by Lucile Adler, plus *The Lightning Tree Southwestern Appointment/Engagement Calendar*. This and subsequent editions, renamed *The Lightning Tree Annual Southwestern Reader*, were far more than simple calendars. Here was a book-style collection of fifty-three historical and literary selections, with facing pages for daily notations, running 112 pages. Marta Weigle, a respected folklorist, gathered the selections.

IN
CELEBRATION
OF THE BOOK
Literary New Mexico

DWIGHT and CAROL MYERS, Editors

The New Mexico Book League
The Lightning Tree
Co-publishers
Albuquerque and Santa Fe, New Mexico

THE LIGHTNING TREE
Title page, *In Celebration of the Book: Literary New Mexico*,
hand set and printed at the Lightning Tree, 1982.

Marketing got cranked up early the following year. The Lightning Tree's first catalog, a small folded flyer, listed seven titles. *Publishing in the West: Alan Swallow* (1974), edited by William Claire, revealed the remarkable man who first published Frank Waters, Anaïs Nin, and Allen Tate. Lyon himself wrote *Tools That Started the Twentieth Century* (1976), a unique "collector's browser" illuminated by cuts and descriptions from a pair of post–Civil War hardware catalogs. *The Willow Farm Pickle Book* by Vermont pickling guru John McKinney appeared in 1973, the first of several cookbooks offered by the press. Lightning Tree cookbooks, comb bound with durable Kivar covers, were sold in both softcover and hardcover versions. Lightning Tree books were sent out for binding. Once stock of first hand-set and printed editions ran out, subsequent runs were often contracted to offset printers, using hand-printed proofs as repro copy.

The occasional *Lightning Tree Journal* provided healthy dashes of personal philosophy. In the first issue, Jene Lyon wrote that Lightning Tree books would address "themes and issues which are coterminous with the social, biological and ecological force arrayed against mankind—the assembly in the camp of the unknowing, uncaring, unfeeling, the troops of the self-serving and greedy," but mixed with occasional works that are "simply fun to do and read, on the theory that there has got to be a tomorrow."[23] After Peter van Dresser built the first intentional solar energy house in Santa Fe and became widely respected as a pioneer of environmenally conscious dwellings, the Lightning Tree published his *A Landscape for Humans* in 1972, as well as *Homegrown Sundwellings* five years later.

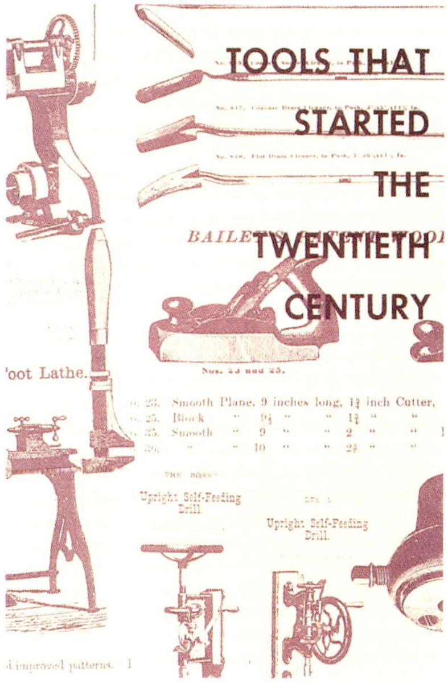

THE LIGHTNING TREE
Tools That Started the Twentieth Century,
the Lighning Tree, 1976.

In 1980, Dwight and Carol Myers approached the Lyons about marking the tenth anniversary of the New Mexico Book League with a finely produced book of memoirs and articles by the most respected experts in book printing, production, publishing, and collecting in the region. Dwight was one of the Southwest's most knowledgeable publisher sales reps. Carol edited the league's *Book Talk*, a reviewing publication that had chronicled New Mexico's publishing scene since 1971. *In Celebration of the Book: Literary New Mexico* would be printed in the finest bookmaking tradition: marbled endpapers by Pamela Smith, handmade paper interleaves by Kathy Gurwell, cloth slipcases, Warren's Olde Style Wove text paper, and "defying every electronic trend in the book publishing industry, with every word handset in real foundry type . . . worthy of Gutenberg and Caxton."[24]

Lyon enthusiastically embraced the project, to be copublished by the Lightning Tree and the Book League. Obstacles appeared almost immediately. He found that Caslon, a handsome and once-common typestyle, was the only classic face still available in a complete set of sizes and ligature characters from American Type Foundry, formerly the colossus of lead type. Out of stock at ATF, full sets of Caslon had to be cast just for this book. After the first eight pages were set, a letter count revealed another sobering surprise. Instead of the planned 160 pages, the book would run to 278 pages. In response to an appeal for help setting all that 14-point Caslon, Dick Fleming, an amateur printer, drove out to the Cerros Negros to meet Jene. Their meeting led to a most fruitful professional and personal relationship. Jetta called Fleming "Dead Eye Dick," and it stuck.[25] Dick Fleming and Jene Lyon typeset and printed the entire book on the Kelly B press at the Lightning Tree. By September 1982, all 500 copies of *In Celebration of the Book* had been presold.

The Squaw Tree: Ghosts, Mysteries and Miracles of New Mexico (1978), by Alice Bullock, wife of sometime Rydal Press owner Dale Bullock, proved a perennial bestseller. *The F. Stanley Story*, a biography and bibliography of a grassroots historian/priest who had self-published some 170 historical books and booklets, won a Southwest Book Award when it came out in 1985.

Angelica and Other Cats by puppeteer Paul McPharlin, an "alphabetical array" of twenty-six cats depicted in paper silhouettes, each with a verse, is considered the Lightning Tree's graphically most interesting book. Appearing in 1986, the limited edition of 200 copies was printed on the Lightning Tree's newly acquired Vandercook proof press, the fine machine favored by many craft printers. Sudden health problems would hobble Jene's productivity for the next two years. But he wasn't done yet. A special slipcased reprint of Erna Fergusson's *Murder and Mystery in New Mexico*, designed by Merle Armitage, came out in 1991 in a 100-copy edition.

In 1991 Jene Lyon received the first Jack D. Rittenhouse Award for lifetime contributions to book publishing in the region from the Rocky Mountain Book Publishers Association. He was a popular choice for the honor, having been the association's spark plug and first president. "In 1976, I was conned into organizing the organization," Lyon told the audience, admitting that his "blind persistence" may have set its tone and kept it going.[26]

A N G E L I C A

AND OTHER CATS

An alphabetical array

Rhymes and cut paper pictures by

Paul McPharlin

With an introduction by Marjorie Batchelder McPharlin

THE LIGHTNING TREE—*Jene Lyon, Publisher* POB 1837, Santa Fé, NM 87504-1837

THE LIGHTNING TREE

Angelica and Other Cats, title page, the Lightning Tree, 1986.

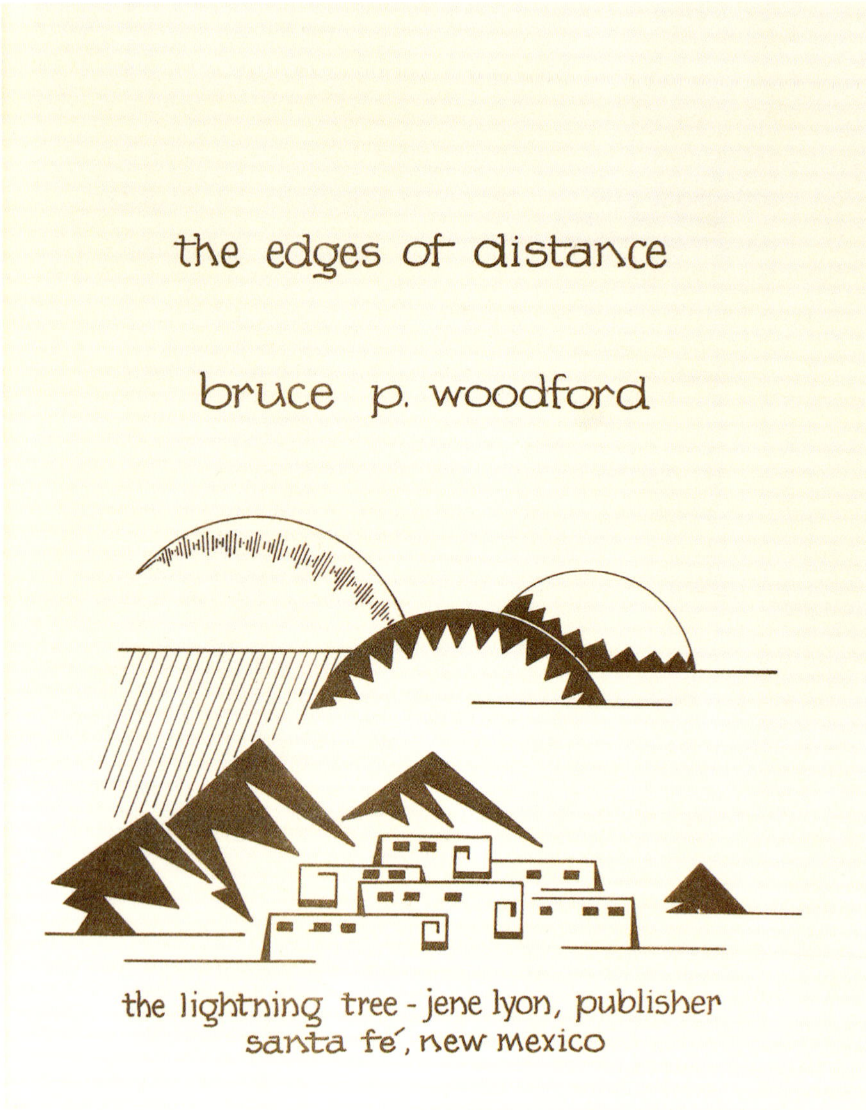

the edges of distance

bruce p. woodford

the lightning tree - jene lyon, publisher
santa fe´, new mexico

THE LIGHTNING TREE

Poet Bruce P. Woodford designed the title page of his book, with calligraphy by Dorothy A. Davidson for the Lightning Tree, 1977.

"One day about a year ago, or one night, during a period of high wind, the tall ponderosa we called the Lightning Tree crashed to the ground, unheard," Jene wrote to clients and friends later in 1991. "Somehow, the fall of the eponymous tree seemed to us a signal that the time has come for us and the press we had named for it to part company."[27] The decision to quit after nineteen productive years became final when Jene's health once again faltered. In October 1991 the business was sold to a friend, Gerald Keenan of Boulder, Colorado. During almost two decades of life in Santa Fe, the Lightning Tree produced fifty-five titles.

Jene Lyon outlasted the tree by a couple of years, until April 1993. Jetta stayed on through the 1990s. Her last published article, "A Sort of a Love Affair," appeared in 1999 in a New Mexico Book Association directory, recounting the Lightning Tree publishing story. She died at home in December 1999.

Vinegar Tom Press

PASSION FOR WESTERN HISTORY was high on the list of Andy Gregg's eclectic interests—play writing, quirky comedy, and the history of magic among them— so in the mid-1960s he and his wife Fay left Wisconsin to settle in Albuquerque. Gregg first worked as a photographer at the *Albuquerque Tribune* and wrote a weekly newspaper column on Western lore, but in 1968 he got a serious injection of printer's ink and the urge to print books himself. With Stagecoach Press proprietor Jack Rittenhouse as inspiration, he set up the Vinegar Tom Press.

Andy Gregg at his Kelsey press, ca. 1970.

Through the Westerners, a club of dedicated history enthusiasts and writers, Gregg connected with Rittenhouse and Philip St. George Cooke III, whose divergent approaches to producing books would influence the unique offerings of the Vinegar Tom. Rittenhouse used frontier technology to produce Stagecoach Press editions and was a perfect mentor in the skills and nuances of letterpress printing. Phil Cooke, grandson of a colorful Civil War general of the same name, was publishing a series of western history booklets as the Press of the Territorian, by commercial offset, in Santa Fe.

Rittenhouse suggested that a small Kelsey hobby press, being portable and easy to secure parts for since the company was still in business, might be suitable for what Gregg wanted to do. He came up with a very old 5 × 8 Kelsey Excelsior, added a few parts, and sold it to Gregg at cost. With Rittenhouse's help, he secured type fonts and furniture and had the old ink rollers recast ("They looked like dried prunes").[28] Setting up the shop in his converted garage in Albuquerque, Gregg was ready to print books, a page at a time, as the curious and delightful Vinegar Tom Press.

The original Vinegar Tom was the "familiar," or companion, of a sixteenth-century English witch, eventually hanged for her vocation. Prowling through Reginald Scot's *Discoverie of Witchcraft*, Gregg came across an engraving with Vinegar Tom, a "curly-tailed greyhound type dog with horns," which he thought would make a great press mark. Not only did it become the name of the press, but Gregg also transposed it to Tom Vinegar, one of his handful of pen names.[29]

The business plan was to bring to market small hand-printed and hand-bound hardcover books cheaply—for $1.50 to $2.50 retail—quite a feat even in the late 1960s. It may be hard to imagine now, but Vinegar Tom was actually intended to make a profit, to be "something other than vanity publishing."[30] Fortunately for collectors, Vinegar Tom produced fifteen memorable titles before reality set in. Subject matter reflected Andy Gregg's enthusiasm for history, magic, and humor.

Proverbs for Today came out as Vinegar Tom's first real book in 1969, a forty-four-page hardcover edition of about 300. Johnny Carson read parts of it on *The Tonight Show* but failed to mention where to find the book.

Gregg found clever ways to make Vinegar Tom books inexpensive to produce—if the arduous hours of setting and breaking down type, hand feeding pages one side at a time, and hand binding each book were not included. He discovered that vinyl wallpaper made great cover material when cut and imprinted on the Kelsey, adhering well to binders' boards without additional glue. When a roll of a particular pattern ran out, he might cover the rest of the

VINEGAR TOM PRESS
Vinegar Tom as depicted in *Discoverie of Witchcraft*, originally published in 1584.

a tour of the pueblo, ending at a home where there are prayers and other rites.

Then come the *Shalako*, the agents of the rain gods, for this whole ritual is a plea for rain. They are grotesque figures nine feet tall, with flapping beaks and rolling eyes controlled by strings. Inside each figure is a man stepping nimbly and carefully to avoid falling.

Dances, blessings and prayers go on through the frigid night while Indians watch impassively and half-frozen visitors wander in and out of the houses.

These ceremonies last until dawn, but most of the palefaces have left by then. The cold drives them out, for the temperature is usually below freezing at this altitude of 6,400 feet. (Visitors are advised to dress *very* warmly.)

The ceremony continues for four more days, but few outsiders see these. They usually come only for the big night when the *Shalako* arrive.

Those who endured the discomfort will have seen an unforgettable ritual out of prehistoric America.

8

The *Shalako*, from an illustration in *Century* Magazine, February, 1883.

9

VINEGAR TOM PRESS

Text and illustration from *A New Mexico Christmas*, Vinegar Tom Press, 1969.

edition with a different pattern. His hand-printed pages served as repro proofs for offset versions when, and if, the first printing sold out.

Christmas Customs Along the Río Grande, a reset magazine article by novelist Richard Bradford, came off the press next in an edition of 400 copies and sold briskly in September 1969. Still having time to hit the same market before Christmas, Gregg himself wrote and illustrated *A New Mexico Christmas*, printed the first 1,000 copies on the Kelsey, bound them by hand, and rushed them over to local craft shops and bookstores. Then, to meet the demand, he had a second run of 1,000 produced offset, with a notation that it was a reproduction of the handmade first printing.

Vinegar Tom brought back short, colorful, historically significant writings that had long been out of print. *Here Comes Elfego!*, an autobiography by one of the West's more famous lawmen, Elfego Baca, first appeared as a pamphlet to promote Baca's run for district judge in 1924 and was reprised by Vinegar Tom in 1971. Three richly descriptive articles by historian and ethnographer Charles F. Lummis, written in the late nineteenth century, were published as

VINEGAR TOM PRESS
Harvey Girls' Recipes cover,
Vinegar Tom Press, 1971.

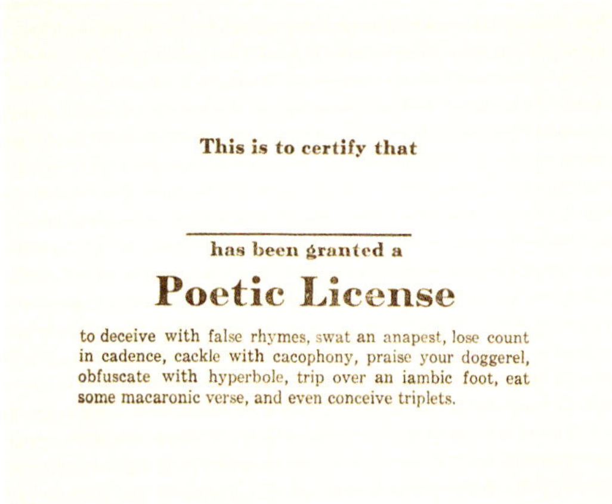

This is to certify that

has been granted a

Poetic License

to deceive with false rhymes, swat an anapest, lose count in cadence, cackle with cacophony, praise your doggerel, obfuscate with hyperbole, trip over an iambic foot, eat some macaronic verse, and even conceive triplets.

VINEGAR TOM PRESS
"Poetic License," Vinegar Tom Press, 1971.

The Southwestern Wonderland in an edition of 500 hardbound books. The first 100 copies or so have an eyebrow-raising error on the last page. Instead of "man or woman," they read "man *on* woman." The rest of the books were corrected by scratching out the right leg of the offending "n." *Harvey Girls' Recipes* came out in a Kelsey-printed, twenty-four page hardbound edition in 1971, at $1.50 retail, and was reprinted offset the following year, priced at a quarter less.[31]

In 1970 the Vinegar Tom reissued *Town Ordinances of Albuquerque, New Mexico 1863*. These twenty-five laws were intended to bring civility to a wild burgeoning town. "Making water under porches" might get you a $5 to $50 fine or five days in jail, and similar punishments awaited "street embarrassments" and "disorderly houses." Magic got its share of attention in *The Little Black Book of Spells: Magic for Power, Health and Love*, by Bill G. Douglas.

Finding markets was a serious endeavor for Vinegar Tom's publisher. Review copies went to newspaper columnists in the West, and simple folded catalogs announced new books as they were added to the list. In his home territory, Gregg hit the sidewalks with a basket of books, paying calls on book and gift shops. He offered the usual 40 percent trade discount but found consignment also useful. Stores would have to pay for books that were gone. They were, he admitted, a handy size for shoplifters.

Vinegar Tom books weren't always examples of meticulous presswork. "Some people bought them because they were cute and handmade. If a page was printed a little crooked, that was OK, because it showed that it was hand-done," Gregg said. "There might be an inky thumbprint on a page," another sign of Vinegar Tom authenticity.[32]

Scraps of leftover paper stock were turned into curious ephemera: A "Poetic License," allowed one "to deceive with false rhymes, obfuscate with hyperbole, and even conceive triplets," and an "Unofficial Travel Permit for the State of New Mexico" could be stuck on a car windshield.

"By 1972, what was supposed to be a moneymaking business seemed more like an obsession," Gregg recalled. After printing fifteen books, "a pretty good score" for three lively years, he sold the Kelsey press and rights to the Vinegar Tom Press name to Spencer Maxwell but kept his Tom Vinegar *nom de plume.* No further books were produced on the Kelsey. In 1991, Maxwell and Sally Armstrong published an annotated bibliographic checklist of Vinegar Tom Press books, an edition of 40 copies under the Maxwell Press imprint.

Just prior to his own private press adventure, Gregg wrote *New Mexico in the 19th Century: A Pictorial History*, published in 1968 by University of New Mexico Press and reprinted several times.[33] After his Vinegar Tom years, he wrote magazine articles, children's fiction, and a dozen plays. Andy Gregg died in Albuquerque in 2004. He is recalled as a serious historical writer and unusual humorist, as well as for making and selling books on a basis that would be hard to imitate now. "Even if I hadn't decided to quit, inflation would have stopped the press," he wrote for the Maxwell Press checklist. "Books sold for $1.50 then would probably be at least $5 today. And who would pay that much?"[34]

San Marcos Press

FOR PROPRIETOR ERNEST W. TEDLOCK, a longtime University of New Mexico English professor, the idea of producing new literary voices held enough intrigue to merit acquisition of an A. B. Dick 350 offset press in 1968. Thus the publishing project took form in the family room of his Albuquerque home, the press displacing a pool table along with a few other Tedlock interests. Until the early 1980s San Marcos Press turned out some thirty-seven titles, most of them soft-covered booklets of regional poetry and history.

Tedlock came to Albuquerque with his family in 1941, following a scholarly path that started at the University of Missouri and continued with graduate work at the universities of Chicago and Southern California. Two years later he started teaching at the University of New Mexico, a career that would span more than thirty years. Here he became a recognized authority on D. H. Lawrence, authoring four substantial books on the well-known British writer, along with additional works on John Steinbeck and Dylan Thomas.

Though he developed considerable experience in the publishing world, contributing to regional magazines in addition to his books, the fifty-eight-year-old professor's decision to become involved in private press work came as a surprise even to his own family. "I was mystified when he wanted to start printing," his son David recalled. "My father was not particularly mechanical and spent many days and evenings frustrated with press problems."[35]

Nevertheless, Tedlock claimed to be fascinated with the process and produced the first San Marcos publication in 1968. A reprint of a story he wrote and published in *New Mexico Quarterly* some years prior, *The Little Engine That Went Backwards* was a pamphlet billed as a "child's story for grownups" and featured black-and-white illustrations by Tedlock's wife Agnes.

Ernest and Agnes Tedlock, ca. 1965.

The first of three best-selling books by Marc Simmons, a young New Mexico historian, followed the inaugural publication and marked the beginning of Tedlock's many collaborations with University of New Mexico colleagues. *Two Southwesterners* (1968) is an account of the friendship between Charles F. Lummis and Amado Chaves, illustrated with late nineteenth-century Lummis photographs of Pueblo Indians and Penitentes. The second Simmons book, *Yesterday in Santa Fe*, appeared the following year, and the third, *The Fighting Settlers of Seboyeta*, came out in 1971.

The story of pioneering Spanish families, *The Fighting Settlers of Seboyeta* was the second title in the San Marcos *New Mexico*

SAN MARCOS PRESS
The Fighting Settlers of Seboyeta, San Marcos Press, 1971.

Heritage series. It was preceded by *No Fire for the Forge* (1971), a collection of bilingual student writings edited by Sabine Ulibarri, and followed in 1973 by *Abiquiú and Don Cacahuate*, a folk history of a northern New Mexico village by Gilberto Benito Córdova. The series, edited by Simmons, ambitiously aimed at promoting a better understanding of the state's varied cultures, but it ended after the release of the first few volumes.

By the summer of 1970, the Tedlocks and their press were newly established on a small ranch twenty miles south of Santa Fe, near the town of Cerrillos. The property, purchased several years earlier, had been the focus of weekend family efforts. The San Marcos name and press mark had been adapted from a nearby Pueblo ruin. Now the publishing firm occupied a one-room electricity-less cabin at the ranch, a factor that further challenged Tedlock's mechanical skills. The A. B. Dick machine was powered by a generator, and the lights were fueled by propane — even at its best a strain on the printer's trifocal-assisted eyes.[36]

Despite these handicaps the San Marcos Press issued a number of notable titles in the early Cerrillos years, among them *Ten Versions from Trilce* (1970), a collaborative translation of the work of Peruvian poet César Vallejo by British writers Charles Tomlinson and Henry Gifford, and in 1973 *Southwestern Spanish Proverbs*, a collection compiled by University of New Mexico professor Rubén Cobos.

The San Marcos Press was a family effort, with Tedlock as the printer and typesetter, Agnes the designer, illustrator, and binder, and son David in charge of marketing. Type was set on a VariTyper, the word processor of the predigital age, and offset printing plates were produced by local firms.

The softcover San Marcos books were utilitarian, put together with saddle clips and perfect bindings, but they reflected a certain enthusiasm for the craft of bookmaking. Papers were carefully chosen and easily expended in the pursuit of crisp printing. Tedlock would often go through hundreds of sheets in an attempt to resolve printing glitches.[37] Most of the books and broadsides were embellished with photographs and drawings. Typography, though far from stunning, showed thoughtful consideration.

Cover, *The Little Engine That Went Backwards*, San Marcos Press, 1968.

Perhaps, in part due to this sense of quality, San Marcos Press was awarded grant funding from the National Endowment for the Arts between 1975 and 1980. With the support of the endowment, the press published a lengthy anthology of contemporary Western fiction along with collections of work by young poets, including Colorado writer Marc Weber, Canadian Bert Almon, and New Mexico's Karen McKinnon, along with others. The anthology, titled *The Far Side of the Storm*, was edited by California writer Gary Elder and appeared in 1980.

In true private press fashion, Tedlock's publishing agenda was dictated by his heart rather than his pocketbook. He delighted in working with young writers and artists but was less inspired by the marketing end of the business. Slow-moving books piled up as orders trickled in, while the reprinting of brisk-selling publications took a low priority.[38] Annual losses were offset by Tedlock's continued teaching, though he had officially retired in 1973.

Sometime in the early 1980s the Tedlocks gave up the struggles of country living and returned to Albuquerque. Though the printing press had been left behind, the San Marcos Press continued to publish a few poetry pamphlets before closing its doors. Agnes died in 1984, Ernest in 1987, and with them the San Marcos Press.

Rini Templeton

TAOS ACTIVIST RINI TEMPLETON brought a powerful new voice to the relatively tame world of New Mexico small press publishing. She had all the passion, skill, and do-it-yourself mentality of a private publisher, although her work was anything but private. She dedicated her life to bringing about social change and her considerable talents to furthering the causes of her convictions. She never officially set up her own press and gave it a name, but she produced hundreds of broadsides, fliers, and pamphlets and taught others how to do the same. Her aim was to demystify printing production, to empower the disempowered with the ability to speak out in print. She produced pamphlets on pamphlet making and set up graphic arts workshops where she taught the process of silkscreening.

Something of a peripatetic illustrator, Templeton spent more than ten years of her life coming and going from the Taos area in the 1960s and 1970s. She traveled from Cuba to Mexico and from Central America to the southwestern United States, working on behalf of land reform, peasant organizations, prisoners' rights, and striking laborers, among other causes.

"Typically, she participated in an event—a march or picket line or rally—and made rough sketches on the spot, which she finished that same night and turned over unsigned the next day for immediate use in a flyer, poster, or banner."[39] She preferred pen and ink to capture the raw emotions of the moment but also used silkscreen, linoleum and woodblocks, and metal engraving techniques to produce strong black-and-white imagery. A one-woman production plant, she carried all the tools she would need to illustrate these journeys.

Her knowledge of the printing arts developed over a period of years, beginning in Chicago in the late 1940s. There at age thirteen she hand set the type for and bound a limited-edition collection of her own poetry titled *Chicagoverse*. The booklet was issued in 1949 under the family's private press imprint—the Water Tower Press. That same year she learned photography and built her own darkroom. These were not unusual accomplishments for Templeton, a child prodigy who took part in the NBC *Quiz Kid* program from 1947 to 1949, specializing in Shakespeare, opera, and baseball.[40] Later she edited both her high school and university newspapers and apprenticed with a Chicago illustrator and printer.

In Taos she found work as an art editor at the newspaper *El Crepúsculo* before leaving for a three-year stay in Cuba, where she worked in the Literacy Campaign and helped set up a Havana printmaking workshop.[41] By the mid-1960s she was once again living in the Taos area, practicing her own art while she continued to devote time to projects for social justice, including the Rio Arriba People's Clinic and the Agricultural Cooperative of Tierra Amarilla, as well as two liberal newspapers, *El Grito del Norte* and the *New Mexico Review*. She was a staff artist at the *Review*, where she became associated with John Nichols, later illustrating his popular 1974 novel *The Milagro Beanfield War*.

Rini Templeton, ca. 1972.

RINI TEMPLETON
Rini Templeton pen-and-ink drawing from protests of the 1960s and 1970s.

In 1973, in the aftermath of political upheaval in Chile, she produced perhaps her most lasting publication, a large-format portfolio of artwork and Pablo Neruda poetry, designed to raise funds for the people of that beleaguered country. *Homage to Neruda, A Folio from New Mexico for the Chilean Poet and His People* contains eight 12 × 19-inch poetry broadsides illustrated by Templeton and painter John DePuy, along with commentary by New Mexico author Stan Steiner. The portfolio carries no private press name, though it asks that donations be sent to *Prensa Crepuscular* in Pojoaque, New Mexico. Nevertheless, *Homage to Neruda* is distinctly the work of Rini Templeton, possibly produced on equipment that occupied her living room, much like any other piece of furniture.

One year after the portfolio appeared, in 1974, she moved to Mexico City, where she joined the *Taller de la Gráfica Popular* and went on creating artwork to bring about social change. She died there in 1986.

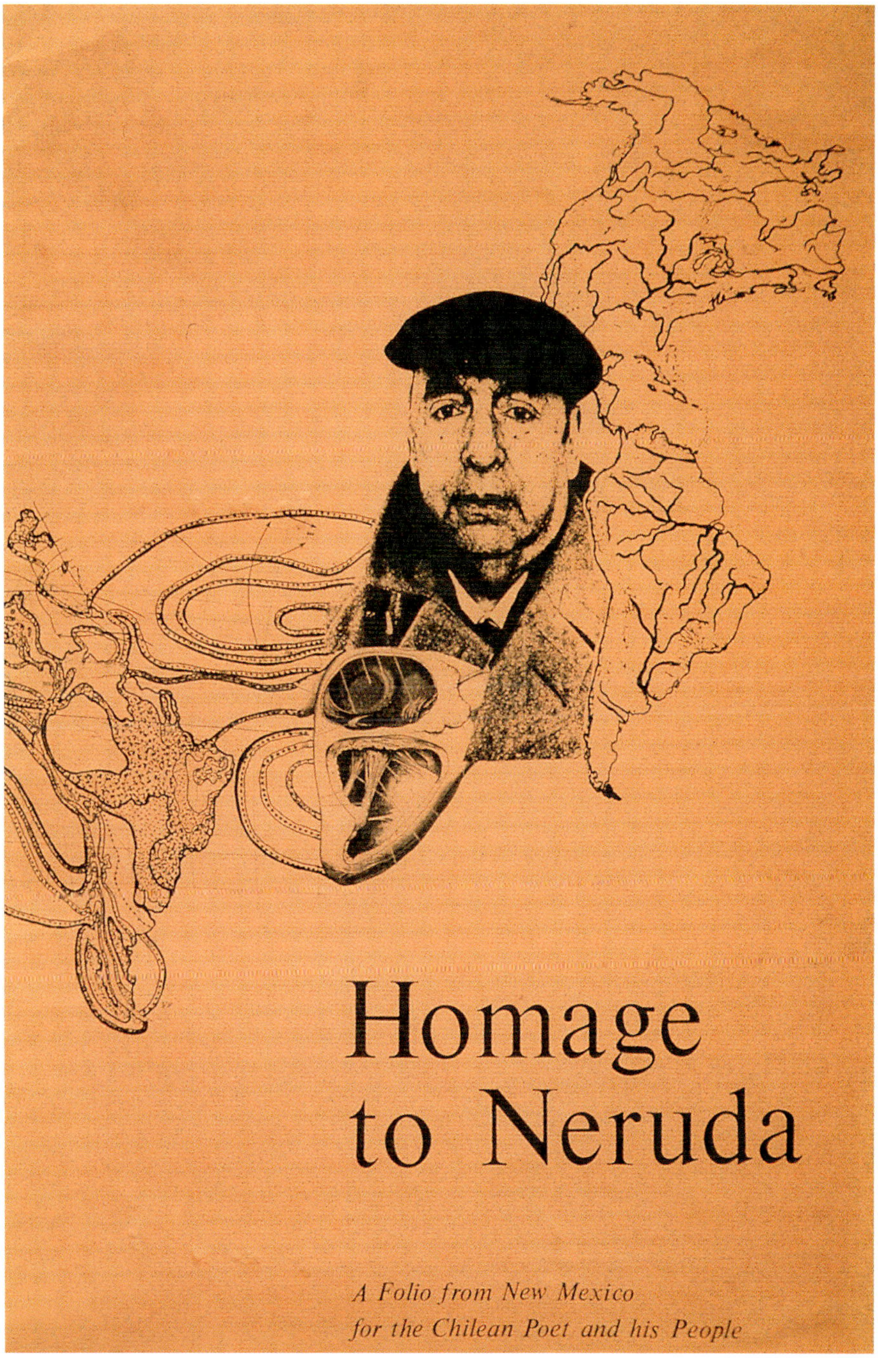

RINI TEMPLETON

Homage to Neruda, A Folio from New Mexico for the Chilean Poet and His People,
produced by Rini Templeton in 1973.

Jason Kellahin at an Albuquerque type exhibit, 1986. Photograph by Mark Holm.

Thistle Press

THE ESTABLISHMENT OF THISTLE PRESS in Santa Fe in 1973 marked Jason Kellahin's return to his first love — the world of letterpress printing. What had been a profession for Kellahin became a hobby, tended to in the hours away from his work as a prominent Santa Fe attorney.

He was an early initiate of the publishing world, starting out around 1919 as a paperboy and then a printer's devil at Roswell's weekly *Southwestern Dispatch*. Later he moved up at the newspaper, operating printing presses and a Linotype machine in the after school hours. He continued the work at the University of New Mexico Press during his student years in the early 1930s and, after graduating from the university, returned to printing as a livelihood throughout the lean Depression years. In time, he left back shop work for the editorial side of publishing, became a reporter, and eventually editor of the *Roswell Morning Dispatch*. Law school brought a departure from all that in 1949.[42]

Though Kellahin had established a successful law firm in Santa Fe by 1954, he never really lost his taste for the printing arts. With platen presses and a Linotype machine acquired locally, Kellahin set up a shop adjacent to his

A Lament On

Tsankawi Mesa

By PEGGY POND CHURCH

THISTLE PRESS
Santa Fé, New Mexico

Title page from the Thistle Press printing of
A Lament on Tsankawi Mesa, 1980.

home and, like hundreds of other hobbyists, printed for the sheer pleasure of it. He produced *La Gaceta*, a periodical issued by a group of western-history buffs, books of poetry for family and friends, an annual publication for his wife's sewing club, and tickets for church benefits. His single most important contribution to New Mexico literature is a limited-edition printing of *A Lament on Tsankawi Mesa*. The lengthy verse by celebrated New Mexico poet Peggy Pond Church was released in a small, unadorned pamphlet format in 1980 and was reputed to have sold out in one afternoon.[43]

Thistle Press continued to turn out good-quality ephemeral work through the late 1980s and was closed after Kellahin's death in 1997.

The Bobcat Press

In a period marked by uncommon private press ventures, the Bobcat Press was perhaps the most unconventional. Set up in Cedar Crest, New Mexico, in the early 1970s by artist Dick Hicks, it was more about the building of printing presses than the use of them.

Hicks discovered the Common press, an early eighteenth-century wood hand press, just as the hazards of sculpting with fiberglass began to threaten his health. "I found the press that Ben Franklin apprenticed on in Boston. I was fascinated with it," he said.[44] Inspired by the precision of the handcrafted Common press, Hicks acquired a reprint of one of the first manuals on printing techniques (originally published in England in 1683) and set out to replicate the press. He brought considerable experience to the task. Descendant of a long line of shipbuilders, Hicks had previously worked with wood: ten years of creating muzzle-loading rifles and another ten of industrial model and pattern

Dick Hicks at work on his Bobcat printing press, ca. 1978.

The Bobcat press

Made and sold by
Richard Hicks
Box 457 Cedar Crest, N. M. 87008
Telephone 1-505-281-3397

About the Press

The Bobcat Press is a fine handcrafted working replica of the Common Press used from the time of Johann Gutenberg until the early 1800's. The frame and the type-chest stand are made of selected Honduras mahogany. The fittings, including the press screw, are made of cast bronze. The finished appearance is that of a well cared for, but usable hand tool of our colonial period. This press can be used to print any number and variety of hand prints. It will need a few drops of oil on the irons and rounce bearings and some wax on the wood frame to keep printing happily for thousands of prints.

THE BOBCAT PRESS
Advertising flier produced on the Hicks press, 1975.

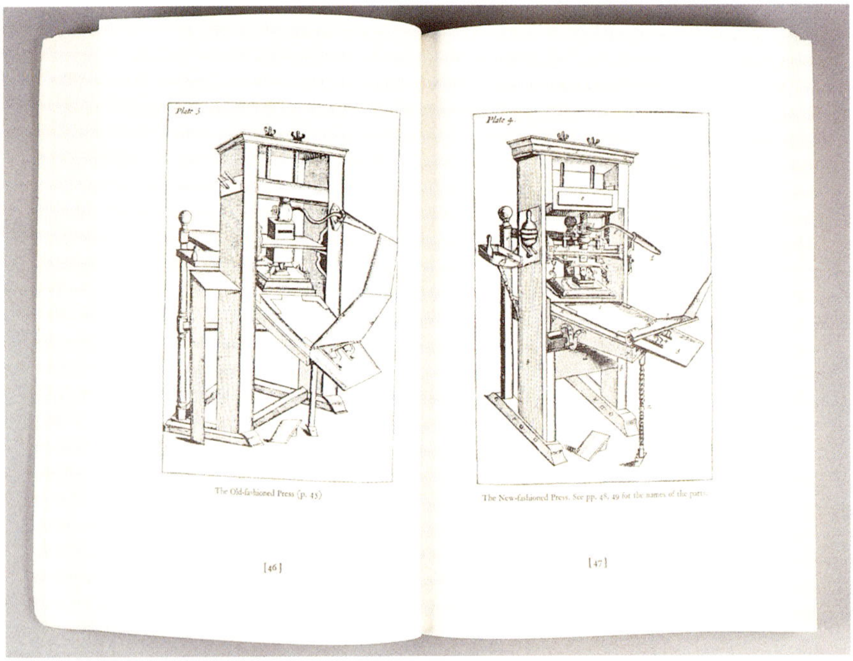

THE BOBCAT PRESS
Common press models from Joseph Moxon's *Mechanick Exercises on the Whole Art of Printing*, first published in 1683.

making. He also had a special interest in the printing arts and since childhood had owned a small Kelsey table model press, which he would continue to use at his Cedar Crest studio along with a Chandler & Price platen press.

The manual, Joseph Moxon's well-known *Mechanick Exercises on the Whole Art of Printing*, detailed the parts and operation of the Common press, information that Hicks dutifully followed. "The plans were very good," he commented, "and once I figured out the seventeenth-century language I began to make progress."[45]

In addition, he built his own foundry and again relied on Moxon to guide him through the casting of bronze fittings for the press. He made the frame of Honduras mahogany and the center screw from maple, which he turned on a large lathe. For nearly a year he worked pushing aside his sculpture projects and tackling one setback after another. The bronze pitted and was irregular in color. The plaster metal molds cracked and leaked, demolishing the mold and running molten bronze over the ground. Parts didn't fit and needed to be redesigned and patterned once again.[46] Progress was slow, but persistence paid off. In 1975, Hicks completed his first Bobcat printing press.

His advertising flier modestly claimed that the appearance of the press "is that of a well cared for, but usable hand tool of our colonial period." Indeed, the finished product was an example of superb craftsmanship. A later bench model sat on a handsome, eight-drawer mahogany type chest. For a little extra, printing aficionados could purchase one of Hicks's handmade ink blocks[47] with accompanying ink balls, hand tools used to apply ink before the advent of rollers.

Between 1975 and 1993 he made thirty Bobcat printing presses and sold them all, both in this country and abroad. His own model went to the Center for the Book at the Albuquerque Public Library. Though his clients put their presses to good use, Hicks himself found little time for such activity. Plans to produce a Bobcat Press book on how to build and print with a Common press were lost in a flurry of fliers, broadsides, advertising pamphlets, and other ephemeral material. Nearly ten years after completing his last press, Hicks still fantasized about reviving his Bobcat Press work. "I'd like to build one more press," he said, "so that I could print into eternity."[48]

Running Women Press

Collaged illustration from *Perspectives*, Running Women Press, 1986.

Chapter 5

Past Meets Present in the Age of Technology

1976–2005

By 1990 Santa Fe had become a cosmopolitan city with a broad spectrum of cultural offerings—opera, film production, chamber music festivals, Shakespeare in the Park, an expanded museum system, and more than two hundred galleries to serve a thriving art market. Los Alamos, the once-secret city of atomic research, had grown into an international scientific community along with Sandia National Laboratories in Albuquerque, attracting educated brainpower from around the globe.

In turn, New Mexico's ever-expanding population of artists began to reflect this worldliness in a wider range of creative endeavors, including crafts and performing arts. The same was true of the private press. After 1975 independent publishers settling in New Mexico, many of whom came with highly evolved printing skills and experience, began introducing a whole new level of sophistication both in the subject matter and artistry of the book.

Linnea Gentry had apprenticed at San Francisco's renowned Grabhorn Press, had helped found *Fine Print*, an international journal of the book arts, and had established a reputation as a successful letterpress printer by the time she moved her Amaranth Press to Santa Fe in 1980.[1] Another member of the Bay Area private press world, Clifford Burke, came to New Mexico in 1989 to become a partner in the Desert Rose Press. His impressive credentials included work in the job printing industry, ten-year proprietorship of the San Francisco–based Cranium Press, and an apprenticeship with Adrian Wilson, one of the West Coast's most respected designer/printers.[2]

Eleanor Caponigro worked in the publishing industry in the East but made her reputation as one of the country's most talented photographic book designers after she settled in New Mexico in the mid-1970s. Here she designed books and portfolios for New York publishers that featured the work of Laura Gilpin, Eliot Porter, Alfred Stieglitz, and Andy Warhol, among others. In 1989, her own Morris Press published *Meditations in Light* with photographs and text by her former husband Paul Caponigro.[3] Although the book was the only title produced by the Morris Press, Caponigro went on contributing to fine printing in New Mexico, establishing impeccable standards of typographic design.

In the early 1990s, book artist Kathy Kuehn brought her Salient Seedling Press to Albuquerque. Although her stay was brief (1992–1997), she influenced the small press community with her fresh approach to the handmade book and her mastery of the printing arts. During the late 1970s, as a University of Wisconsin student, she got her introduction to the book arts and went on to work with Walter Hamady at the Perishable Press in nearby Mount Horeb. She learned to make her own paper and developed her hand as a bookbinder. Later, in New York, her printing skills were finely honed at Pace Editions, where she worked collaboratively to produce the etchings and relief prints of contemporary artists. Here in New Mexico she taught workshops, worked on projects with the Tamarind Institute, a center for fine art lithography at the University of New Mexico, and published a few Salient Seedling Press titles.[4]

Along with this influx of skilled book artists came a whole new world of technology. Paula Hocks turned to the photocopier for reproduction of her collaged Running Women Press books, while Desert Rose and Weaselsleeves presses began combining traditional letterpress work with computer-generated text and digital imagery. The Vandercook proof press, a development of the twentieth century, replaced earlier platen and hand presses as the preferred piece of equipment for fine printing.

Subject matter exploded into a wider realm of topics, focusing on everything from medieval Latin hymns to women's liberation issues. Not everyone embraced the changes. In response to this departure from traditional New Mexico themes, a few revivalist efforts sprang up. In 1985, Clark Kimball reestablished the defunct Rydal Press as a publishing house for classic Southwest writings. After a forty-year hiatus, Willard Clark returned to his work as a woodcut artist in 1982, resurrected his Clark Studio imprint, and ten years later produced early recollections of his adopted home in a limited-edition volume titled *Recuerdos de Santa Fe*.

Blending the old with the new, in recent years New Mexico's private publishers have turned out exceptional examples of the handmade book. Though they remain few in numbers, they continue today to quietly affect the look, feel, and tone of New Mexico literature.

Tooth of Time Books

AMONG THIS NEW GENERATION of private publishers was a young Californian with an armload of poetry and a 1909 Rotary Neostyle Mimeograph machine. John Brandi brought his family and his small press publishing venture to an isolated Mora County, New Mexico, canyon in 1971. He settled into a log cabin he built by hand and continued printing poetry broadsides and booklets under the Nail Press imprint, which he had used in Monterey, California, with his partner Fred Marchman. Later, on his own, Brandi rechristened the press Tooth of Time Books, after a rock formation in the wilderness near his new home.

John Brandi with his Rotary Neostyle Mimeograph machine, Guadalupita, New Mexico, ca. 1978.

Like others, he had come out of a "longing for paradise, or a need to create some utopia in a world gone awry."[5] He found it in the mountain-ringed valleys where farmers still plowed their land by hand and built their homes of sun-baked mud-and-straw bricks.

Adapting to the local lifestyle, Brandi typeset his publications on a recycled 1915 Underwood typewriter and printed them on an outmoded mimeograph machine. He hand-colored his drypoint illustrations and bound the work with the aid of a treadle operated sewing machine. Sometimes he hired himself out as a laborer to pay for the work. Distribution, according to the fledgling publisher, was "by hand, foot, word of mouth, horseback, jet and transcendental magic."[6]

TOOTH OF TIME BOOKS
Brandi's first printing/publishing effort, *A Nothing Book*, an offset pamphlet featuring his poetry and illustrations, California, 1964.

Such dedication to the book had been nurtured since Brandi's Los Angeles childhood. Following family excursions into deserts and mountains, he was encouraged to draw his impressions or record them in writing and was then assisted in stapling the work into booklets. At age twelve he was given a small rotary printing press on which he produced neighborhood news and, long before most, realized that books are "magic entities not to be taken lightly."[7]

At San Fernando College (now California State University at Northridge), he further pursued his publishing interests, studying graphic arts and printing his own poetry. He collaborated on major literary productions, including *Interchange* (1964), an experimental Jack Hirschman poem presented in a boxed, architectural format and dedicated to John Cage, as well as *Kline Sky* (1965), an essay also by Hirschman which Brandi designed and printed using enlarged fragments reproduced from Franz Kline's paintings.

But it was a hermit of the Andes named Johnny Lovewisdom who provided the young poet with his greatest inspiration. While serving as a Peace Corps volunteer in the mid-1960s Brandi met Lovewisdom in Ecuador, where the forty-eight-year-old ex-Californian had fled after suffering partial paralysis from pesticide contamination. He was living in the Valley of Vilcabamba, which he claimed to be a radioactive-free area, quietly regaining his health as he tended a small garden, practiced yoga, and spent his afternoons hand cranking an antiquated mimeograph machine on which he printed his *Universal Life Newsletter*. These personal and philosophical offerings were done in editions of 300 and mailed out to friends and acquaintances around the world.

As their friendship solidified, Lovewisdom learned of Brandi's frustrations in attempting to publish his own writings and invited him to make use of his printing setup. "Don't wait for the world to move," he urged. "Move it yourself. Not in editions of three but in three hundred. As many pages as it takes! Use my treadle sewing machine. Bind the pages, make books."[8]

In return he asked only that Brandi donate paper and help him retrieve old crankcase oil which was collected by local bus drivers for Lovewisdom's use as a printing ink. Brandi took him up on the offer and soon found himself yoked with five-gallon cans of used oil as he struggled uphill on his visits to the hermit's hut. There Brandi's detailed letters to family and friends turned into prose poems, which were mailed out to literary publishers throughout the United States and eventually reprinted in magazines and newspapers.

Returning to California in 1968 with increased confidence in his writing skills, Brandi authored several books on his Latin American experience, all published by notable Bay Area small presses. The care and craftsmanship that went into creating these works further influenced his decision to take an active role in the production of his writings. It wasn't long before he had his own mimeograph machine, a five-dollar flea market find that became the cornerstone of Tooth of Time Books in New Mexico.

TOOTH OF TIME BOOKS
Dark Horses and Little Turtles, first Tooth of Time Books publication, 1974.

At the Mora County cabin Brandi began by publishing his own poetry, two volumes in 1973: *The San Francisco Lastday Homebound Hangover Highway Blues* and *A Partial Exploration of Palo Flechado Canyon*, both done under the Nail Press imprint. The following year he introduced Tooth of Time Books with the release of *Dark Horses and Little Turtles*, a poetry collection by Tucson ethnobotanist Richard Felger. The booklet was the first in an intended series of quarterly reviews dedicated to "exploration, meditation, and narration of astral and biographical hemispheres"[9] and was partially funded by the Coordinating Council of Literary Magazines in New York.

Through the 1970s he produced six Tooth of Time reviews, some printed on the mimeograph machine, sewn together on the treadle-operated stitcher, and funded through the fruits of Brandi's physical labor. Other editions, assisted by the Coordinating Council, were shipped out to local job shops for printing. The books were collaborative efforts. Like Lovewisdom, Brandi urged inquiring authors to join him in New Mexico, to design, type, bind, or help in whatever way possible to produce their books on his equipment. Though this

Brandi hand-colored illustration from *Only the Ashes, 1981.*

practice eliminated some, it drew what he considered the right kind of people for his publishing interests — interdisciplinary artists who combined their writing with visual arts and technology. The initial work was crude but showed a concern for aesthetics with artwork in the form of calligraphy, drawings, and hand coloring.

In 1981, when he received a major grant through the National Endowment for the Arts (NEA) Assistance to Small Presses Program, Brandi's little log cabin publishing house changed drastically. He moved out of the isolated canyon into La Canova, a somewhat more populated northern New Mexico village. Tooth of Time editions, in a uniform 6 × 9-inch format, were all sent off to the West Coast Print Center in Berkeley to be printed and bound and editions jumped from 200 copies to at least 750. One exception was a handsome book of haiku translated by Steve Sanfield. *Only the Ashes* (1981) was printed letterpress by Linnea Gentry at the Amaranth Press and featured hand-colored Brandi illustrations.

With poetry still the emphasis, the Tooth of Time publisher sought to use his newfound resources to provide a forum for unknown Southwest writers. "I wanted to give them the opportunity to get their work out into the world so that they could be discovered by larger publishers. I couldn't wait for New York to catch wind of these people," he said.[10] He looked for poets who brought regionalism out of provincialism and into a universal setting.

ON MOUNTAINS' BREATH

Poetry & Drawings
by Harold Littlebird

TOOTH OF TIME BOOKS

On Mountains' Breath by Harold Littlebird, 1982 Tooth of Time edition.

Through the early 1980s Brandi published, among others, the poetry of Nanao Sakaki, a Japanese wanderer living in a school bus in the Taos mountains; Pueblo poet Harold Littlebird; Luci Tapahonso, a Navajo writer from Shiprock, New Mexico; and Arthur Sze, a rising star on the national poetry scene.

His fine eye for literature earned Tooth of Time Books a national reputation, but it came at a price. NEA required Brandi to establish a board which would oversee his publishing activities. Although he selected respected and sympathetic writers as members, the new arrangement brought an end to his autonomy. By 1987 the NEA influence on his annual list of titles created an impasse. Brandi's plan to produce Bengali poets, Nicaraguan women poets, prison writings, and an anthology of children's verse was met with resistance by the federal agency, which had every intention of funding Tooth of Time but requested a revision in the proposed program. "Right then I knew Tooth of Time was done," Brandi said. "It was no longer my press; it was NEA's."[11]

Although Brandi tried to turn down the grant and hang on to his agenda, he ended up scrapping his plans in favor of books that might expediently fulfill his obligation to the endowment. But his private press venture was over, along with the excitement of discovery. He suspended Tooth of Time work for nearly twelve years, reviving the imprint in 2000 with his haiku journey through northern Vietnam titled *Stone Garden*. His editions number fewer in copies now, reflect a more personal and handcrafted nature, and carry no government subsidy. "I ended up coming full circle," Brandi concluded, "back to an uncompromised position."[12]

Running Women Press

NOT LONG AFTER John Brandi began his work in New Mexico, artist Paula Hocks introduced her Running Women Press in Santa Fe. She arrived in the mid-1970s, after studying art and working as a sculptress in both Colorado and California.

A forerunner of her book work, Hocks's sculptures often made use of familiar three-dimensional objects modified, re-created from unusual materials, or placed in unfamiliar settings, as a means of startling the viewer into a new way of seeing.[13] They were shown in major American cities, as well as in Europe and England.

In Santa Fe she soon discovered the handmade book, a convenient vehicle for her broad range of artistic interests, including poetry, architecture, and photography, in addition to painting and sculpture. The medium would engage her talents for the next thirty years and lead to some of the most unusual work in New Mexico private press history.

Her introduction to book work came through an association with Santa Fe publisher William Gannon and his wife Virginia, a skilled hand bookbinder. Already a confessed book lover, Hocks was influenced by the Gannons' dedication to producing quality reprints of classic Southwest literature and began to put her own work into book form. These initial attempts were small photographic studies of her sculpted clay figures. Though somewhat crude at first, they were enough to capture her enthusiasm for the bookmaking process.

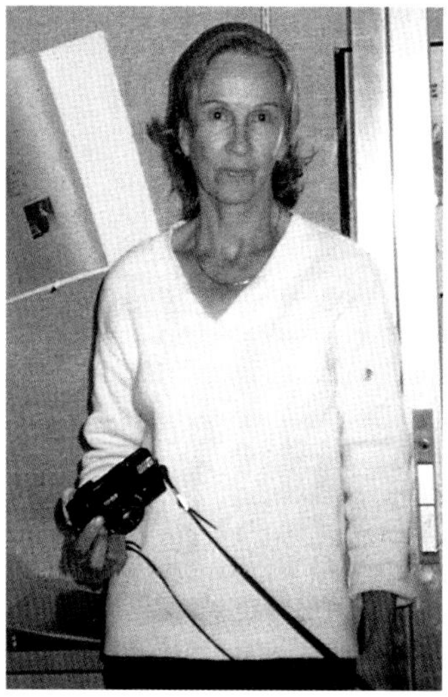

Paula Hocks, 1984. Photograph by Priscilla Spitler.

It was the opportunity to control both form and content that excited her. "I was delighted by the idea of making a book that would be an artwork on its own, and by the sculptural aspects of putting it together. The material for the work would be beautifully presented, the paper and the bindings as much a part of it as the artwork. It seemed to me my horizon was almost limitless."[14]

Before long she began to shape her first major publications, blending her own collage work, prose, and poetry to produce a three-book series titled *Heads and Bodies*. A study of the human face and figure in various emotional settings, the *Heads and Bodies* series was done between 1978 and 1980 and set the pace for future Running Women Press books. All were professionally bound by Virginia Gannon (now Virginia Westray) and represented for Hocks the making of a miniature gallery—"one to hold in the hand and carry along at lunch time."[15] Each page was a fresh canvas on which she applied her imagination.

Like her sculpture, Hocks's books are full of visual surprises, startling the reader with uncommon relationships of elements. "I created hidden treasures in a cohesive subject matter," she explained.[16] Unlike many artists who have tried their hand at making books, Hocks incorporated a healthy respect for traditional private press standards in her own creative efforts. She established herself as Running Women Press, a name inspired by the work of nineteenth-century photographer Eadweard Muybridge. Her publications adhered to a familiar codex format and usually appeared in small, slightly varied editions, but any further resemblance to classic design ended there.

Without access to printing equipment and with no desire to master hand printing techniques, she turned instead to the Xerox machine, or what she liked to call "electrostatic printing." As a result, her books exude a spontaneity seldom found in traditional letterpress work. Images tumble over and after one another in a kaleidoscope of pages. Text, produced by Hocks or freely quoted from other sources, was handwritten, typed, or clipped from printed material and formed a close bond with her artwork, which appeared at angles, in layers, and from collages. Even omissions and corrections became part of the finished work.

Printing was done on an array of papers. Though limited to the use of a stock conducive to the photo duplicating process, Hocks's work often surprised the reader with a blank sheet of sumptuous handmade paper or colored tissue interleaved among a book's more utilitarian text pages.

Her bindings varied. Some were done in conventional materials, such as leather, book cloth, or marbled papers, while other more playful copies are embellished with inset mirrors, gold foils, Mylar, and Plexiglas. Hardcover editions were generally executed by skilled artisans. Though untrained, Hocks used her ingenuity to create fanciful soft covers for her chapbooks and had some spiral bound by commercial firms.

Before her death in 2003 Hocks produced more than thirty New Mexico editions with content built on the classics, surrealism, and dadaism. They feature her own writing, photography, and collaged imagery all loosely organized around a particular theme or story line. As philosophical as they are poetic and visual, they represent a journey through the mind of their maker.

With a grant from the National Endowment for the Arts, in 1979 she produced *Etruscan Lunches* as a sequel to her *Heads and Bodies* series. That same year she met Santa Fe bookbinder Priscilla Spitler, an association that would lead to a long and fruitful collaboration.

Hocks's ardent interest in architecture became a theme running throughout Running Women Press works. *Columns of Santa Fe*, a 1982 chapbook, was inspired by her discovery of limestone Ionic columns that once graced New Mexico's State Capitol building. *Perspectives*, done in 1986, was drawn from the seventeenth-century treatise of draftsman Jan Vrederman de Vries. It creates a kind of psychology of space with collages overlaying images of de Vries engravings.

Hocks returned to the subject again in the late 1980s with a series of works focusing on Barcelona. Beginning with *A la Ciutat de Barcelona* (1986), the collection celebrates the architectural marvels of the Spanish city.

Like other Running Women Press imprints, the Barcelona books were a result of Hocks's travels abroad and her love affair with the cities she visited. After a season in London in 1983 and 1984, she produced *The English Book*, recalling her experiences in collaged fragments of everything British. An open umbrella fans out across the cover of the book, which originally came packaged in a rain bonnet.

Other Running Women Press books sprang entirely from the artist's agile imagination. *Ariadne's Thread and the Language of the Minotaur* (1982) is a retelling of the Greek myth based on conversations between Ariadne and the monster and presents a reversal of roles. "In this later, less-known version of the Ariadne legend the thread is used by Ariadne herself, Theseus being away on his endless errand," she states in the author's note. Alone, Ariadne makes her way through the labyrinth. Hocks considered this her best book. She produced 20 signed and numbered copies, one handsomely bound by Spitler in leather and painted Plexiglas.

Nuns on Horseback (1984) is another product of the artist's storytelling talents. It recounts the escape of nuns from a small convent near the city of Sarajevo and their subsequent difficulties in dealing with freedom. Somewhat autobiographical, the story hails back to Hocks's brief stay in a convent in northern California. On the advice of Trappist monk Thomas Merton, a poet, spiritual writer, and longtime Hocks friend, she went to find solace during an emotionally trying period of her life but left the convent after two months. *Nuns on Horseback* is what Hocks called "a neglected chapter in the history of women."[17]

Her most ambitious work, however, appeared toward the end of her career, a grand finale of art, literature, and music. *The Cry from Bomarzo: A Study of*

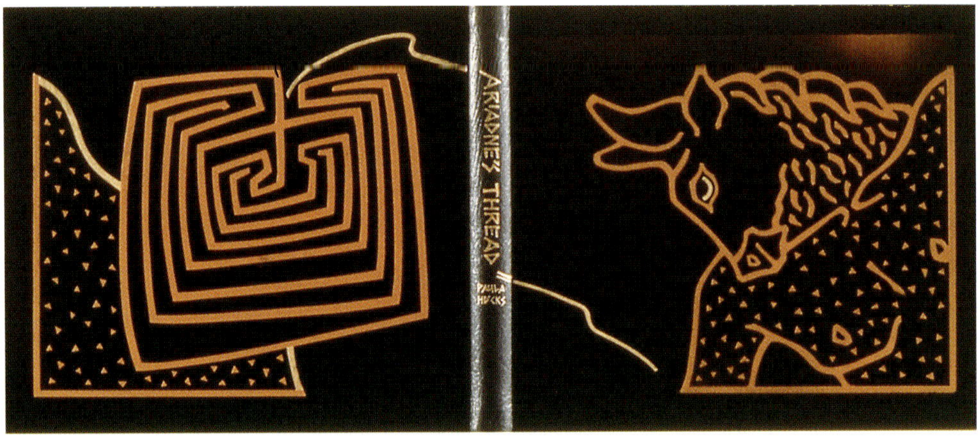

Running Women Press

Painted Plexiglas binding created in 1989 by Priscilla Spitler for *Ariadne's Thread and the Language of the Minotaur*, Running Women Press, 1982.

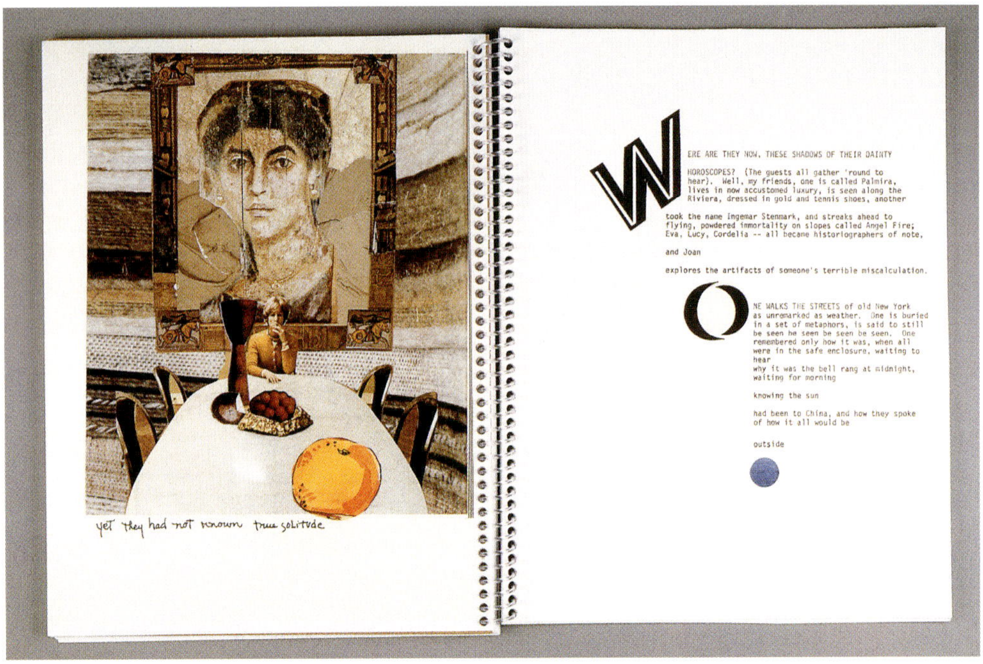

Running Women Press

Nuns on Horseback, Paula Hocks collaged illustration, 1984.

Running Women Press

The Cry from Bomarzo, cover illustration, Running Women Press, 2001.

Language (2001) is Hocks's homage to communications, a subject that runs throughout her Running Women Press imprints. It was inspired by her interest in a little-known sixteenth-century garden near Viterbo, Italy. Intrigued by the monstrous stone sculptures that haunt the garden, she began to search for clues to unlock the secrets of the gargoyle-like creatures. In the silence of their contorted forms she found a longing to be heard and understood, a desire she associates with all art forms. *The Cry from Bomarzo* blends historic and contemporary photos with Hocks's own essays and the commentary of other artists who have speculated on the mysteries of the ancient garden. Though she produced two more autobiographical works before her career ended, none rivaled her ten-year dedication to the production of *The Cry from Bomarzo.*

Amaranth Press

ALONG WITH OTHER small press publishers of the period, Linnea Gentry came to New Mexico with a strong background in the book arts. In San Francisco, where she had established her Amaranth Press in the mid-1970s, she was a respected member of the fine printing community. She was a book world "blue blood," the niece of Helen Gentry, one of the seventy most influential women in publishing, according to a 1987 Women's National Book Association Award citation.[18] Her uncle Bruce Gentry was a widely recognized book designer and printer and a second uncle, David Greenhood, a notable poet, novelist, and one-time editor at New York's Holiday House.

Linnea Gentry at the Amaranth Press, Santa Fe, 1982. Photograph by Richard Scholnik.

She launched her own book career in 1970 in the Children's Book Division of the EP Dutton firm in New York, working as an assistant to the art director before finding her way to San Francisco in 1973. There she followed in the footsteps of her accomplished aunt.

Persistence paid off for both Gentrys. With newfound enthusiasm for the art of the book, Helen

Gentry set out in 1925 to find work with the Grabhorn Press, one of San Francisco's most reputable fine printing firms. Despite Edwin Grabhorn's discouragement and warnings that printing would "spoil her hands," she returned until she was hired to sort used type back into cases.[19] By 1929 she opened her own shop at the corner of Commercial and Montgomery streets in San Francisco.

Nearly fifty years later, the younger Gentry had a similar experience. With an aim to set up her own fine printing business and a need to gain experience, she too came knocking at the Grabhorn doors. By this time the press was in the hands of former Grabhorn partner Andrew Hoyem and was soon to be renamed Arion Press. But the policy on women printers had not changed.

"It took a while to convince Andrew to take me on as an apprentice," Gentry said.[20] Eventually she became a typesetter for Hoyem and was encouraged to try her hand at bookbinding. Her determined interest in letterpress printing, however, was not to be redirected. In spare moments she learned to operate the machines under the guidance of Hoyem's printers. By 1976 she had her own Amaranth Press, an operation that fell somewhere between a private and commercial business.

Along with her partner Will Powers, Gentry produced finely printed work for a discriminating clientele. Among the clients were Crown Point Press, one of the most influential etching workshops in the country; chef Alice Waters, founder of Berkeley's Chez Panisse Restaurant; and established Bay Area book organizations, including the Book Club of California, the state's oldest and largest; and the Roxburghe Club of San Francisco.

In the mid-1970s, she helped found *Fine Print*, a review for the arts of the book. This widely recognized magazine was edited and published through the 1980s by former librarian and rare-book enthusiast Sandra Kirshenbaum. Gentry took over as production manager, contributed a column called "On Type," and printed the journal at the Amaranth Press.

Over time she became a well-known figure in the Bay Area book community. Her own work was exhibited at the San Francisco Public Library. She was inducted into the Roxburghe Club, a men's organization until Gentry and Helen Lee of the Mackenzie-Harris Type Foundry joined in 1979. In 1978 she spearheaded a nationwide gathering of book artists, dubbed a "Wayzgoose"

Amaranth Press
Title page from *New Mexico Santos*, printed at the Amaranth Press in 1983.

Amaranth Press
"San Isidro," Gustave Baumann woodcut print from *New Mexico Santos*, a 1983 Amaranth Press printing.

after a medieval printers' celebration. The conference included lectures, panel discussions, and social events that brought the congenial group together for the first time.

Despite her West Coast success, by 1980 Gentry had relocated Amaranth in Santa Fe. It was a city she had grown familiar with after years of family visits. Throughout the 1940s and 1950s her aunt Helen, along with uncles Bruce and David, were part-time residents of Santa Fe and settled there after 1965. The younger Gentry's move also was motivated by her marriage to Courtney Sheehan, an accomplished restoration bookbinder who had set up shop in Santa Fe and whom Gentry met on one of her trips to the area.

She installed her Vandercook and Colt's Armory platen presses in the restored quarters of a once-popular Canyon Road nightspot called Claude's Bar. There she continued on a course she had established for herself in California. She hired St. John's College student Richard Scholnick as a helper.

Together the two produced finely printed commission work, much of it with a Southwest flavor. They printed for the Symposium Press in Los Angeles, the Navajo Community College (now Diné College) in Tsaile, Arizona, and for Portfolio Editions in Oklahoma City, in addition to printed books, broadsides, and portfolios for Santa Fe artists and writers.

Notable among these works is *New Mexico Santos*, a suite of previously unpublished woodblock prints by Gustave Baumann. The portfolio of eight multicolored images was published in 1983 by the artist's daughter, Ann Baumann. Though five of the woodblocks used to print the series were left unfinished at the time of the artist's 1971 death, they were completed for the folio by Willard Clark. Gentry herself did the ink making to match the artist's distinctive palette.

One ongoing job, started in San Francisco and continued in Santa Fe, involved design and text printing for an ambitious project planned by the Classic Gravure Corporation of Santa Fe. Using contemporary photogravure prints made from original intaglio copper plates, the firm set out to reproduce *The North American Indian*, written, illustrated, and published in the nineteenth century by well-known photographer Edward Curtis. Though Classic Gravure planned to do a four-volume series, work on the mammoth undertaking came to a halt in the early 1980s with the completion of only two volumes.

Aside from her commission work, Gentry published one Amaranth book during her New Mexico years. A masterful example of fine bookmaking, *Cantus Sanctus* (1981) celebrates sacred verse with a presentation of six medieval hymns. Each appears in the original Latin, along with English translations dating from the sixteenth to the twentieth century. For Gentry, a student of history and classics, the book represented a labor of love. She lavished the production with handmade papers from the Twin Rocker mill in Indiana and hand-colored decorative initials by California calligrapher Mark Livingston. A deluxe, full-vellum binding was executed by Sheehan on 10 copies, and the remainder of the 130-book edition was bound in a combination of vellum spines and printed papers.

Less than two years later Gentry closed the Amaranth Press, thus ending abruptly her fine printing career. The struggle of keeping a small press alive in a failing economy coupled with the responsibilities of a growing family sent

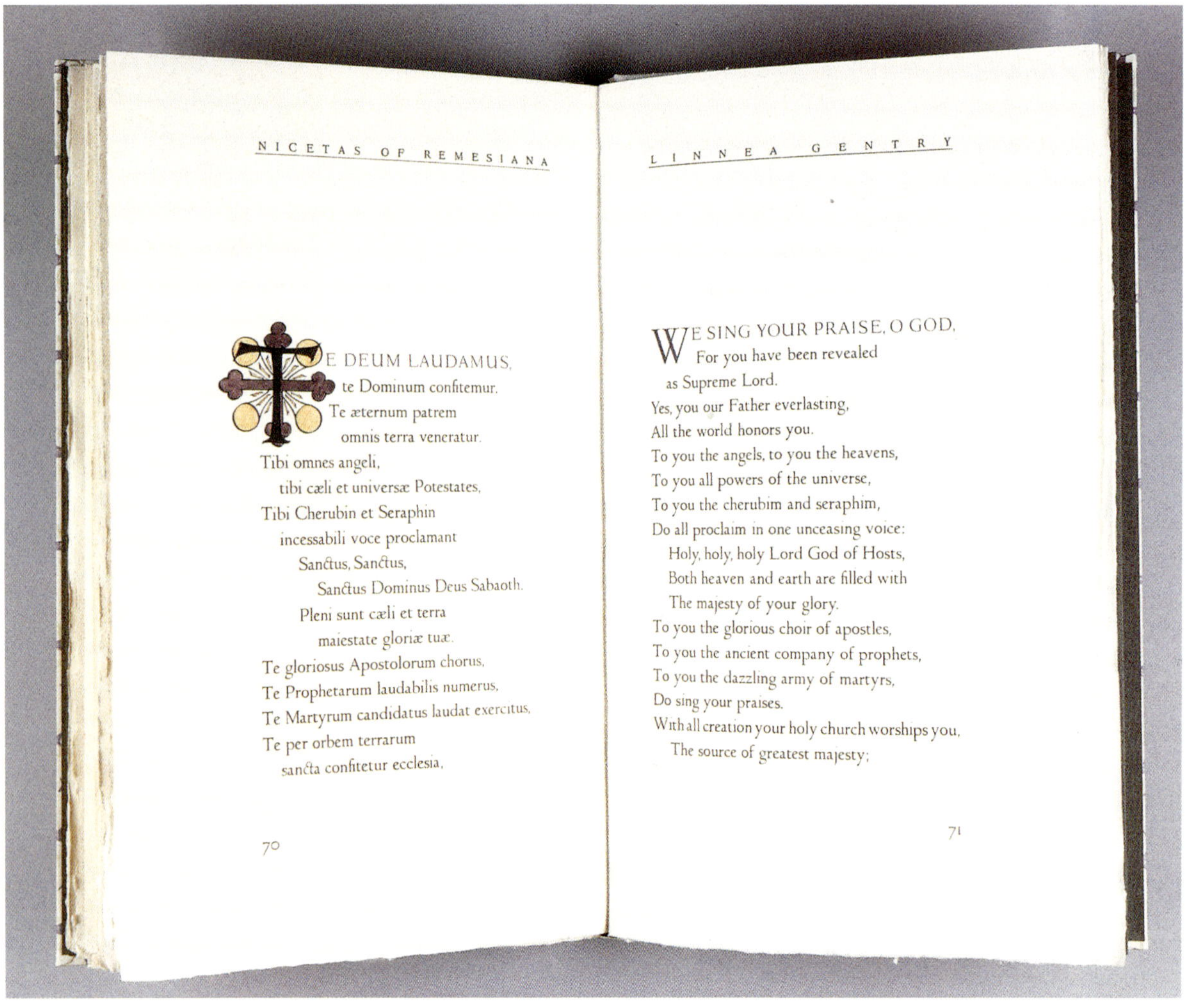

Amaranth Press

Cantus Sanctus text pages with decorative initials by Mark Livingston, Amaranth Press, 1981.

Cantus Sanctus, Amaranth Press, 1981.

her back to the world of commercial publishing. In 1983 she took a position as book designer at the University of Arizona Press.

Press of the Palace of the Governors
from the personal recollections of author Pamela S. Smith

WHILE MANY NEWLY ESTABLISHED small publishing houses of the period departed from regionalism to introduce a broader spectrum of subject matter, some, in response to a rapidly changing cultural climate, chose to focus on preserving the best of New Mexico's literary past. For the Press of the Palace of the Governors, a forerunner in this literary revivalism, such a traditional approach is a mission rather than a choice.

Founded in the late 1960s as a project of the Museum of New Mexico, this living history exhibition is on the courtyard of Santa Fe's Palace of the Governors, the oldest public building in the United States. Now under the direction of Colorado book artist Tom Leech,[21] the press hosts thousands of visitors annually at the same time that it produces award-winning limited-edition books.

Tom Leech at the Press of the Palace of the Governors, 2005. Photograph by Jim Howard.

It all began with a gift of the J. L. Hollenbeck family of Albuquerque. In 1969, Elvira Constant Hollenbeck, daughter of Estancia, New Mexico, newspaper publisher Jacob Constant, offered the museum equipment from her father's long-padlocked *Estancia News Herald* printing plant. Established in the early 1900s, the newspaper flourished as the little town of Estancia grew in the wake of the railroad but closed in the early 1940s when the boom was over and a war was in progress.

Fired by the enthusiasm of Peter Wells, an exhibits preparator in the history division, and Richard Polese of the Museum of New Mexico Press, museum administrators accepted the gift and began plans for a working exhibition. Wells was placed in charge of the new operation. Though he had no previous experience with letterpress printing, he had an innate sense of the mechanical. He was an accomplished blacksmith, understood the basic principles

Inside the Press of the Palace of the Governors, 1994.

of metal tools and equipment, and perhaps inherited some of his letterpress skills from a grandfather and great-grandfather, who both worked as pressmen.[22]

With the help of volunteers, he opened the exhibit to the public in 1970 and began printing a few ephemeral pieces — replica "wanted" posters along with poetry and prose quotations. Much of his time was spent restoring the machinery that had sat idle in Estancia for nearly thirty years. Work on the presses, along with the massive task of organizing thousands of type pieces and spacing material, kept Wells busy until he left the Museum of New Mexico less than a year after the printing equipment had been installed.[23]

I arrived two years later to find an exhibit rarely opened since Wells's departure. A refugee of the urban Midwest, I came to New Mexico, like many others, seeking the freedom of open spaces and a more relaxed lifestyle. With me I brought skills as a writer and a desire to work with my hands. I had studied journalism, written art and architecture feature articles in Chicago for the University of Illinois Public Information Office, and had done a fair amount of typographic design. In the saturated Santa Fe job market, I managed to find work in production at a tabloid shopper called the *Santa Fe News* — not exactly the kind of hand work I had in mind. I found offset paste-up a fussy business in which snippets and slivers of paper bearing type lines were constantly escaping me, clinging to my sweater sleeves and falling to the floor.

A tip from a fellow printing enthusiast came just in time. I was looking for a letterpress apprenticeship in which I might set metal type and operate hand presses. Unfortunately, I was looking in the wrong historic period. Though unions fought the changes, most printing firms had long ago moved into the realm of photographic type and offset printing. When I was told about the museum exhibit and the need for a printer, I applied immediately, signed on as a volunteer, and three months later was hired to direct the living history exhibition on a part-time basis. Like Wells, I spent a good deal of my time sorting and cleaning hundreds of metal type fonts, many stored in paper bags and boxes that split apart and carpeted the floor with their metal contents.

One of the Estancia platen presses and a small Colt's Armory press that had once belonged to Jack Rittenhouse were already in operation when I started out, and Wells was finishing restoration on a prized Washington hand press that had come to the museum from Hatch, New Mexico, in 1971.[24] Charged with being somewhat self-sufficient, I enthusiastically put the presses to use, creating greeting and postal cards to sell to museum visitors, along with replicas of old-time newspapers. I produced menus, invitations, and exhibit labels for various museum divisions and taught children's printing classes through the Museum School.

Pamela Smith at the Press of the Palace of the Governors, 1989. Photograph by Kitty Leaken.

A corps of volunteers headed by amateur printers Cecil Carnes and his son John proved invaluable in making additional press repairs, cleaning type cases, and building storage units. In time, the project became a permanent exhibition of the Museum of New Mexico History Division. My job evolved into a full-time position with the regal sounding title of "Palace Printer." Additional employees were funded by the Comprehensive Employment Training Act (CETA).

Although I began with little background in the arts of the book, I augmented on-the-job experience with occasional trips to workshops and fine printing conferences.

F OR ALL TRUE *Southwestern bibliophiles, the name Lawrence Clark Powell needs no introduction. As a distinguished librarian, educator, author, and lecturer, he has in the course of a career spanning more than*

PRESS OF THE PALACE OF THE GOVERNORS
Willard Clark woodcut in *My New Mexico Literary Friends*, Press of the Palace of the Governors, 1986.

As my skills developed so did my interest in printing high-quality limited-edition books. In 1976 the shop introduced the first in a succession of finely printed works. *Spirals. Five Songs of the Mountain Trail*, a poem in five parts by Santa Fe writer Leslie Bottorff, was a cooperative effort. Bottorff recruited students for a letterpress printing class which I taught, focusing on the production of her book as a learning experience. Five students hand set the type and printed the 150-book edition illustrated with Bottorff's woodcuts. It was bound by Santa Fe hand bookbinder Mina Balleydier (now Mina Yamashita).

After Kirk Hughey, an accomplished painter and draftsman, joined the staff in 1980, the press published *The Sena Family: Blacksmiths of Santa Fe* (1981) by Marc Simmons and a portfolio titled *New Mexico Wildflowers* (1982). A meticulous artist and craftsman, Hughey created a number of linoleum block illustrations for both publications. The wildflower portfolio alone required sixty-one blocks for the printing of fourteen four-color images and a five-color title print. Binding of the portfolio box and accompanying text pamphlet was done

Press of the Palace of the Governors

New Mexico Wildflowers, Press of the Palace of the Governors, 1982.

by Priscilla Spitler, a graduate of the London College of Printing who had joined the staff shortly before Hughey left in 1982.[25]

Spitler, all six feet of her, towered close beneath the low-lying *vigas* of the print shop's traditional ceiling. In one small corner she managed to set up an entire workshop where she bound Press of the Palace editions — *New Mexico Wildflowers*, as well as *Tales of the Mountain Men* (1984) compiled by Barton Barbour and illustrated by Santa Fe artist Andrew Burns, and a lecture by Southwest bibliographer Lawrence Clark Powell titled *My New Mexico Literary Friends* (1986).

While the work of publishing went on, the shop continued to develop as a printing history exhibition and hosted a steady stream of museum visitors, including many who recalled their printing experiences. It became a center for revival and pursuit of traditional book arts and sponsored an Annual Book Arts Festival from 1980 through 1984 to inspire interest in book work and literature. In turn, the shop's reputation as a center of fine printing attracted more talented employees — hand binders Diana Bynum, Patrick Alvarez, Rosalia Galassi, Bill Sneeburger, and Gordon Fluke; cartoonist Sarah Laughlin, who created whimsical drawings for a 1987 Press of the Palace production titled *Broncho* [*sic*] *vs Bicycle*, and typographic designer Judy Herzl.[26]

Like most book productions, Press of the Palace editions are collaborative efforts, drawing upon the skills of poets and authors, illustrators, editors, and bookbinders, among others. Along with input from print shop staff, I selected manuscripts produced during my tenure at the museum, as well as designed and printed each of the books. Text was most often set in Monotype by typographers in various parts of the country, then printed on the shop's hand- and foot-operated presses. Later an automated inking Vandercook proof press was put into operation.

In keeping with the Press of the Palace mission to preserve New Mexico literary history, these titles continued to highlight area writers and publishers: *Bulletin in Bold Characters* (1990), the story of the Seton Village Press; *The Journal of José Salaíces, 1789–1818*, the diary of a Spanish colonial translated and annotated by Museum of New Mexico curator Diana DeSantis (1998); and Saul Cohen's *Southwest Writer Harvey Fergusson* (2001).

Perhaps the most ambitious undertaking during my years at the Press of the Palace was a portfolio that strayed from this literary focus. *New World Saints*,

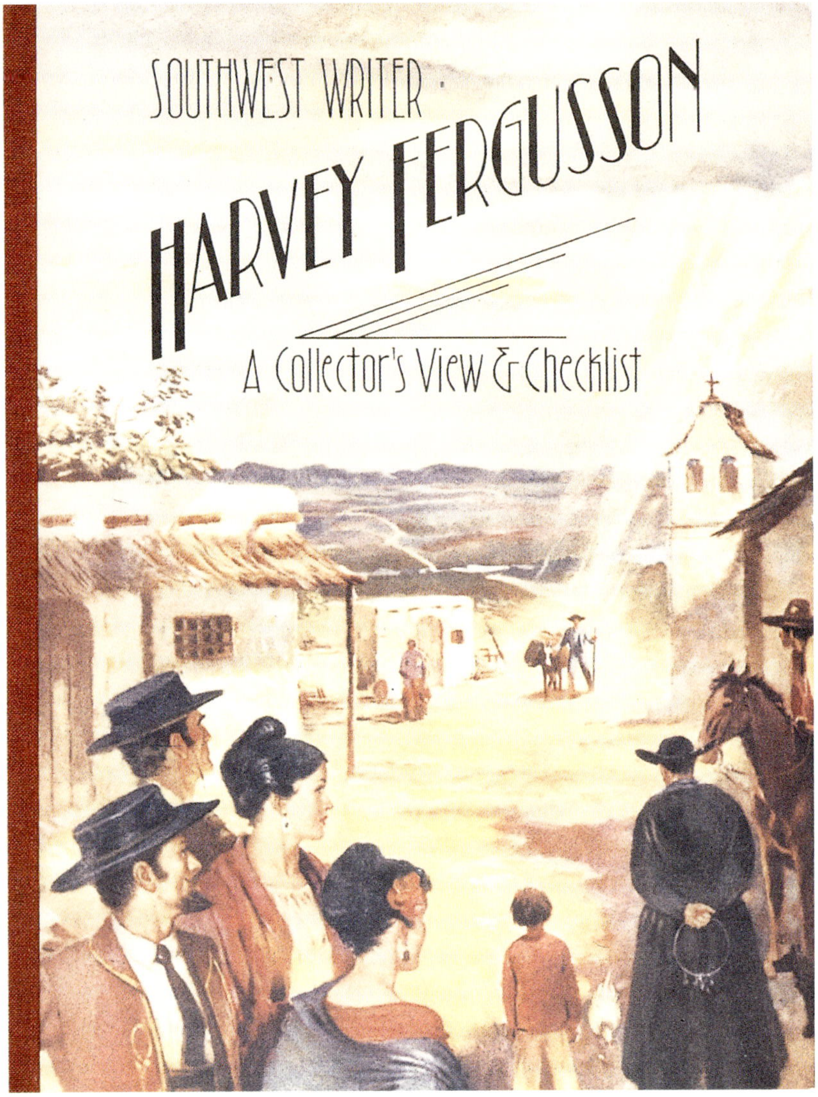

Press of the Palace of the Governors

Southwest Writer Harvey Fergusson, Press of the Palace of the Governors, 2001.

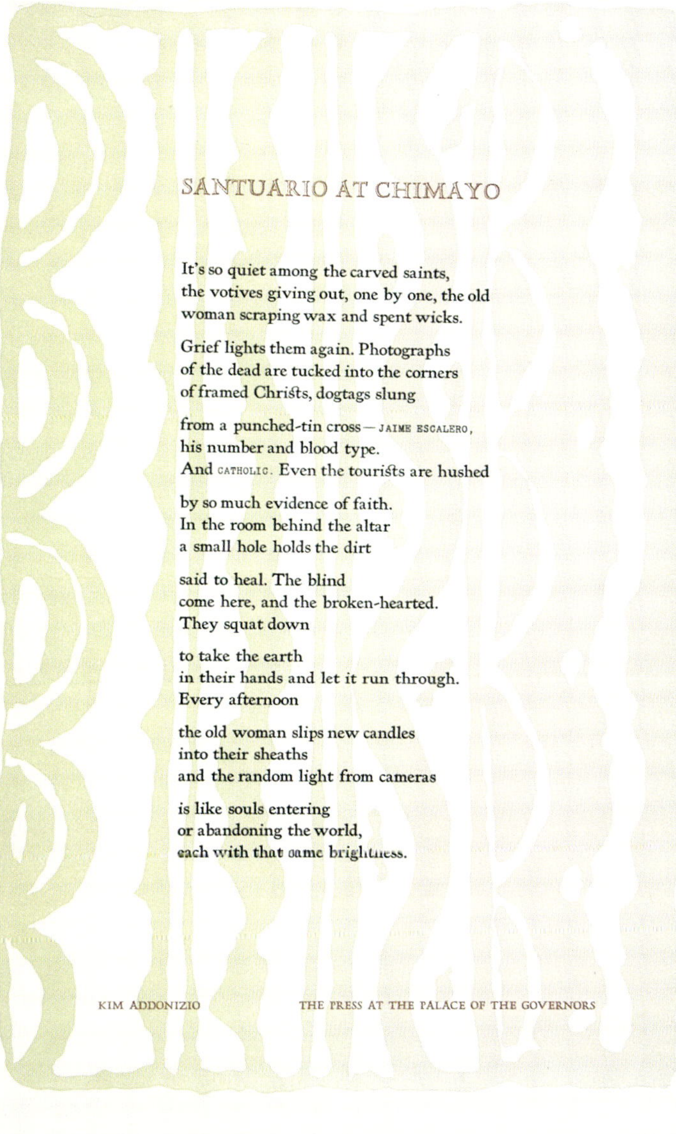

SANTUARIO AT CHIMAYO

It's so quiet among the carved saints,
the votives giving out, one by one, the old
woman scraping wax and spent wicks.

Grief lights them again. Photographs
of the dead are tucked into the corners
of framed Christs, dogtags slung

from a punched-tin cross—JAIME ESCALERO,
his number and blood type.
And CATHOLIC. Even the tourists are hushed

by so much evidence of faith.
In the room behind the altar
a small hole holds the dirt

said to heal. The blind
come here, and the broken-hearted.
They squat down

to take the earth
in their hands and let it run through.
Every afternoon

the old woman slips new candles
into their sheaths
and the random light from cameras

is like souls entering
or abandoning the world,
each with that same brightness.

KIM ADDONIZIO THE PRESS AT THE PALACE OF THE GOVERNORS

PRESS OF THE PALACE OF THE GOVERNORS
Santuario at Chimayo by Kim Addonizio, with linocut illustration
by Lee Marchalonis, poetry broadside from *Word Art*,
Press of the Palace of the Governors, 2004.

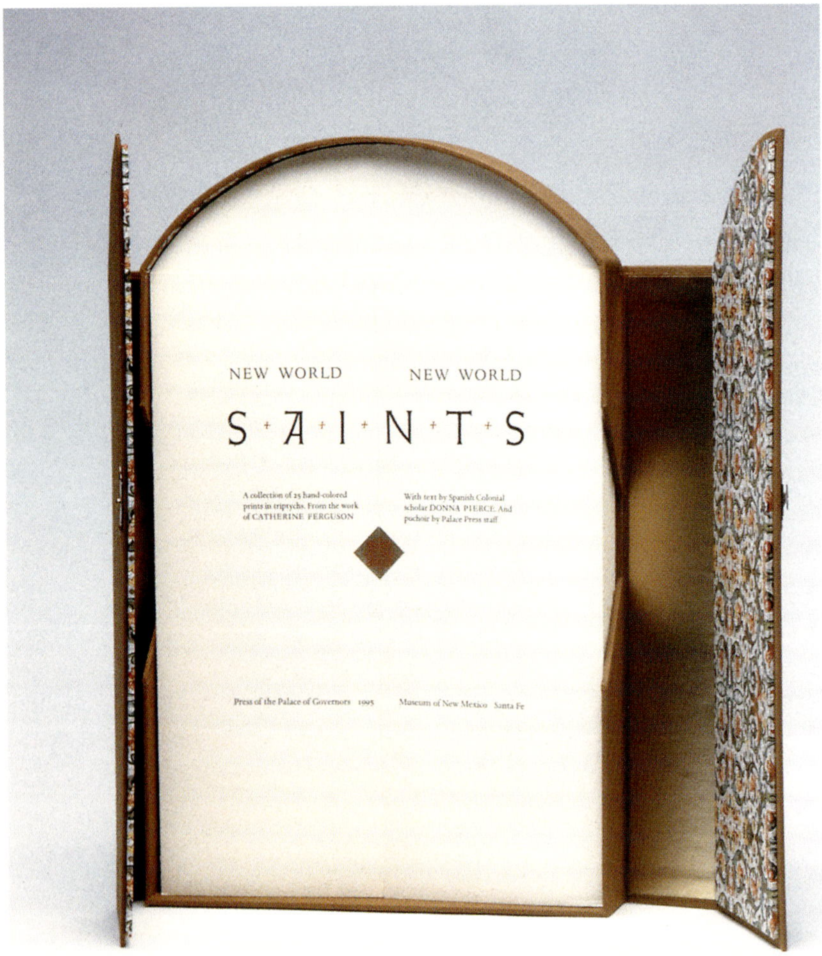

PRESS OF THE PALACE OF THE GOVERNORS
New World Saints, title and portfolio box, Press of the Palace of the Governors, 1995.

a collection of artwork by Catherine Ferguson and text by Spanish Colonial Arts scholar Donna Pierce, was released in 1995. It includes twenty-five hand-colored prints of saints housed in die-cut paper triptychs that carry the text. The 140-copy edition was a five-year project (two years alone for the hand coloring) involving print shop staff and a dedicated corps of volunteers. The portfolio was one of seven Press of the Palace of the Governors publications to capture a coveted American Association of Museums design award.

In 2001, after my retirement from the museum, Leech took over the helm of the Press and, with the help of letterpress printer James Bourland, now directs what has become New Mexico's longest continually operating fine printing establishment. Following the shop's tradition of crafted literary works, in 2005 he completed a colorful collection of illustrated poetry broadsides, printed on his own handmade paper. *Word Art* is a collaboration with contemporary writers edited by Santa Fe poet Gary Mex Glazner.

Future titles promise more literary treasures. In the works as of this writing is *Jack Thorp's Songs of the Cowboys*, originally printed at the Estancia newspaper plant in 1908. The book of lyrics, some written and others collected by Nathan Howard "Jack" Thorp, is touted as America's first folklore collection of cowboy songs. Also in production is a reprint of a rare 1923 illustrated poetry edition titled *Sun and Smoke*. Produced by Holling Clancy Holling, an artist inspired by visits to New Mexico in the early 1920s, the book features Holling's charming hand-colored woodcuts.

Rydal Press Revival

CLARK KIMBALL'S PURCHASE of the Rydal Press imprint in 1985 represents another of the period's revivalist efforts. Rydal had a long Santa Fe history, described in Chapter Two. It was brought here from Pennsylvania in 1933 by proprietor Walter Goodwin. Though the enterprise flourished and won national recognition for its handsomely printed volumes, by 1941 Goodwin had left the business to become a photographer.

In the hands of the new owner, longtime newspaperman Dale Bullock, Rydal continued to produce quality Southwest writing through the 1960s but began to focus more on commercial job printing and less on publishing. Bullock's books reflected little of Goodwin's elegant typography or the handcrafted flare he brought to each edition.

In 1976, the Rydal Press, a Santa Fe institution by this time, changed hands once again, and the lofty ideals upon which the reputable old press had been established slipped even further from view. The new owners, Andrea Dewey, Jonathan Carleton, and Richard Davis, exchanged letterpress equipment for high-speed offset presses and moved the business from its longtime Canyon Road location to a strip mall not far from the plaza. Though they published a few books, including *The Hospital at the End of the Trail* (1977), a photographic history of St. Vincent Hospital by Clark Kimball and Dr. Marcus J. Smith, the new owners brought a quick print flavor to Rydal and turned their attention to satisfying a commercial printing market. By 1980 the Rydal Press had closed. It was just three years shy of a half century of continuous operation.

Enter Clark Kimball, a Santa Fe bookseller and bibliophile to the bone. Kimball was well schooled in Rydal Press history and had a special appreciation for Goodwin's fine printing. He taught typography while studying at Cornell University. At the University of North Carolina he earned a graduate degree in writing. From there he went on to Columbia University, where he received a master's degree in Library Services and Rare Books. Following his student years he was associated with the Pierpont Morgan Library in New York.[27]

Clark Kimball, 1986. Photograph by Kitty Leaken.

In Santa Fe he was part owner of Great Southwest Books, an antiquarian concern established in 1975. With his partner Jackie Stone he had already tested the publishing waters. In 1981 the two produced *Witter Bynner's Photographs of D. H. Lawrence*, a Kodak documentation of the poet's 1923 trip to Mexico. Among Bynner's traveling companions were Lawrence, Lawrence's wife Frieda, and his former student and current secretary Willard "Spud" Johnson. Four of the snapshots appeared in Bynner's 1951 account of the vacation titled *Journey with Genius*. However, twenty-six previously unpublished photos turned up sixty years after the trip to be acquired by Kimball and Stone.[28] Great Southwest Books published a limited-edition photo album with images reproduced from original negatives. The 50 boxed copies featured calligraphed text by Stone.

Success of the publishing project coupled with Kimball's special appreciation of the Rydal Press led him to acquire the imprint shortly after the business closed. "The old press was going down the tubes with a black eye," he said. "Though I didn't know what I was going to do with it, I couldn't let that happen." Kimball claimed he purchased the Rydal name for one silver dollar.[29]

In resurrecting the Rydal imprint, the new proprietor made a commitment not only to reviving one of New Mexico's most important small publishing houses but also to producing classic Southwest literature for which the press had become known. By relying on skilled artisans for typographic work, illustrating, printing, and binding, he hoped to restore the Rydal reputation for beautifully crafted books.

Under the Sangre de Cristo, by Pulitzer Prize—winning author Paul Horgan, appeared late in 1985 under the Rydal imprint. True to his word, Kimball's first book was a handsome collector's edition printed letterpress at the reputable Meriden-Stinehour Press in Vermont and hand bound with original marbled papers. The book includes episodes of Horgan's *From the Royal City*, which first appeared in the *Yale Review* and were reprinted by Goodwin for Villagrá Book Shop in 1936,[30] along with excerpts from Horgan's *Taos Valley*. The *Santa Fe Reporter* praised the book, saying "It belongs on the shelf with all good New Mexico things . . . ."[31]

A year later he produced *Flight From Fiesta*, an unpublished novel by Frank Waters, one of the Southwest's most beloved chroniclers. The book is bound in paper wrappers featuring a multicolored woodblock design by Willard Clark. The 200-copy edition again was printed letterpress at Meriden-Stinehour.

Kimball went on to publish three more books by Southwest literary titans Edward Abbey, John Sinclair, and N. Scott Momaday. Abbey's *Vox Clamantis in Deserto* (*A Voice Crying in the Wilderness*) came out in 1989. It is a collection of notes selected from the secret journals of the widely published naturalist, a manuscript completed only weeks before Abbey's death in March of that same year. For this book Kimball veered slightly from his handcrafted standards. *Vox Clamantis* was printed offset and commercially bound but featured hand lettering by Santa Fe book artist Mina Yamashita. He followed this

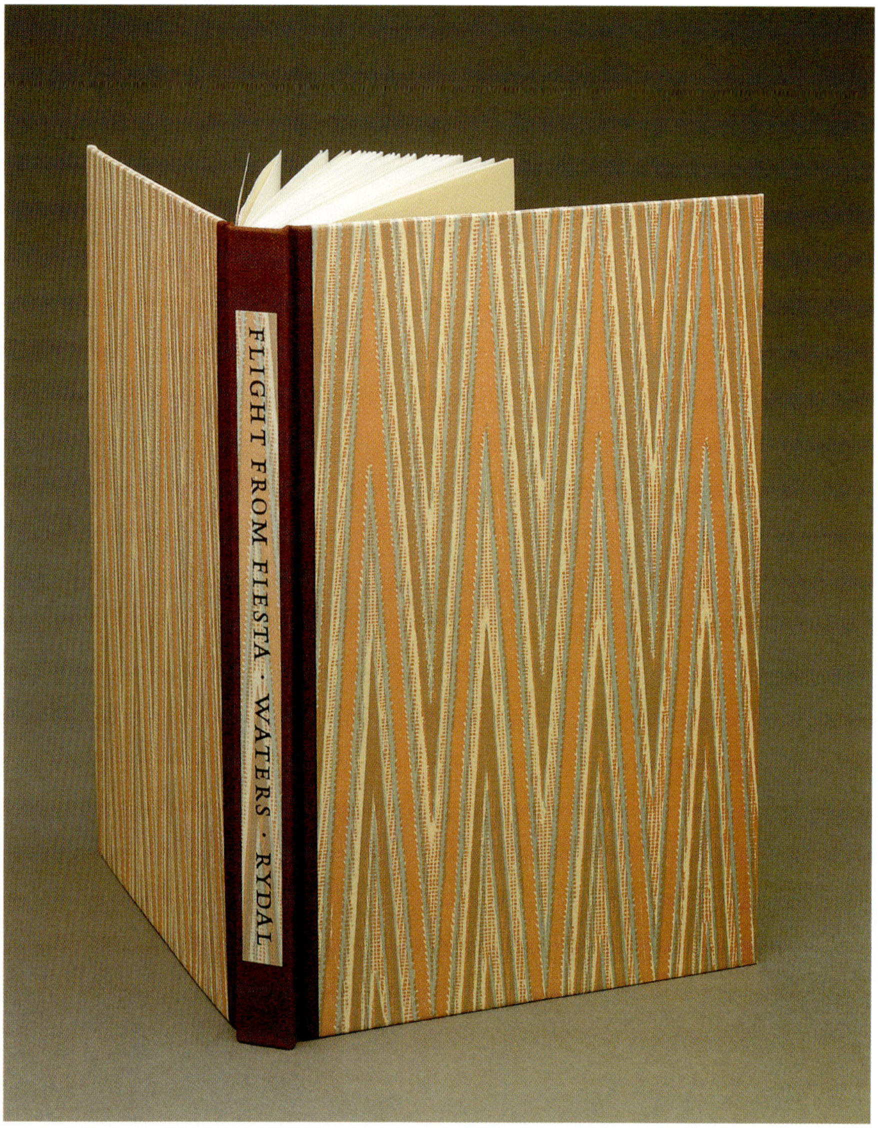

THE RYDAL PRESS-CLARK KIMBALL
Flight from Fiesta with covers by Willard Clark, Rydal Press, 1986.

The Floating Feathers Shield

When Gai-talee was still a boy, learning how to hunt, he had a wonderful dream. In it he saw a great bear on the side of a mountain. The bear stood still for a long time, waiting in the shadow of a high stone ridge near timberline. Then a shape hurtled on the ridge, and the bear reared suddenly and took in his claws an eagle from the air. For a moment there was an awful frenzy; then again the stillness, and dark feathers floating and fluttering down on a little wind.

Gai-talee told Many Magpies of the shield he wanted, and it was made according to his dream. Gai-talee raided many times in Mexico, and he carried his shield with him. They say that Gai-talee's shield is well known below the Llano Estacado.

THE RYDAL PRESS - CLARK KIMBALL

"The Muddy Horses Shield" from *In the Presence of the Sun*, Rydal Press, 1992 work in 1991 with *The Night the Bear Came Off the Mountain* by New Mexico cowboy writer John L. Sinclair, again featuring Yamashita's artwork.

His greatest effort, *In the Presence of the Sun, A Gathering of Shields*, appeared in 1992. The work of another Pulitzer Prize recipient, N. Scott Momaday, the book includes drawings of sixteen Plains Indian shields accompanied by prose poems in the Kiowa tradition. Kimball produced 140 copies of the book, set by M&H Type Foundry in San Francisco and printed letterpress at Okeanos Press in Oakland. Twenty-six deluxe copies are slipcased and highlighted with hand-colored prints.

By the late 1990s Kimball was beginning to experience difficulties in finding the kind of literature he wanted to produce. This challenge, coupled with the heavy demands of private press publishing, led him to reconsider his Rydal Press proprietorship. "I was proud to be the caretaker, to have been entrusted with the work for a brief time, but felt I could no longer continue being a worthy proprietor," he said.[32] In 1998 he sold his interest in the press to Santa Fe bookseller Spencer Maxwell, who produced two titles before his Rydal publishing efforts went into a holding pattern.[33]

Clark's Studio Revival

WHILE CLARK KIMBALL was busy revitalizing Walter Goodwin's Rydal Press, Santa Fe woodcut artist Willard Clark was in the process of staging a comeback of his own. He had closed the doors to Clark's Studio in 1942, sold his equipment, and given up the successful job printing business to take a position at the atomic laboratory in Los Alamos.[34] Influenced by a nationwide movement to join in the war effort and a need for a consistent means of support for his family, he became a tool and die specialist at the laboratory. His gouges and gravers went into storage, and the hallmark Clark's Studio imagery ceased to flow.

During his thirty-year career in Los Alamos, Clark produced no woodcuts. Instead, he satisfied his craftsman yearnings by painting and taking up jewelry making on his own time. When he retired in 1974, it didn't take him long to find his way back to his artistic roots. He took over his daughter's DAS

Gallery on Canyon Road, where he specialized in Asian art and also sold his own custom-designed jewelry.[35] Later he moved the business to his home on Sosaya Lane.

Willard Clark at work, 1992.
Photograph by Joanne Rijmes.

By the early 1980s Santa Fe was changing far too rapidly for those who valued the Old World quality of life that had persisted there through the first half of the century. Growth of population brought an end to the town's village-like atmosphere. An increased number of businesses sprawled into shopping malls, which sprang up on the outskirts of Santa Fe. The plaza, once the economic heart of the town, had been taken over by high-end tourist related shops. It was no longer a place where friends and neighbors might meet and relax for a chat but instead became a place where strangers gathered in large numbers.

As tradition slipped further from view, Clark's charming wood-engraved images of the past took on new significance. His wood-laden burros, adobe casitas, and picturesque chapels resting in a landscape devoid of condominiums were suddenly in demand. He gathered a portfolio of work from his Clark's Studio days and began marketing the prints. Soon he became sought after for his remarkable work.

Under the direction of Pamela Smith, the Press of the Palace of the Governors at the Museum of New Mexico began a decade-long collaboration with the woodcut artist. The versatile relationship involved everything from press repair to mentoring and book illustration. In 1982 Clark's work was exhibited at the Press of the Palace's Annual Book Arts Festival. Two years later he designed the festival poster and produced artwork for a Lawrence Clark Powell lecture, *My New Mexico Literary Friends*, delivered at the gathering and published by the Press of the Palace in 1986.

Marta Weigle and Kyle Fiore's 1982 book *Santa Fe and Taos, The Writer's Era, 1916–1941*, carried a dust jacket designed by Clark along with his woodcut illustrations. He worked with Linnea Gentry at Amaranth Press to complete unfinished Gustave Baumann woodblocks for a 1983 portfolio titled *New Mexico Santos*. And he was deluged with visits from aspiring wood engravers, small press printers, collectors, writers, and admirers.

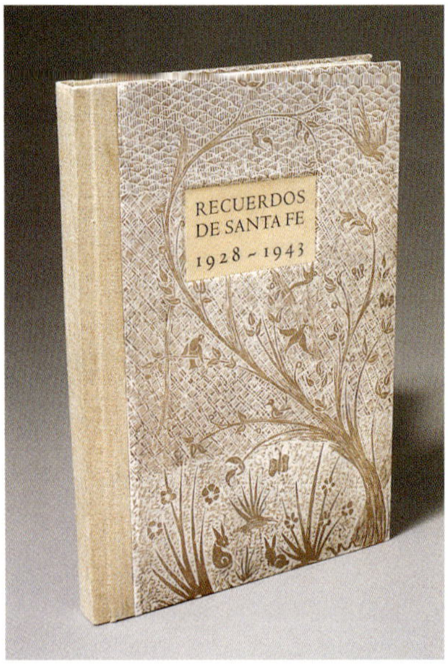

CLARK'S STUDIO REVIVAL
Recuerdos de Santa Fe, with Willard Clark printed cover papers, 1990.

Despite his newfound success, Clark was not content to rest on his laurels. "All my life I've wanted to see how fine a block I could cut, and now I have time to do that, since I don't care when I get done," he said in 1992.[36]

At the new Clark's Studio, unencumbered by the need to satisfy paying clients, Clark began creating complex, fine-line imagery in as many as eight colors. Although in his seventies by this time, his hand was still steady enough for the task. As he worked, he started teaching his grandson Kevin Ryan some of his finely honed skills—how to fabricate wood-engraving tools and the process of grinding pigments for making ink. He purchased a 1910 Potter proof press and customized the machine to fit his needs. Now, however, the Clark's Studio output went into a fine art portfolio, the work of a master printmaker rather than the product of a creative job printing shop.

In 1985 he set himself yet another challenge, perhaps the most ambitious project of the Clark's Studio revival. In response to what he considered regrettable changes to his adopted hometown, he planned to produce a book of wood engravings and text recalling his earliest impressions of the area. *Recuerdos de Santa Fe, 1928–1943* was five years in the making. Though Clark entertained the idea of collaboration, in true private press spirit he took on the entire task, first writing, then illustrating the book. When his health began to fail, he relied on his grandson to help with the printing, binding, and marketing of the 100-copy edition. The book's forty-six wood engraved images, together with Clark's brief prose, depict an era in New Mexico when the pace was slower and the wide-open spaces much wider.

Recuerdos was met with an enthusiastic response. Copies sold as fast as Clark could bind them, and a trade edition quickly followed the deluxe handmade version.

Two years later he was named a Santa Fe Living Treasure. His work was featured in a one-man show at the Museum of Fine Arts. And the never-idle craftsman, by this time in his eighties, was ready to go on to his next book. He

Clark's Studio Revival
"Santuario," woodcut print from *Recuerdos de Santa Fe, 1928–1943*,
Clark's Studio, 1990.

designed *The Simple Life* with a format similar to *Recuerdos*. It would be made up of wood engravings accompanied by short descriptive text. Only four of the planned illustrations were completed when Clark died in December 1992.

In the hands of his grandson, Kevin Ryan, the work of Clark's Studio goes on today with reprints from the portfolio of the master craftsman.

The Weaselsleeves Press

JANET RODNEY lived and traveled throughout the world before settling in New Mexico in the early 1980s and establishing her Weaselsleeves Press. Like other recent arrivals, she brought fresh ideas to blend with Southwest themes and a sense of adventure to traditional letterpress technique.

Rodney had an international upbringing. She lived in France, Taiwan, then in Spain for eighteen years, and later in Guatemala, with travels to England, Austria, and Italy, as well as Japan and the Philippines. Her multicultural experiences as a child led to an early fascination with language, and she began writing poetry in her adolescent years.[37] After studies at Middlebury College in Vermont, Universidad Menéndez Pelayo, and the European Division of the University of Maryland, she became a literary scout and reader for Farrar, Straus & Giroux in Madrid and went on to work as a journalist and magazine editor there.

Janet Rodney at the Weaselsleeves Press, ca. 1989. Photograph by Nathaniel Tarn.

Again it was language that motivated a return to the United States in 1974. "I was tired of being an expatriate. I wanted to get back to the American idiom, to the spoken English language of my roots," she said.[38] After her return to the U.S. she spent several years at Rutgers University, where she took a master's degree in comparative literature and briefly taught Spanish as an adjunct.

Despite academic interests, Rodney felt a need to explore new directions as part of her literary activities. She wrote and published books of poetry, grew familiar with the small press world, began associating with book artists and printers, and became intrigued with the visual quality of the written word. For approximately two years she traveled almost daily from Pennsylvania to New York, where she apprenticed at the Grenfell Press with Leslie Miller, one of the East Coast's most prominent fine printers. As a printer's devil, Rodney was smitten with letterpress printing and gradually learned the process.

Eventually she began to accumulate tools and equipment of her own. From New York's disappearing letterpress industry, she salvaged metal type and type cases, storing them in her garage in Pennsylvania.[39] In 1985, Rodney and her husband, poet Nathaniel Tarn, moved the weighty collection to the Santa Fe area, where the two took up residence and the Weaselsleeves Press was born.

Weaselsleeves printer's mark.

The inaugural 1989 Weaselsleeves Press announcement reads:

> *Janet Rodney, having decided to establish a small printing press at Lot 27 on the old Las Dos Homestead, about nine miles northwest of Santa Fe, New Mexico, where all kinds of printing have been duly performed this last year with accuracy, dispatch, and upon moderate terms, is pleased to announce that she is ready to begin to print chapbooks by carefully chosen authors and artists under the imprint of The Weaselsleeves Press.*

With this printed card Rodney declared her intentions as a private press publisher, maintaining the right to determine editorial focus. Her longtime passion for experiment and language was a major factor in manuscript selection and created a focal point for Weaselsleeves books, the first of which appeared in 1990.

The Guatemalan folk tale *Grandmother Sweat Bath* is told in English by Martin Prechtel, with words from the language of the Tzutujil Maya woven throughout. It was illustrated by Prechtel and printed on Rodney's Vandercook press. Bound in a soft cover of handmade paper, the book marked the beginning of a decade-long collaboration between the Weaselsleeves Press and talented Santa Fe bookbinder Martha Little.[40]

In *Grandmother Sweat Bath*, Rodney began to demonstrate her adeptness with artwork. She brought Prechtel's bold line drawings of the Maya to life, printing them full page size in a reddish-brown earth color over soft backgrounds of turquoise, pink, and gray. Intermingled with the text, the five images work to enhance the story's village setting.

Her second book, *Incloser* by Susan Howe (1992), is a testimony to both the visual and provocative power of language. Based on Howe's studies of the autobiographical manuscript of seventeenth-century Evangelical preacher Thomas Shepherd, the book examines the extraordinary language of recorded revelations by women seeking membership in the religious community. Large graffiti-like illustrations, adapted from Shepherd's own script, accompany the text and appear almost to shout out from the page. Rodney created imagery using an enlarged photographic copy of a manuscript page and then had zinc engravings made of the work. By printing the script in layers and thoughtfully registering it on colored backgrounds, she brought a painterly quality to the prints. The 60-copy edition was bound by Martha Little in both quarter leather and quarter cloth.

Unlike many fine printers, Rodney interjects a sense of risk into her work. She first prints the text, then experiments with the artwork on the finished pages, eventually achieving an eye-catching unpredictability. Spontaneity in the printing process, the "happy accident," is what she is looking for.

This adventuresome quality is most evident in her third Weaselsleeves book published in 1995. *Two Stein Talks* is two essays in which poet Lyn Hejinian relates the term "realism" to Gertrude Stein's writings. Rodney echoes the text, set in Gill Sans Light, with what she calls a "geometry of language"—bold linoleum block forms printed in sharp blacks and brilliant primary colors. Inspired by Russian constructivists of the 1920s and 1930s, the illustrations are like a Joseph Albers exercise in which colors and shapes appear to change depending upon their interaction.

Between productions of limited-edition books, Rodney produced one-of-a-kind broadsides and artist books that gave her further opportunity to try out new materials and techniques. In 1994 she made a series of four "prayer flag" books. Drawn from her travels in Tibet, the *Himalayan Windows* series is made up of Xerox copies of photographs on handmade papers which are painted, then pasted and sewn onto fabric pages. *Oh, Say Can You See*, focusing on the Bill Clinton/Monica Lewinsky scandal, followed in 1998. Stars and stripes printed

Weaselsleeves Press

Two Stein Talks, title page and portfolio box, Weaselsleeves Press, 1995.

Weaselsleeves Press

Oh, Say Can You See, Weaselsleeves Press, 1998.

from linoleum blocks provide an American flag backdrop for the book's pages, which carry snatches of commentary from the media and a female figure that appears to tumble throughout. Rodney produced only 3 copies of the book, which is sewn on an accordion spine and fans out in a star shape.

By 2001, when the most recent Weaselsleeves offering appeared, Rodney's fascination with new technique had led her into the rapidly developing world of computers. *Younger-Older Ones*, a story by Rina Swentzell about the people of Santa Clara Pueblo, combines traditional letterpress work with computer-generated text and graphics. Using newly acquired Photoshop skills, Rodney composed and printed finely textured collaged images of clouds, rock formations, and cave paintings to accompany the book's story line. The text was printed from polymer plates at Digital Letterpress in Austin, Texas, and hand bound at the studio of Martha Little.

Though Rodney has produced no new letterpress titles since 2001, her commitment to keeping the bookmaking process fresh and alive suggest future innovative works from the Weaselsleeves Press.

Desert Rose Press

"IT ALL STARTS with a love of letters, and of books."[41] That's how Clifford Burke described the origins of his fine printing career. Like Janet Rodney, he settled in New Mexico after more than thirty years of experience in the literary world. From a politically turbulent Berkeley of the 1960s and early 1970s, his path led him back to his roots in the Skagit Valley of Washington State and finally to the village of Galisteo, where he formed a partnership with Virginia Mudd at the Desert Rose Press in 1990. Since that time the combined efforts of these two seasoned fine printers has produced a body of work that blends handcrafts and digital technology to promote environmental and spiritual awareness.

In 1989 when the two first met, Mudd had been a student of the book arts at Mills College in Oakland and was working as an apprentice at Wesley Tanner's successful Arif Press in Berkeley. A self-published book about her 1978 cross-country bike trip initially sparked her enthusiasm for the process of bookmaking. In 1987 she launched her formal studies of the book arts at Mills, printing at the school's Eucalyptus Press and producing her first Desert Rose book titled *Earth Tones, Heart Tones*. Before long she began to accumulate equipment of her own. Her clear and determined plan called for a return to recently purchased property in New Mexico where she intended to "live as a hermit and print for the rest of her life."[42]

By this time, Burke was a semi-retired veteran of the venerable San Francisco private press world. He started out in high school, working in his spare time at the production plant of a local newspaper, later developing solid skills as an employee in the job printing industry. In 1966 he opened his own Cranium Press in the heart of the flower power movement—the Haight Ashbury district—and produced his first commercial job for a neighboring business called the Psychedelic Shop.[43] Two years later he discovered San Francisco fine printer/designer Adrian Wilson, an association that would have a profound effect on his letterpress career.

Inspired by Wilson's classic manual *The Design of Books* (1967), Burke set out to meet the esteemed print world figure and ended up working with him off and on for the next eight years. At the press in Tuscany Alley, he printed books designed by Wilson for discerning clients like the Sierra Club, the Book Club of California, and the Roxburghe Club of San Francisco. Under the tutelage of the master printer, he learned to operate a cylinder press, developed a refined hand for the meticulous craft, and became steeped in the rich tradition of San Francisco fine printing.

Clifford Burke and Virginia Mudd at the Desert Rose Press, Galisteo, New Mexico, 1991.

When he wasn't involved in Tuscany Alley projects, he was busy working at his own Cranium Press, where his special interest in poetry determined a focus for finely printed editions. He produced established West Coast poets such as Gary Snyder, Richard Brautigan, and Lawrence Ferlinghetti, as well as a younger generation of writers. Some of the publications appeared under the Cranium imprint, while others were taken on as commissions. Notable among the ten-year Cranium output is the *Maya Quarto* series that appeared between 1969 and 1971. Edited by David Meltzer and Jack Shoemaker, the 12 soft-bound booklets featured fresh new talent from the Bay Area poetry circle, among them John Brandi, Jack Hirschman, and Bill Bathurst.

As the protest movements of the 1960s and 1970s spiraled around him, Burke supplemented poetry with politics. He produced fliers for the War Resisters League and taught others how to put their concerns into print. He wrote *Printing It!*, a guide to simple and economical techniques for mass-produced information. Released by Wingbow Press in 1972, the paperback book spoke to novices, among them student activists who had little access to the world of commercial publishing.

By the mid-1970s, however, the outcry of the 1960s began to fade. Times had changed. Populist printing efforts, including Burke's Cranium Press, were suddenly competing with large grant-funded operations. Feeling the economic squeeze that too often accompanies private press ownership, Burke closed his press and left California for the Northwest in 1976.[44]

Printing It! by Clifford Burke, with cover illustration by Chuck Miller, 1972.

The Skagit Valley, bounded by the glacial peaks of the Cascades and coastal waters of Puget Sound, provided a nurturing ground for his environmental interests and inspired the poetry he wrote and gathered into volumes titled *Sacred Places* and *Ten Poems from Downriver Skagit*. Though his printing equipment remained in storage, his writing activity increased. In 1980 he completed what has been called one of the most appealing manuals of the letterpress craft. In *Printing Poetry* Burke revisited a technical realm he introduced in *Printing It!* This time, however, he guided the reader through traditional hand processes for the crafting of beautiful books and addressed concept as well as construction. An elegant production, *Printing Poetry* was designed and printed by Burke at Spring Valley Press in Langley, Washington.

Nine years later *Printing Poetry* sparked a correspondence between Burke and Virginia Mudd that ultimately led to their marriage and partnership in the Desert Rose Press. By 1990 the two had combined type and printing equipment and set up shop in Galisteo, New Mexico. Their mutual concern for the environment provided a focus for publications, as clarified in this statement from a 1992 Desert Rose catalog: "While the Book was the art that brought us together and led to the building of the Press, it became clear from the beginning

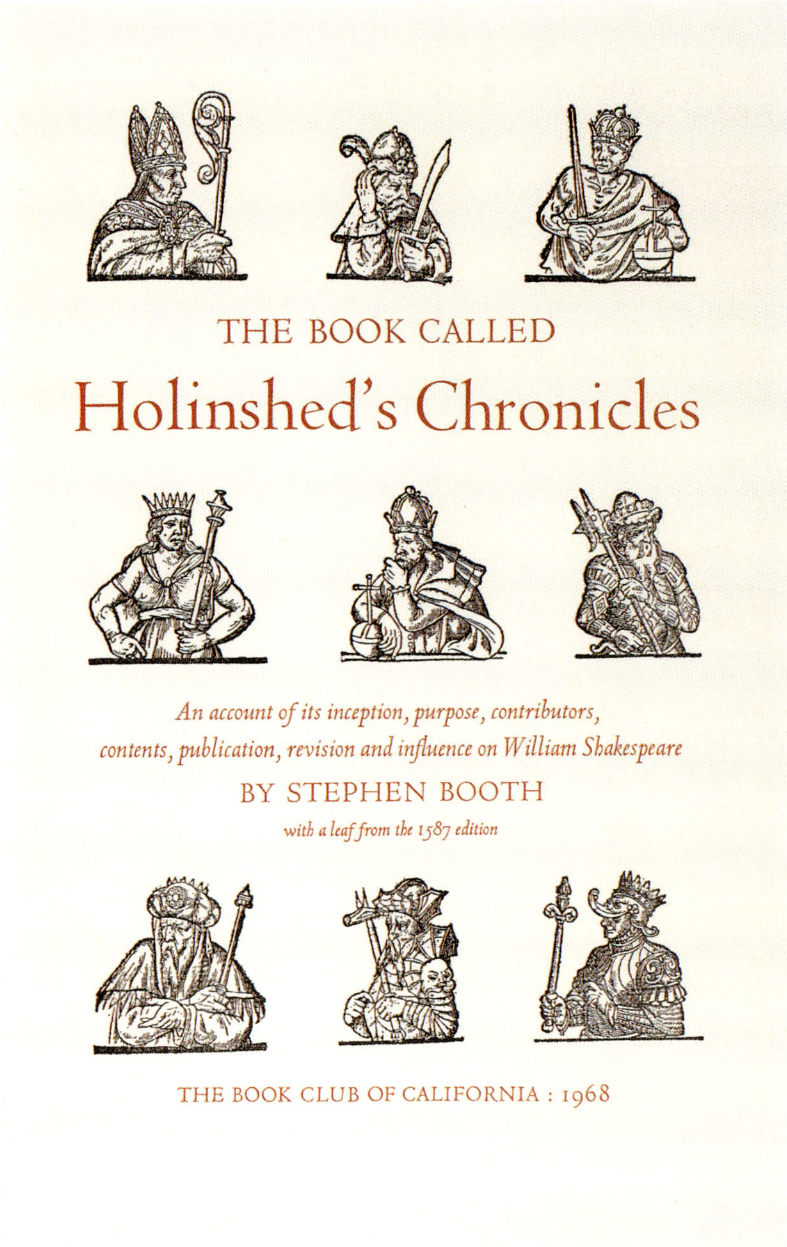

THE BOOK CALLED

Holinshed's Chronicles

An account of its inception, purpose, contributors, contents, publication, revision and influence on William Shakespeare

BY STEPHEN BOOTH

with a leaf from the 1587 edition

THE BOOK CLUB OF CALIFORNIA : 1968

DESERT ROSE PRESS

The Book Called Holinshed's Chronicles, a 1968 Book Club of California publication printed by Clifford Burke at the Tuscany Alley Press.

SOME OF THESE DAYS

POEMS *BY* PHILIP WHALEN

DESERT ROSE PRESS

Some of These Days, Desert Rose Press, 1999.

DESERT ROSE PRESS
"Be Praised, My Lord," hand-painted illustration from *Canticle of the Sun*,
Desert Rose Press, 1991.

that we had a larger purpose than the art of the book; that we could use our skills and the work of our hands to express the emerging consciousness of our Earth as a holy being."

With the environment as a focal point, the two have produced poetry and other texts in the form of books, broadsides, and greeting cards; beginning with an *Earth Day* series created by Mudd for the twentieth anniversary of this event in 1990. The set of eight cards features original monoprint illustrations.

A small and vibrant edition of St. Francis of Assisi's *Canticle of the Sun* appeared the following year. The age-old prayer pays homage to the earth, its elements and its creatures. Mudd enhanced the ten text invocations with original gouache paintings and created unique bindings for the copies with her own decorated papers.

In exploring alternative formats, the two have created accordion-fold booklets as well as strong "typographic prints," or broadsides, that enshrine the text in artwork. Among these one-sheet offerings are *Song for Salmon Babies*, a poem by Burke featuring a monoprint border, and his haiku *Gravity* encircled with a brush-drawn gesture suggestive of Japanese calligraphy.

Five years after Desert Rose was established in Galisteo, Burke and Mudd reaffirmed their commitment to silence, solitude, and nature,[45] moving their home and studio to a remote tract of land in a wilderness area southeast of Santa Fe. Despite the isolated setting, the one-time activists have found new ways to make themselves heard. With the help of a computer, they now participate in a virtual community without having to leave their mountain retreat. The Desert Rose web site reaches hundreds of people on a day-to-day basis and establishes an ongoing dialogue in a way books are unable to do.[46] In addition, the two have relied on digital technology to generate typography, reproduce imagery, and even to print a 1995 Desert Rose booklet titled *Skull Drawings and Bone Songs*.

Although the computer has been added to the inventory of Desert Rose tools, there is little danger of it overshadowing Burke and Mudd's dedication to handcrafted limited-edition works. Their laser-printed *Skull Drawings and Bone Songs*, a revised edition of Claire Van Vliet's 1992 Janus Press printing, was hand bound in letterpress-printed wrappers. A book of Philip Whalen poetry titled *Some of These Days* (1999) is hand set in Goudy Italian Oldstyle types, masterfully printed on a Vandercook press, and hand bound by Martha Little. Powerful black-and-white woodcut imagery accompanies Burke's "Nineteen Tiny Poems" in a 2003 Desert Rose printing titled *Out of Nowhere*. The woodcuts, from *Ten Thousand Square Ideas*, a work in progress, enclose interrupted brush strokes in cubicle frames.

As Burke points out, "To a typographer the challenge of new techniques is unavoidable." But the future of Desert Rose Press lies in the delicate balance between the worlds of art and technology. "Because," he explains, "we feel that in an age of fugitive information, the work of the hand, the things an artist makes, take on value far beyond commerce: a thing of beauty to come back to and to share, perhaps to keep the record of our best hopes and dreams."[47]

Press of the Palace of the Governors

Portfolio box, *Word Art*, Press of the Palace of the Governors, 2004.

Afterword

THE MAKING OF BOOKS has become a popular pastime for craft enthusiasts across the country and a means of expression for artists working in a wide variety of media, but the arduous task of letterpress printing remains in the hands of a dedicated few. Faced with the closure of type foundries and the disappearance of hand press and tool manufacturers, artisan printers still cling to the centuries-old craft. They defied the age of industrialism and now the digital age, ingeniously adapting twenty-first-century technology to fit their needs rather than surrender to it. Computer-generated type becomes a raised surface photopolymer printing plate, digital imagery accompanies letterpress printed text, and the precision of a laser beam takes the place of the time-honored die cutting process. As British type designer Eric Gill observed in 1931, the power of industrialism and the humanity of craftsmanship can coexist. For the work of the hand is a primal urge, an "indestructible and permanent need in human nature," distinct from the work of machines.[1]

Despite the proliferation of information via the Internet, the book remains the primary source for the preservation of human knowledge. As long as there are people to make them, there will be an audience of readers to enjoy the deliciously intimate experience that books offer. As for the handmade book, its future is assured by its irreplaceable tactile quality, its feast of color and design, and the unmistakable spirit of its maker communicated on each page. In New Mexico, where the muse is seldom absent and the independent spirit of the West prevails, there will always be a place for the work of the private press.

Notes

INTRODUCTION NOTES

1. Blumenthal, *The Printed Book in America*, x.
2. Lyon, Jetta Carleton, "A Sort of a Love Affair," 5.
3. Burke and Mudd, *Desert Rose Press Catalog*, 5.

CHAPTER ONE NOTES

1. Pino, *Exposición Sucinta y Sencilla de la Provincia del Nuevo Mexico*, 94. "Pedro Bautista Pino had traveled to Spain in 1812 to represent the province of New Mexico in the newly formed Spanish *Cortes*, his aim being to bring attention to conditions in the province and to obtain aid for New Mexico from a newly reorganized government. In a concise report, Pino laid out the problems affecting New Mexico, pointing to the lack of schools, teachers, and the means to prepare *Nuevomexicanos* for entering professions." Meléndez, *So All Is Not Lost: The Poetics of Print in Nuevomexicano Communities, 1834–1958*, 15.
2. Barreiro, *Ojeada Sobre Nuevo México*, 95.
3. Martínez, *Relación*, 328–29.
4. Chávez, *But Time and Chance*, 51–53.
5. In January of 1847 a mob of Taos insurgents rose up against the newly established American government, killing the provisional civil governor Charles Bent along with his brother-in-law Pablo Jaramillo, Narciso Beaubien, and other local officials. Though American forces quickly put down the rebellion, false accusations naming Martínez as a secret instigator persisted for years. Chávez, *But Time and Chance*, 82–85.
6. Chávez, *But Time and Chance*, 27.
7. Gregg, *Commerce of the Prairies*, 142.
8. Gibson, *Journal of a Soldier Under Kearny and Doniphan*, 222. In all actuality this printing press was an ideal model for New Mexico. It was built of wood and metal, was inexpensive, lightweight, and easily transported. Most importantly, it was an uncomplicated piece of equipment that could be repaired by almost anyone with a mechanical sense. Philadelphia manufacturer Adam Ramage, who produced printing equipment from the early 1800s through the middle of the century, catered to the printing needs of the remote West and became known, more than any other press maker, as a pioneer in spreading the process of printing. Moran, *Printing Presses*, 47.

9. Under Mexican law publishers were required to produce both an *aviso*, a printed notification announcing the establishment of a press, and a list of citizens who would act as jurors in the event of libel suits.
10. *The New Mexican*, April 21, 1876.
11. Wagner, "New Mexico Spanish Press," 11–13.
12. Chávez, *But Time and Chance*, 156.
13. Banker, "Presbyterian Missionary Activity in the Southwest," 55.
14. Ibid.
15. Menaul to John C. Lowrie, December 12, 1871, ZL.
16. Menaul to John C. Lowrie, January 9, 1873, ZL.
17. Stewart, *Sheldon Jackson*, 228–29.
18. Fraser, "Indian Mission Printing in New Mexico," 311. Menaul, *Third Annual Report of the Laguna Mission*, 16, LMPP.
19. *Third Annual Report of the Laguna Mission*, 17, LMPP.
20. Ibid., 16, LMPP. The Washington was among a new breed of all-metal printing presses that began to evolve in the late eighteenth century. Thought to be a high-speed press, instead of the center screw common to older wood presses it had a variety of toggle-joint mechanisms. American Samuel Rust is credited with developing an American version that found commercial use in New Mexico through the early part of the twentieth century. Moran, *Printing Presses*, 79.
21. Menaul, *Laguna Indian Translation of McGufeyf's [sic] New First Eclectic Reader*, Introduction.
22. Banker, "Presbyterian Missionary Activity in the Southwest," 58.

CHAPTER TWO NOTES

1. Bynner, "A City of Change."
2. White, *The Taos Society of Artists*, 1–2.
3. Robertson and Nestor, *Artists of the Canyons and Caminos*, 25.
4. Gregg, *Commerce of the Prairies*, 105.
5. Weigle and Fiore, *Santa Fe and Taos*, 10.
6. Udall, *Spud Johnson & Laughing Horse*, 38–39.
7. Santa Fe's Palace of the Governors, seat of New Mexico governments since the seventeenth century, was refurbished in 1909 and became the home of a territorial museum, later a part of the Museum of New Mexico. Tobias and Woodhouse, *Santa Fe*, 48–52.
8. Krause, *Gustave Baumann: Nearer to Art*, 13–14.
9. Baumann, "Concerning a Small, Untroubled World," 22.
10. *The Santa Fe New Mexican*, April 2, 1961.
11. Baumann, "Unpublished Autobiography," 46, ABC.
12. Acton, *Hand of a Craftsman*, 21–23.
13. Baumann, *Chips an' Shavings*; Krause, *Gustave Baumann*, 60.
14. Sze, "The Gustave Baumann House," 2.

15. "Gustave Baumann of Santa Fe," by Laura Daby (unpublished manuscript) 12, MFL; Baumann, *Frijoles Canyon Pictographs.*
16. Interview with Willard Clark, ca. 1984.
17. *Albuquerque Journal*, September 17, 1991.
18. Characterized by its clamshell action, the platen press was designed to do small job printing and evolved over a period of time beginning in the early nineteenth century. Equally popular among commercial printers and amateurs, jobbing platens varied in size from large standing models to a smaller table size press used by hobbyists. They were originally treadle operated and hand fed but later motorized.
19. Farmer, *Willard Clark, Printer & Printmaker*, 2.
20. A woodcut is printed from the surface that remains after areas have been carved away. In the intaglio process, the shallow incised areas hold the ink while the surface is wiped clean before printing; thus the printed image lifts out of these recessed areas.
21. Clark, "Great Impressions: The Art of Willard Clark," 24–25.
22. Clark, *Recuerdos de Santa Fe, 1928–1943*, 40.
23. Farmer, *Willard Clark*, 21–22; *The Santa Fe Plaza*, July 31, 1937, WCP.
24. Clark depicted two roosters coming together in "Combination rather than Competition" on this 1937 flyer "Announcing the Combination of the printing facilities of the Rydal Press & Clark's Studio," WCP.
25. Interview with David Allen, October 17, 2001; Farmer, *Willard Clark*, 39.
26. Like many Santa Feans at the time, Dr. Harry P. Mera wore more than one hat. His career as a physician was eclipsed by his enthusiasm for anthropology. Dr. Mera's design for the state's distinctive "Zia symbol" flag was adopted by the State Legislature in 1925.
27. Margaret Hale was the daughter of renowned Latinist William Gardner Hale, a co-founder of the University of Chicago.
28. Ralph Pearson to Gracia Alling, February 18, 1921, ACHL.
29. Ralph Pearson to Emma Pearson, December 8, 1920, ACHL.
30. Ralph Pearson to Carl J. Smalley, December 12, 1920, ACHL.
31. Ralph Pearson to George A. Nelson, September 6, 1921, ACHL.
32. Vancil Foster to Gretchen Hercz, July 27, 1922, ACHL.
33. Cuthbertson, *Nobody Said Not to Go*, 52–53.
34. *The Taos News*, July 18, 1985.
35. Ibid.
36. Ibid.
37. Sommers, "Thomas Benrimo," 29.
38. *Albuquerque Journal*, November 15, 1992.
39. Udall, *Spud Johnson & Laughing Horse*, 4–5.
40. Johnson, "The Seven Years Between, an Autobiographical Fragment," HRC.

41. Witter Bynner was a Harvard-educated poet whose work brought him into contact with the great writers of his generation. After teaching a popular literature course at Berkeley, he became one of Santa Fe's pioneer literary colonists, settling there in 1922. His longtime association with Johnson, his secretary/companion in the years following his arrival, lasted until his death in 1968.
42. Johnson, "The Laughing Horse," 162.
43. Ibid., 164.
44. Ibid., 165.
45. Johnson, *Laughing Horse*.
46. Morrill, *A Taos Mosaic*, 133.
47. Johnson, *Laughing Horse*.
48. *Arrow Editions, first catalogue 1933–1936*, RPC.
49. Goodwin and Long, "The Rydal Press of Santa Fe, New Mexico: A Brief Account of Its History and Purpose." This eight-page article was typeset and printed with six small woodcuts by Willard Clark, for placement in *The Colophon: The Annual of Bookmaking* in 1938. The piece is a splendid example of the typographic excellence and good page design that characterized the Rydal Press.
50. Rittenhouse, "Southwest Imprints—Writers' Editions," 3.
51. Goodwin and Long, "The Rydal Press." Within this account of the Rydal Press, Haniel Long describes the complete Writers' Editions vision and framework, colorfully expressing an enduring conviction: "For the *belles-lettres* the private press can serve the same function as the senate filibuster: it can allow a minority to go on expressing itself as long as the minority cares to."
52. Rittenhouse, "Southwest Imprints," 4.
53. Long, *Interlinear to Cabeza de Vaca*, ix–xi. Fanny Bandelier, wife of the pioneering southwestern archaeologist Adolph Bandelier, translated Núñez Cabeza de Vaca's letter for *Interlinear*.
54. Church, "Writers' Editions," 5; Anton V. Long to Walter Goodwin, December 31, 1975, GFP.
55. Goodwin and Long, "The Rydal Press."
56. W. David Laird to Jack D. Rittenhouse, December 18, 1975, GFP.
57. Church, "Writers' Editions," 4.
58. Ernest Thompson Seton dedicated his life to introducing others to the wonders of nature. In his lifetime, he lectured throughout the world and wrote some sixty books, in addition to nearly four hundred magazine articles. He was born in England in 1860 and raised in Canada. An accomplished artist, he trained in Ontario, London, and Paris before working as an illustrator in New York in the 1880s and studying part time at the Art Students' League. Through early associations with indigenous peoples of Canada, Seton developed a special appreciation for a native way of life, including rituals and a reverence for nature. Later he incorporated idealized notions of his experiences into his youth organizations. Anderson, *The Chief*, 3–17.

59. The Woodcraft movement started in 1902 as an attempt by Seton to curb a wave of trespassing and vandalism at his Connecticut estate. He set up weekend camps, inviting neighborhood boys of twelve years and older to participate in outdoor activities. They became the first members of his Woodcraft "tribe." Somewhat older than the Boy Scouts of America, which Seton helped introduce into this country in 1910, the Woodcraft League shared many of the same goals. Through lectures, publications, and outdoor programs, the youth organization offered an education in wilderness skills and Indian lore, with contests, awards, and insignias as incentives. Though headquartered at the village, the league was an international movement that counted thousands of members. In his youth, Maurice Taylor himself had been a Woodcrafter and carried the values into his adult life. Anderson, *The Chief*, 184–97.
60. The College of Indian Wisdom was an outgrowth of the Woodcraft League, modeled after training courses Seton previously offered for youth organization leaders. It was part of his grand plan to promote outdoor activities as a path to "spiritual refreshment." The first session took place at Seton Village in 1932. Held during the summer months, the program drew as many as 150 students from all over the world to participate in arts and crafts, as well as nature and Indian lore studies. Fully accredited by the American Association of Colleges, through New Mexico Normal College (now New Mexico Highlands University), the classes were taught by a faculty of forty-two instructors. The impressive roster included Edgar L. Hewett, chair of the Anthropology Department at the University of New Mexico, and Clyde Fisher of the American Museum, among others. Sessions were held until 1940 when loss of personnel to World War II forced closure. Anderson, *The Chief*, 220–21.
61. Anderson, *The Chief*, 219–20, 224.
62. Taylor, *Bulletin in Bold Characters*, 11.
63. Taylor, "Prospectus," 5–6.
64. Designed for the American Type Founders Co. by Warren Chappell, Lydian is a bold sans serif type with a calligraphic appearance. Introduced in 1938, it became highly popular as a display and advertising type. Lawson, *Anatomy of a Typeface*, 327.
65. A Midwesterner by birth, Roy A. Keech lived in Albuquerque and studied at the University of New Mexico before settling in Santa Fe. In addition to poetry, he wrote books for young people and other fiction.
66. Pop Chalee was one of the first Native American women to achieve national recognition in the arts. She was born in 1906, the daughter of Taos Indian Joseph Lujan. Later she studied under Dorothy Dunn at the Santa Fe Indian School, where she graduated in 1937. She became well known for her paintings of traditional Indian dances.
67. Taylor, *Bulletin in Bold Characters*, 38.
68. Ibid., 50.

CHAPTER THREE NOTES

1. Chappell, *A Short History of the Printed Word*, 231.
2. Frank Hamilton Cushing came to New Mexico in 1879 under the auspices of the Federal Bureau of Ethnology. He lived with the Zuni Indians four and a half years and was adopted into a family at the pueblo. Following his research, he published several works focusing on the Zuni culture, beginning with *My Adventures in Zuñi* (1882). Fowler, *A Laboratory for Anthropology*, 107, 117–18, 125.
3. Adolph Bandelier, anthropologist, historian, archaeologist, and explorer, was among the first to study Indian cultures of the Southwest. Five years after his work began in New Mexico he made Santa Fe his home base. In an attempt to popularize his studies, in 1890 he wrote a classic tale of twelfth-century Anasazi life titled *The Delight Makers*. Fowler, *A Laboratory for Anthropology*, 172–80.
4. The School of American Research was established as a center for the study of archaeology and ethnology of the Southwest and was associated with the Museum of New Mexico until 1959. Still based in Santa Fe, SAR continues to encourage scholarly work in the area of Native American studies.
5. Tobias and Woodhouse, *Santa Fe*, 189.
6. Minutes of the Eighth Annual Meeting of the Laboratory of Anthropology Board of Trustees, March 1, 1935, MIAC/LAL.
7. The Public Works of Art Project was established in 1933 under a grant from the Civil Works Administration, a New Deal employment program. Before it closed in June 1934, the project provided work relief for 3,600 artists nationwide, including more than fifty from New Mexico. Along with Arizona, New Mexico constituted Region 13, directed by Jesse Nusbaum and locally coordinated by Gustave Baumann. Weigle, *New Mexico in Cameo and Camera*, 215.
8. Campbell, "Louie Ewing," 123.
9. The Federal Art Project, 1935–1939, was a New Deal work relief program designed to employ artists, along with skilled and unskilled people associated with the arts. Participants produced paintings and sculpture, offered lectures, taught art classes, and produced exhibitions, among other projects. Along with Arizona, Colorado, Utah, and Wyoming, New Mexico was in Region 5, locally directed by Russell Vernon Hunter. The Works Progress Administration, created in 1935, was responsible for coordinating and implementing the work relief programs as a whole. Weigle, *New Mexico in Cameo and Camera*, 213–14, 216.
10. Louie Ewing interview with Sylvia Loomis, January 1964, AAA.
11. Ibid.
12. Armitage, *Merle Armitage: Book Designer*.
13. Annual Report of the Laboratory of Anthropology Director, November 1, 1946, MIAC/LAL.
14. Armitage, *Merle Armitage: Book Designer*.
15. Ibid.

16. Director's Memorandum to the Executive Committee of the Laboratory of Anthropology Board of Trustees, December 9, 1946, MIAC/LAL.
17. Cassidy, "Art and Artists of New Mexico," 25.
18. *San Francisco Chronicle*, August 21, 1964.
19. "Binding 400 Folios," 1667.
20. *San Francisco Chronicle*, October 18, 1931.
21. Kimball, "Edward McLean — Bookman," 6.
22. *San Francisco Chronicle*, April 8, 1951.
23. Ibid.
24. Choice of the Merrymount Press indicates Dreis's discriminating taste. The press was set up in 1893 by Daniel Berkeley Updike, one of America's most distinguished and able printers, and was known for its impeccable commercial work standards. Chappell, *A Short History of the Printed Word*, 204.
25. *San Francisco Chronicle*, August 21, 1964.
26. *Rocky Mountain News*, September 14, 1982.
27. Ibid.
28. Ippolito and Kopatz, "Alan Swallow, Platten [*sic*] Press Publisher," 477, 478.
29. Ibid.
30. Claire, *Publishing in the West*, 57.
31. Ippolito and Kopatz, "Alan Swallow," 478.
32. Claire, *Publishing in the West*, 57.
33. Ibid.
34. Ibid.
35. Ippolito and Kopatz, "Alan Swallow," 480.
36. Interview with Judson Crews, January 29, 2002.
37. Crews, "Shoe-String Publisher," 9.
38. Anderson, *The Heart's Precision*, 12–13.
39. Ibid., 15–16.
40. Crews, "Shoe-String Publisher," 10–15.
41. Ibid
42. Ibid.
43. Patrocinio Barela, who had come to northern New Mexico from Arizona at an early age, was involved with the WPA Federal Arts Project during the 1930s and created a large body of artwork. He was a natural sculptor whose untrained efforts and uncomplicated forms captured the interest of the wider arts community. His carvings were acquired by museums throughout the country, among them the Museum of Modern Art in New York City. He died in 1964 in a fire that burned his ramshackle studio to the ground.
44. Crews, "Shoe-String Publisher," 11.
45. Ibid., 14.
46. Dietrich, *A Book about D.N.S.*

47. Dietrich, *New Mexico Recollections Part II*, 5. Bryn Mawr educated Margretta Dietrich was a suffragist, active in Nebraska where she headed the state's Women's Suffrage Association and later worked for the National League of Women Voters. After settling in New Mexico she became a well-known advocate for the rights of Native Americans, participating in the Indian Arts Fund and the New Mexico Association on Indian Affairs (later the Southwest Association on Indian Affairs).
48. Dietrich, *A Book about D.N.S.*
49. Interview with Jean Buchanan, January 2002.
50. Ibid.
51. Ibid.
52. Dietrich, *A Book about D.N.S.*

CHAPTER FOUR NOTES

1. Jon Webb to John Martin, August 7, 1965, Black Swallow Press papers, SPC.
2. Jon Webb to John Martin, August 15, 1965, Black Swallow Press papers, SPC.
3. Wilder Bentley, "the Elder," worked with Porter Garnett at the Laboratory Press, Carnegie Institute of Technology, in the early 1930s before establishing first the Acorn and then the Archetype Press in San Francisco beginning in 1934.
4. Interview with Jim DeKorne, May 2002.
5. Interview with Richard Polese, October 2001.
6. Myers, *Jack D. Rittenhouse, 1912–1991*, 6.
7. Interview with Charlotte Rittenhouse, September 13, 2001.
8. Myers, *Jack D. Rittenhouse, 1912–1991*, 8.
9. Invented by Merrit Gally and first produced in 1869, the Gally Universal (Colt's Armory) press was unique among platen presses in that it solved the problem of uneven impression. Unlike common "clamshell" presses, the Gally's platen was articulated to meet the type form exactly parallel. After Gally's patent expired, his popular design was made and sold by several builders, including Colt's Patent Firearms Company of Hartford, Connecticut. "For perfect presswork and fine work using woodcuts, it has never been surpassed by any other platen press." Williams, "Colt's Armory Press," 1–3.
10. The Mergenthaler Linotype used magazines (fonts) of brass matrices to cast full lines of type in lead. Operated by a keyboard that dropped each letter in place, its maze of moving cams, gears, and levers produced lead "slugs" that were locked into forms for printing, then could be melted down for reuse.
11. Hendrix, *Writings and Publications of Jack D. Rittenhouse*, 3.
12. The Vandercook Universal proof press was originally designed by Robert O. Vandercook of Chicago as an engraver's test press. Electrically inked, but with each sheet of paper hand cranked along a cylinder over the type, it proved ideal for the small press craftsperson of this era. The tedium of spreading ink properly and the faulty registration of old platen presses were no longer a challenge, and serious

craft publishers flocked to the Vandercook. The basic design was made from 1925 until 1976. Williams, "The 'Vandy' A Splendid Press!" 1, 2.

13. Chernofsky, "The Book Worlds of Jack D. Rittenhouse," 1–3; Rittenhouse, *First Fifty: A Checklist of the Stagecoach Press*, 5.
14. Rittenhouse, "New Mexico Bibliographies," 1–10.
15. Myers, *Jack D. Rittenhouse, 1912–1991*, 11.
16. Andrus, "Santa Fe's Stagecoach Press," 76.
17. Lyon, Jetta Carleton, "A Sort of a Love Affair," 3–5.
18. Lyon, Jene, "The Lightning Tree," 1, 2.
19. Lyon, Jene, "What It's All About," 1; Interview with Sam Larcombe, February 2, 2002.
20. Lyon, Jene, "The Lightning Tree," 2.
21. The Kelly B was a fairly common sheet-fed (17 × 22-inch) book-capable flatbed cylinder press made from 1914 to 1937 by American Type Foundry. The Kelly at the Lightning Tree had a gas drying device that was supposed to dry the ink "somewhat" as paper came off the impression cylinder. "Now and then a piece would get away from us, and we'd have to douse the blaze," typesetter Dick Fleming recounted. Fleming, "My Friend Jeno," 4.
22. Lyon, Jene, "Report from the Mountain," 2. The Lightning Tree first acquired a Monotype machine. Unlike a Linotype, which produces lines of type in lead, each Monotype letter is cast individually. However, no operator could be found who knew the Monotype's mechanical mysteries. The far more ubiquitous Mergenthaler Linotype was a more practical solution for rapid hot type composition.
23. Lyon, Jene, "What It's All About," 1.
24. Lyon, Jene, "Why the Celebration Will Be a Little Late This Year," 4. With chapters by Rittenhouse, Marc Simmons, Alice Bullock, Jack Potter, F. Stanley, C. L. Sonnichsen, Lawrence Clark Powell, and others, *In Celebration of the Book* is a rare gem of writing finesse and regional book knowledge.
25. Fleming, "My Friend Jeno," 4.
26. Jene Lyon speech accepting Rittenhouse Award, October 25, 1991, NMSUL.
27. Lyon, Jene, Letter to "Friends, Authors, Business Associates," 9.
28. Jack Rittenhouse recounted his role in the beginnings of Vinegar Tom Press in a 1991 letter to Spencer Maxwell, with thanks for sending him a copy of the Maxwell Press's fine little bibliography of the press. Gregg wrote to the Kelsey Company in 1968 to inquire about his particular machine and learned that "the press you have is an old timer, having been made somewhere between 40–70 years ago." The first item printed by Gregg on the press may have been *Southwestern Chuckles*, done for the local chapter of Westerners. Jack D. Rittenhouse to Spencer Maxwell, May 15, 1991, PPG; C. E. Mosher of the Kelsey Company, Meriden, Connecticut, to Andy Gregg, May 14, 1968, PPG.
29. Gregg, "The Tale of Vinegar Tom," 4, 5.

30. Interview with Andy Gregg, ca. 1998, PPG.
31. Maxwell and Armstrong, *Vinegar Tom Press: A Bibliographic Checklist*, 14–18.
32. Interview with Andy Gregg, ca. 1998, PPG.
33. Gregg, "The Tale of Vinegar Tom," 5.
34. Maxwell and Armstrong, *Vinegar Tom Press*, 10–11.
35. Interview with David Tedlock, August 2002.
36. Ibid.
37. Ibid.
38. Interview with Marc Simmons, October 2001.
39. Martínez, *The Art of Rini Templeton*, 10.
40. Ibid., 204.
41. Ibid., 206.
42–43. Interview with Linnie Kellahin, October 2001.
44–45. Interview with Dick Hicks, February 2002.
46. *Albuquerque Tribune*, August 28, 1975.
47. The block created by Hicks provides a flat surface for spreading ink to a thin, even consistency in preparation for applying it to raised surface type and artwork.
48. Interview with Dick Hicks, February 2002.

CHAPTER FIVE NOTES

1. Interview with Linnea Gentry, October 2002.
2. Interview with Clifford Burke, January 2002.
3. Interview with Eleanor Caponigro, January 2002.
4. Interview with Kathy Kuehn, September 2004.
5. Brandi, *Reflections in the Lizard's Eye*, 69.
6. Brandi, *San Francisco Lastday Homebound Hangover Highway Blues*, colophon.
7. Brandi, *Reflections in the Lizard's Eye*, 172.
8. Ibid., 175.
9. Felger, *Dark Horses and Little Turtles*, colophon.
10. Interview with John Brandi, November 2001.
11. Ibid.
12. Ibid.
13. Wooding, "Communicating in a Different Medium," 6.
14. Ibid., 7.
15. Hocks, *Heads and Bodies II*.
16. Interview with Paula Hocks, November 2001.
17. Ibid.
18. "Helen Gentry, 1897–1988," 100.
19. Ibid.
20. Interview with Linnea Gentry, October 2002.

21. Tom Leech got his introduction to printing in junior high school, where he learned to set metal type and later expanded upon these skills as an employee in the commercial offset printing industry. Following studies in printmaking and sculpture, he began making paper in Colorado Springs in 1978. For nearly a decade his San Miguel Paper Workshop turned out handmade sheets for artists and printers in addition to supplying the Press at Colorado College, a fine art press then under the direction of James Trissel. His broad interest in the art of the book led him to begin acquiring printing equipment in 1979, with which he established his own Fine Mess Press (later called Smokebrush Press). A few years later the multitalented Leech had begun to master the art of paper marbling and was offering the decorated sheets for sale along with his handmade paper and letterpress printings. Before relocating in New Mexico in 2001, he helped found Paper Road/Tibet and was instrumental in bringing about a revival of the hand papermaking craft in that country. Interview with Tom Leech, September 2004.
22. Interview with Peter Wells, March 2002.
23. After leaving the museum in 1970, Peter Wells settled in El Rito, New Mexico. There he did blacksmithing and, inspired by the work of fine printer Wilder Bentley, established his own Sunflower Press. Two years later he moved to Sandia Park, New Mexico, and continued until 1990 to do commercial letterpress printing in the area. Interview with Peter Wells, March 2002.
24. Built by the Cincinnati Type Foundry, this Washington hand press was used throughout southern New Mexico in the later half of the nineteenth century. Legend has it that the press was used to print one of the state's earliest and most important newspapers, the *Mesilla Times*, and later followed a trail of mining camps throughout the Black Range before ending up in Hatch, New Mexico, in 1925. In the hands of editor Manley Miles, the Washington press was used to produce the *Río Grande Reporter* from 1926 through 1929 when the name was changed to the *Hatch Reporter*. By the 1940s the press was retired and eventually stored in a barn for thirty years before being brought to the museum in pieces.
25. Priscilla Spitler left the museum in 1986 and eventually established her own fine bookbindery in Austin, Texas. Hands On Bookbinding, now located in Smithville, Texas, specializes in finely crafted editions for artists and private presses.
26. Many former Press of the Palace of the Governors employees continue working in the arts of the book in Santa Fe. Rosalia Galassi manages her own fine bindery, and Judy Herzl is a freelance graphic designer. Gordon Fluke, who moved his J. D. Grahame Cracker press from Baltimore to New Mexico before joining the staff in 1997, continues to do letterpress printing for artists in his studio in the Ortiz Mountains south of Santa Fe.
27. Interview with Clark Kimball, September 2001.
28. *Santa Fe Reporter*, August 6, 1981.

29. Interview with Clark Kimball, September 2001.
30. Villagrá Bookshop was opened in 1927 by Roberta Robey. Located on Palace Avenue in Santa Fe's newly remodeled Sena Plaza, the shop was a well-known gathering spot for Santa Fe literati and generated a few publications by regional writers. Weigle and Fiore, *Santa Fe and Taos, The Writer's Era*, 24.
31. *Santa Fe Reporter*, January 8, 1986.
32. Interview with Clark Kimball, September 2001.
33. Spencer Maxwell's Rydal books include a reprint of a 1920 pamphlet by W. D. Sayle titled *A Trip to the Rainbow Arch* (1999) and *Armageddon and New Mexico, Writing for Fun and Profit in the Poorest State in America* (2000) by Taos writer John Nichols. Twenty-six deluxe copies of each book were hand bound by Santa Fe book artist Rosalia Galassi. Interview with Spencer Maxwell, September 2004.
34. Tucked away in the Jemez Mountains northwest of Santa Fe, Los Alamos Scientific Laboratory (later Los Alamos National Laboratory) was established during World War II as the nation's atomic weapons laboratory. The best kept secret of the war years, the Manhattan Project at Los Alamos was headed by Dr. J. Robert Oppenheimer and Gen. Leslie Groves with the aim of developing the first atomic bomb.
35. Farmer, *Willard Clark, Printer & Printmaker*, 40.
36. Clark, "Great Impressions: The Art of Willard Clark," 22–29.
37. Interview with Janet Rodney, November 2001.
38. Ibid.
39. Ibid.
40. Hand bookbinder Martha Little moved her studio to New Mexico in 1987. First located on Camino del Monte Rey in Santa Fe, the bindery later moved to West Alameda, where it remained until she left the area in 2003. A specialist in book and paper conservation, Little had worked at Yale and later set up and headed the University of Michigan Libraries conservation laboratory. In Santa Fe she demonstrated her talent for edition bookbinding, working with the Weaselsleeves Press, as well as with the Press of the Palace of the Governors and Desert Rose Press to produce finely bound volumes. She continues the work in her northern California studio. Interview with Martha Little, August 2003.
41. Burke and Mudd, *Desert Rose Press Catalog*, 5.
42. Interview with Clifford Burke and Virginia Mudd, January 2002.
43. Ibid.
44. Ibid.
45. Burke and Mudd, *Desert Rose Press Catalog*, 3.
46. Interview with Clifford Burke and Virginia Mudd, January 2002.
47. Burke and Mudd, *Desert Rose Press Catalog*, 6.

AFTERWORD NOTES

1. Gill, *An Essay on Typography*, The Theme.

Glossary

Back Shop — Production area of a publishing firm.

Binder's Board — A heavy layered stock used for book covers.

Bookbinder's Press — A small iron screw press used for light and quick pressing, also known as a "nipping press."

Casebound — Common hardcover binding style in which the text block is held to the covers by means of pasted down endpapers and spine linings.

Chapbook — A small pamphlet originally containing tales, ballads, or tracts, sold by peddlers in the years following the invention of printing. A term still used today to refer to small softcover booklets.

Chase — Metal frame into which raised surface type and printing blocks are fixed for insertion into the press.

Codex — Book form of folded and gathered leaves that succeeded the papyrus scroll and became a model for the book as we know it today.

Colophon — Notes on the production of finely printed books, including information regarding printer, binder, type styles, materials, edition size, and so forth. Usually found on the final leaf.

Comb Binding — A commercial plastic binding that allows for a printed spine and pages that lay flat, commonly used for cookbooks, somewhat akin to spiral binding.

Composing Stick — Hand-held, adjustable metal tray into which type may be set and justified.

Cylinder Press — Letterpress machine that makes use of a cylinder to impress paper onto inked type.

Dingbat — A typographical device other than a letter or numeral, often used in text for decorative purposes.

Endpaper — Folded sheets placed on either side of the text block to form a lining for the inside of the cover boards, as well as front and back flyleaves.

Flatbed Press	Letterpress machine in which the printing form rests on a flat surface, usually horizontal.
Folio	Usually a large-format book made up of sheets folded only once.
Font	Complete set of characters of one particular typeface and size made up to a specified weight or number of letters.
Furniture	Pieces of wood or metal placed about the type matter to position it within the chase or inserted within the job itself to create white space.
Galley	Three-sided, shallow metal tray used for transporting and storing set type.
Guillotine	A large volume paper and book-cutting machine with a descending or sliding blade.
Half Title	An abbreviated title, also known as the bastard title, that precedes the full title page of a book.
Hand Press	Printing press on which both the inking and impression are done by hand, such as a Washington press.
Hand Set	Composition process by which individual metal type characters are hand selected for organization into words, lines, and pages.
Headband	A decorative band wrapped in silk, linen, or cotton thread that stretches across the top and bottom edge of a book and rests along the contour of the spine.
Hot Type	Also referred to as foundry type or metal type. Raised surface characters cast from an alloy of lead, antimony, and tin.
Imprint	Name and address of the printer appearing in printed matter.
Intaglio	Printmaking process by which ink is transferred to paper from engraved lines rather than from raised surfaces.
Job Case or Type Case	A wooden tray divided into compartments to hold individual type pieces and spacing material.
Letterpress	Process of printing from raised type and blocks cut or etched in relief.
Ligature	Two or more letters conjoined and cast on one body, such as ff, fi, fl, ffi, ffl.

Linoleum Block — Relief printing block carved from a thin sheet of linoleum mounted on wood.

Linotype — Complex machine for setting and casting raised surface characters on a single line or slug. Makes use of a keyboard and brass dies.

Lithography — The process of printing from a flat stone (nowadays metal) treated by hand or by photography so that only the areas required to print pick up ink. The rest of the plate, receptive to water, remains ink-repellent.

Marbling — Ancient decorating technique by which color patterns are transferred from the surface of a liquid to leather, paper, or book edges.

Monoprint — Single print achieved by hand, with color applied to a nonporous flat surface and transferred to paper.

Monotype — Registered trade name of a mechanical system that produces composed type matter in the form of single metal characters.

Octavo — A size of book page that results from folding each printed sheet into eight leaves, the most common book format.

Offset — A cheaper and faster means of lithography in which the printing surface is a flat metal plate sensitized so that ink is attracted to image areas and repelled by water from non-printing areas. Images are transferred from the plate to a rubber blanket and then to paper, thus the term "offset."

Perfect Binding — A commercial flat spine binding style made up of individual leaves of paper, typical of softcover books.

Photogravure — Printing process in which the type or image is produced from a photographic negative transferred to a metal plate and etched in.

Photopolymer Plate — Plastic printing plate created in relief by means of a photographic process.

Pica Stick — Standard measuring tool of the printer, also known as a "pica pole" or "line gauge."

Printer's Devil — Traditional print shop assistant and scapegoat.

Printer's Mark	Graphic image used as a type of private press logo, often appearing on the title page of printed books along with the press imprint.
Proof Press	Press designed to quickly produce good-quality trial prints from type, blocks, or plates.
Quarter Leather	Bookbinding style in which the spine is covered with leather and the front and back boards with paper or fabric.
Quarto	A page or paper size resulting from folding a sheet into four leaves.
Quoin	Wedges of wood or metal, or mechanically expanding blocks, used to lock printed material into the chase.
Repro Proof	A letterpress print photographically reproduced for the offset printing process.
Serigraph	A silkscreen print.
Signature	Term used synonymously with the word "section," meaning the units of folded leaves comprising a book.
Silkscreen	Method of printing that makes use of a stencil applied to tightly stretched fabric. Ink is forced through the screen onto paper by means of a squeegee and is resisted by the stencil.
Slipcase	A protective and removable bound case often used to enclose special edition books.
Vellum	Lime-cured calf or goatskin, used as a writing material for centuries before the advent of printing and the use of paper.
Web Fed Press	Automated printing press that makes use of a continuous roll of paper stock rather than cut sheets.
Woodblock	A design cut in relief, with gouges and gravers, on the surface of a wood block or plank.

Bibliography

ABBREVIATIONS

AAA	Archives of American Art
ABC	Ann Baumann Collection
ACHL	Angélico Chávez History Library
GFP	Goodwin Family Papers
HRC	Harry Ransom Humanities Research Center
LMPP	Laguna Mission Press Papers
MFL	Museum of Fine Arts Library
MIAC/LAL	Museum of Indian Arts and Culture/Laboratory of Anthropology Library
NMSUL	New Mexico State University Library
PPG	Press of the Palace of the Governors
RPC	Rydal Press Collection
SPC	Small Press Collection
WCP	Willard Clark Papers
ZL	Zimmerman Library

PRINTED MATERIAL

Acton, David. *Hand of a Craftsman: The Woodcut Techniques of Gustave Baumann.* Santa Fe: Museum of New Mexico Press, 1996.

Anderson, H. Allen. *The Chief: Ernest Thompson Seton and the Changing West.* College Station: Texas A&M University Press, 1986.

Anderson, Wendell. *The Heart's Precision: Judson Crews and His Poetry*. Carson, CA: Dumont Press, 1994.

Andrus, Ellen Hill. "Santa Fe's Stagecoach Press." *Western Review* 3, no. 2 (Winter 1966).

Armitage, Merle. *Merle Armitage: Book Designer* (catalog). Austin: Humanities Research Center, University of Texas at Austin, 1963.

Bacon, Lucy. "Seton Village." *New Mexico Magazine* 11, no. 5 (May 1933).

Banker, Mark T. "Presbyterian Missionary Activity in the Southwest: The Careers of John and James Menaul." *Journal of the West* 23, no. 1 (January 1984).

Barreiro, Antonio. [1832] *Ojeada Sobre Nuevo México.* Translated by H. Bailey Carroll and J. Villasana Haggard. Reprint *Three New Mexico Chronicles: The* Exposición *of Pedro Bautista Pino, 1812; and the* Ojeada *of Antonio Barreiro, 1832; and the additions by Don José Agustín de Escudero, 1849.* Albuquerque, NM: The Quivira Society, 1942.

Baumann, Gustave. *Chips an' Shavings.* Santa Fe, NM: Velarde Press, 1929.

———. "Concerning a Small, Untroubled World." *El Palacio* 78, no. 1 (April 1971).

———. *Frijoles Canyon Pictographs.* Santa Fe, NM: Writers' Editions, 1939.

"Binding 400 Folios." *Publishers Weekly* 118, no. 14 (October 4, 1930).

Blumenthal, Joseph. *The Printed Book in America.* Boston: David R. Godine, in association with The Dartmouth College Library, 1977.

Brandi, John. *Reflections in the Lizard's Eye.* Santa Fe, NM: Western Edge Press, 2000.

———. *San Francisco Lastday Homebound Hangover Highway Blues.* Monterey, CA: Nail Press, 1973.

Burke, Clifford, and Virginia Mudd. *Desert Rose Press Catalog.* San Jose, NM: Desert Rose Press, 1997.

Bynner, Witter. "A City of Change." *Laughing Horse* no. 11 (September 1924).

Campbell, Suzan. "Louie Ewing." *Southwest Art* 20, no. 3 (August 1990).

Cassidy, Ina Sizer. "Art and Artists of New Mexico." *New Mexico Magazine* 17, no. 9 (September 1939).

Chappell, Warren. *A Short History of the Printed Word,* Boston: Nonpareil Books, 1980.

Chávez, Fray Angélico. *But Time and Chance: The Story of Padre Martínez of Taos, 1793–1867.* Santa Fe, NM: Sunstone Press, 1981.

Chernofsky, Jacob L. "The Book Worlds of Jack D. Rittenhouse." *AB Bookman's Weekly for the Specialist Book World* (October 7, 1991).

Church, Peggy Pond. "Writers' Editions 1933–1939: Some Distant Recollections." *Book Talk* 11, no. 1 (February 1982).

Claire, William F., ed. *Publishing in the West: Alan Swallow.* Santa Fe, NM: The Lightning Tree, 1974.

Clark, Willard. *Recuerdos de Santa Fe, 1928–1943.* Santa Fe, N.M.: Clark's Studio, 1990.

Clark, William. "Great Impressions: The Art of Willard Clark." *El Palacio* 97, no. 2 (Spring/Summer 1992).

Crews, Judson. "Shoe-String Publisher." *Southwestern American Literature* 11, no. 1 (Fall 1985).

Cuthbertson, Ken. *Nobody Said Not to Go, The Life, Loves, and Adventures of Emily Hahn.* Boston: Faber & Faber, 1998.

Dietrich, Margretta. *A Book about D.N.S.* A memorial booklet. Santa Fe, NM: n.p., 1956.

———. *New Mexico Recollections Part II*. Santa Fe, N.M.: Vergara Printing Co., 1961.

Farmer, David. *Willard Clark, Printer & Printmaker.* Abilene, TX: Four-O Publishing, 2000.

Felger, Richard. *Dark Horses and Little Turtles.* Guadalupita, NM: Tooth of Time Books, 1974.

Fleming, Dick. "My Friend Jeno." *Book Talk* 22, no. 3 (June 1993).

Fowler, Don D. *A Laboratory for Anthropology: Science and Romanticism in the American Southwest, 1846–1930*. Albuquerque: University of New Mexico Press, 2000.

Fraser, James H. "Indian Mission Printing in New Mexico: A Bibliography." *New Mexico Historical Review* 43, no. 4 (October 1968).

Gibson, George Rutledge. *Journal of a Soldier Under Kearny and Doniphan, 1846–1847*. Ed. Ralph P. Bieber. Glendale, CA: Arthur H. Clark Company, 1934.

Gill, Eric. *An Essay on Typography*. Boston, MA: David R. Godine, 1988.

Goodwin, Walter L., Jr., and Haniel Long. "The Rydal Press of Santa Fe, New Mexico: A Brief Account of Its History and Purpose." *The Colophon: The Annual of Bookmaking*. New York: Colophon, 1938.

Gregg, Andy. "The Tale of Vinegar Tom." *Book Talk* 24, no. 4 (September 1995).

Gregg, Josiah. *Commerce of the Prairies* (1st ed., 1844). Ed. Max L. Moorhead. Norman: University of Oklahoma Press, 1954.

"Helen Gentry, 1897–1988." *Fine Print* 15, no. 2 (April 1989).

Hendrix, Art. *Writings and Publications of Jack D. Rittenhouse and His Stagecoach Press*. Commerce, TX: East Texas State University, 1983.

Hocks, Paula. *Heads and Bodies II*. Santa Fe, NM: Running Women Press, 1979.

Ippolito, Donna, and Shirley Kopatz. "Alan Swallow: Platten [*sic*] Press Publisher." *Journal of the West* 8, no. 3 (July 1969).

Johnson, Spud. "The Laughing Horse." *New Mexico Quarterly Review* 21, no. 2 (Summer 1951).

———. *Laughing Horse*, no. 14 (Autumn 1927).

Kimball, Clark. "Edward McLean—Bookman." *Book Talk* 13, no. 1 (January 1984).

Krause, Martin F., Madeline Carol Yurtseven, and David Acton. *Gustave Baumann: Nearer to Art*. Santa Fe: Museum of New Mexico Press, 1993.

Lawson, Alexander. *Anatomy of a Typeface*. Boston: David R. Godine, 1990.

Long, Haniel. *Interlinear to Cabeza de Vaca: His Relation of the Journey Florida to the Pacific, 1528–1536*. Santa Fe, NM: Rydal Press, 1936.

Lyon, Jene. "Friends, Authors, Business Associates." *Book Talk* 20, no. 5 (November 1991).

———. "The Lightning Tree." *Book Talk* 13, no. 3 (June 1984).

———. "Report from the Mountain." *The Lightning Tree Journal* 1, no. 4 (Spring/Fall 1974).

———. "What It's All About." *The Lightning Tree Journal* 1, no. 1 (Fall 1972).

———. "Why the Celebration Will Be a Little Late This Year." *Book Talk* 11, no. 2 (April 1982).

Lyon, Jetta Carleton. "A Sort of a Love Affair." Opening to *New Mexico's Book World, A Resource Guide*. Ed. Richard Polese. Santa Fe: New Mexico Book Association, 1999.

Martínez, Antonio José. [1838] *Relación de Méritos del Presbítero Antonio José Martínez*. Trans. by Cecil V. Romero. Reprint *New Mexico Historical Review* 3, no. 4 (October 1928).

Martínez, Elizabeth, ed. *The Art of Rini Templeton: Where There Is Life and Struggle*. Seattle: Real Comet Press, 1989.

Maxwell, Spencer, and Sally Armstrong. *Vinegar Tom Press: A Bibliographic Checklist*. Santa Fe, NM: The Maxwell Press, 1991.

Meléndez, A. Gabriel. *So All Is Not Lost: The Poetics of Print in Nuevomexicano Communities, 1834–1958*. Albuquerque: University of New Mexico Press, 1997.

Menaul, John. *Laguna Indian Translation of McGufeyf's [sic] New First Eclectic Reader*. Laguna, NM: Laguna Mission Press, 1882.

Moran, James. *Printing Presses, History and Development from the Fifteenth Century to Modern Times*. Berkeley and Los Angeles: University of California Press, 1973.

Morrill, Claire. *A Taos Mosaic: Portrait of a New Mexico Village*. Albuquerque: University of New Mexico Press, 1973.

Myers, Dwight. *Jack D. Rittenhouse, 1912–1991*. A memorial booklet. Albuquerque: n.p., 1991.

Pino, Pedro Bautista. [1812]. *Exposición Sucinta y Sencilla de la Provincia del Nuevo Mexico*. Trans. by H. Bailey Carroll and J. Villasana Haggard. Reprint *Three New Mexico Chronicles: The* Exposición *of Pedro Bautista Pino, 1812; the* Ojeada *of Antonio Barreiro, 1832; and the additions by Don José Agustín de Escudero, 1849*. Albuquerque, NM: The Quivira Society, 1942.

Rittenhouse, Jack D. "New Mexico Bibliographies: A Guide to 157 Guides Dealing Wholly or Chiefly with New Mexico." *Book Talk* 15, no. 2 (April 1986).

———. *First Fifty: A Checklist of the Stagecoach Press*. Santa Fe, NM: Stagecoach Press, 1968.

———. "Southwest Imprints—Writers' Editions." *Book Talk* 4, no. 5 (December 1975).

Robertson, Edna, and Sarah Nestor. *Artists of the Canyons and Caminos: Santa Fe, the Early Years*. Santa Fe, NM: Ancient City Press, 1996.

Rodriguez, Arnold L. "New Mexico in Transition." *New Mexico Historical Review* 24, no. 4 (October 1949).

Sommers, John. "Tom Benrimo (1887–1958), An Appreciation." *Artspace* 8, no. 4 (Fall 1984).

Stewart, Robert Laird. *Sheldon Jackson, Pathfinder and Prospector of the Missionary Vanguard in the Rocky Mountains and Alaska.* New York, Chicago: F. H. Revell Company, 1908.

Sze, Corinne P. "The Gustave Baumann House." *Bulletin of the Historic Santa Fe Foundation* 19, no. 1 (June 1991).

Taylor, Maurice. *Bulletin in Bold Characters*. Santa Fe, NM: Press of the Palace of the Governors, 1990.

———. "Prospectus." *Quest: A Journal of Adventure in Philosophy and Art* no. 12 (Spring 1938).

Tobias, Henry F., and Charles E. Woodhouse. *Santa Fe: A Modern History, 1880–1990*. Albuquerque: University of New Mexico Press, 2001.

Udall, Sharyn R. *Spud Johnson & Laughing Horse*. Albuquerque: University of New Mexico Press, 1994.

Wagner, Henry R. "New Mexico Spanish Press." *New Mexico Historical Review* 12, no. 1 (January 1937).

Weigle, Marta, ed. *New Mexico in Cameo and Camera: New Deal Documentation of 20th Century Lives*. Albuquerque: University of New Mexico Press, 1985.

Weigle, Marta, and Kyle Fiore. *Santa Fe and Taos:, The Writer's Era, 1916–1941*. Santa Fe, NM: Ancient City Press, 1982.

White, Robert R., ed. *The Taos Society of Artists*. Albuquerque: University of New Mexico Press, 1983.

Williams, Fred. "Colt's Armory Press." *Type & Press* (Winter 1983). Available on the Amalgamated Printers Association website: apa-letterpress.org/Files/APA/TP/.

———. "The 'Vandy' A Splendid Press!" *Type & Press* (Winter 1991). Available on the Amalgamated Printers Association website: apa-letterpress.org/Files/APA/TP/.

Wooding, David O. "Communicating in a Different Medium." *The Santa Fean* 7, no. 9 (October 1979).

NEWSPAPERS

Albuquerque Journal
Albuquerque Tribune
Rocky Mountain News
San Francisco Chronicle
Santa Fe New Mexican
Santa Fe Reporter
Taos News

INTERVIEWS WITH PAMELA S. SMITH

David Allen, Santa Fe, 2001.
John Brandi, El Rito, New Mexico, 2001.
Jean Buchanan, Santa Fe, 2002.
Clifford Burke and Virginia Mudd, San Jose, New Mexico, 2002.
Eleanor Caponigro, Tesuque, New Mexico, 2002.
Willard Clark, Santa Fe, ca. 1984.
Judson Crews, Taos, 2002.
Jim DeKorne, El Rito, New Mexico, 2002.
Linnea Gentry, Tucson, 2002.
Dick Hicks, Cedar Crest, New Mexico, 2002.
Paula Hocks, Albuquerque, 2001.
Linnie Kellahin, Santa Fe, 2001.
Clark Kimball, Santa Fe, 2001.
Kathy Kuehn, New York City, 2004.
Tom Leech, Santa Fe, 2004.
Martha Little, Santa Fe, 2003.
Spencer Maxwell, Santa Fe, 2004.
Richard Polese, Santa Fe, 2001.
Charlotte Rittenhouse, Albuquerque, 2001.
Janet Rodney, Santa Fe, 2001.
Marc Simmons, Cerrillos, New Mexico, 2001.
David Tedlock, Tucson, 2002.
Peter Wells, Santa Fe, 2002.

ARCHIVAL MATERIAL

Angélico Chávez History Library, Museum of New Mexico, Santa Fe. Manuscript Collection, Ralph Pearson/Margaret Hale Business Correspondence.

Ann Baumann Collection, Santa Rosa, California. *Unpublished Autobiography*, n.d.

Archives of American Art, Smithsonian Institution, Washington, DC Oral History Interviews, Louie Ewing interview with Sylvia Loomis, January 7, 1964 [microfilm].

Center for Southwest Research, University of New Mexico, Albuquerque. Laguna Mission Press Papers.

Center for Southwest Research, University of New Mexico, Albuquerque. Rydal Press Collection.

Center for Southwest Research, University of New Mexico, Albuquerque. Small Press Collection.

Harry Ransom Humanities Research Center, University of Texas at Austin. Manuscript Collection, Spud Johnson.

Kate Lopez, Santa Fe. Goodwin Family Papers.

Kevin Ryan, Santa Fe. Willard Clark Papers.

Museum of Fine Arts Library, Museum of New Mexico, Santa Fe: Gustave Baumann Papers.

Museum of Indian Arts and Culture/Laboratory of Anthropology Library, Museum of New Mexico, Santa Fe. Manuscript Collection, Laboratory of Anthropology Reports of the Directors.

New Mexico State University Library, Department of Archives and Special Collections, Las Cruces. Manuscript Collection, The Lightning Tree.

The Press of the Palace of the Governors, Museum of New Mexico, Santa Fe. Vinegar Tom Collection.

Zimmerman Library, University of New Mexico, Albuquerque. Microfilm, American Indian Correspondence: The Presbyterian Historical Society Collection of Missionaries' letters, 1833–93.

Credits

Frontis, pp. 161-22, 164-66: © and courtesy Press at the Palace of the Governors, Museum of New Mexico. Pp. 8, 32-33, 36: © Ann Baumann, courtesy Museum of Fine Arts Library and Archives and Ann Baumann. Pp. 12, 45, 47-48 © and courtesy Leona Foster, Ranchos de Taos, New Mexico. Pp. 16, 20: Courtesy Rare Book and Special Collections Division, The Library of Congress, Washington, D.C. P. 19: Daguerrotype image courtesy the Albuquerque Museum, PC1998.27.29. P. 20: Courtesy Harwood Museum of Art, Taos. P. 22: Courtesy Menaul Historical Library, Albuquerque. Gift of Roberta Nicholsen Hickman. P. 23: Courtesy Palace of the Governors (MNM/DCA), Santa Fe. Neg. #16050. P. 24: © 1885 Van Antwerp, Bragg and Co., courtesy Ohio Historical Society. P. 26: Courtesy Laguna Mission Press Papers, Center for Southwest Research, University Libraries, The University of New Mexico, Albuquerque. Pp. 28, 38-39, 42-43: Courtesy Kevin Ryan. P. 31: Courtesy Ann Baumann, Santa Rosa, California. P. 32: © 1912 Bobbs-Merrill Company, courtesy Museum of Fine Arts Library and Archives, Santa Fe, and Ann Baumann. P. 40: © 1930 El Estudio Press, courtesy Kevin Ryan. P. 44: © 1938 Janette Sebring Lowrey, courtesy Kevin Ryan. Pp. 51, 54 75, 90: Courtesy Harry Ransom Humanities Research Center, The University of Texas at Austin. P.53: Courtesy Southwest Collection, New Mexico State Library, Santa Fe. P. 55: Courtesy Fray Angélico Chávez History Library. P. 56: Courtesy Kate Goodwin Lopez, Santa Fe. P. 57: Courtesy Palace of the Governors (MNM/DCA) Neg. # 59757. P. 58: Courtesy Spencer Maxwell, Santa Fe. P .60: © 1938 Pynson Printers, Inc., courtesy Press at the Palace of the Governors, Museum of New Mexico. P. 61: © 1935 John Gould Fletcher, courtesy Center for Southwest Research, University Libraries, The University of New Mexico, Albuquerque. Pp. 63-65, 158-59, 188: Courtesy Press at the Palace of the Governors, Museum of New Mexico. P. 67: © 1941 Aurora Lucero-White, courtesy Bartlett Library, Museum of International Folk Art, Santa Fe. P. 68: © 1940 Clyde I. Price, courtesy Fray Angélico Chávez History. P. 70: © Laboratory of Anthropology, courtesy Museum of Indian Arts and Culture/Laboratory of Anthropology. P. 74: Courtesy of Mark and Martha Ewing, Santa Fe. P. 78: Courtesy Museum of Indian Arts and Culture/Laboratory of Anthropology Library, Santa Fe. P. 79: Courtesy *Publishers Weekly*, New York. P. 80: Courtesy Myron Tanenbaum, Denver. P. 81: © Laboratory of Anthropology, courtesy Museum of Indian Arts and Culture/Laboratory of Anthropology. Pp. 81L, 86: Courtesy University of Denver Special Collections; 81R: © 1942 U.S. Dept. of Agriculture, courtesy Bartlett Library, Museum of International Folk Art. P. 82: © 1941 Edward McLean, courtesy Bartlett Library, Museum of International Folk Art. P. 83: © 1943 Margaret Schevill, courtesy Fray Angélico Chávez History Library. P. 84: © 1947 Edward McLean, courtesy Center for Southwest Research, University Libraries, The University of New Mexico. P. 88: © 1942 Swallow and Critchlow, courtesy Zimmerman Library, The University of New Mexico, Albuquerque. P. 91: © and courtesy Judson Crews, Ranchos de Taos, New Mexico. P. 92: © 1962, 1976 Taos Recordings and Publications, courtesy Harwood Museum of Art, Taos, New Mexico. P. 95: Courtesy Museum of Fine Arts Library and Archives and Historic Santa Fe Foundation. P. 97: © 1933 Dorothy N. Stewart, courtesy Museum of Fine Arts Library and Archives and Historic Santa Fe Foundation. P. 98: © 1953 Dorothy Newkirk Stewart, courtesy Museum of Fine Arts

Library and Archives and Historic Santa Fe Foundation. P. 99: © 1949 Dorothy N. Stewart, courtesy Museum of Fine Arts Library and Archives and Historic Santa Fe Foundation. P. 100: © 1950 Agnes C. Sims, courtesy Museum of Indian Arts and Culture/Laboratory of Anthropology Library. Pp. 102, 131: Courtesy Center for Southwest Studies, University Libraries, The University of New Mexico. P. 105: Courtesy Charlotte Rittenhouse, Albuquerque, New Mexico. P. 107L: © Charlotte Rittenhouse, courtesy Richard Polese, Santa Fe. P. 107R: Courtesy Archives and Special Collections, New Mexico State University, Las Cruces. P. 108: © 1932 Atchison, Topeka and Santa Fe Railway, courtesy Richard Polese. P. 111: © Charlotte Rittenhouse, courtesy Archives and Special Collections, New Mexico State University. P. 112: Courtesy *The Albuquerque Tribune*. P. 114: © New Mexico Book League and The Lightning Tree, courtesy Press at the Palace of Governors, Museum of New Mexico. P. 115: © Jene Lyon, courtesy Archives and Special Collections, New Mexico State University. P. 117: © Marjorie Batchelder McPharlin, courtesy Archives and Special Collections, New Mexico State University. P. 118: © Bruce P. Woodford, courtersy Archives and Special Collections, New Mexico State University. P. 119: Courtesy Fay Gregg, Albuquerque. P. 122: © Fay Gregg, courtesy Press at the Palace of the Governors, Museum of New Mexico. P. 125: Courtesy Marc Simmons, Cerrillos, New Mexico. P. 126: © San Marcos Press, courtesy Fray Angélico Chávez History Library. P. 127: © San Marcos Press, courtesy David Tedlock, Tucson. Pp. 129-30: © and courtesy Rini Templeton Memorial Fund, San Francisco. P. 132: Courtesy *Albuquerque Journal*. P. 133: © Kathleen D. Church, courtesy Linnie Kellahin, Santa Fe. Pp. 134-36: Time Books. P. 143: © Richard Felger, courtesy Tooth of Time Books. Pp. 144, 145: © and courtesy Tooth of Time Books. P. 147: Courtesy Priscilla Spitler, Smithville, Texas. P. 150T: © Priscilla Spitler, courtesy Center for Southwest Research, University Libraries, The University of New Mexico. Pp. 150B; 151: © Priscilla Spitler, courtesy Museum of Fine Arts. Gift of Paula Hocks. P. 152: Courtesy Linnea Gentry, Tucson. P. 154: © Ann Baumann, courtesy Linnea Gentry. P. 156: © and courtesy Linnea Gentry. P. 160: Courtesy Kitty Leaken, Santa Fe. P. 168: Courtesy *The Santa Fe New Mexican*. P. 170: © Frank Waters, courtesy Tal and Marilyn Luther, T.N. Luther Books & Art. P. 171: © 1991 N. Scott Momaday, courtesy Tal and Marilyn Luther, T.N. Luther Books & Art. P. 173: Courtesy Palace of the Governors (MNM/DCA) Neg. from Living Treasures, Inc. Collection. Pp. 174-75: © and courtesy Kevin Ryan. Pp. 176-77, 180: Courtesy Weaselsleeves Press, Santa Fe. P. 179: © Lyn Hejinian, courtesy Weasesleeves Press. P. 182: Courtesy Desert Rose Press, San Jose, New Mexico. P. 183: © Clifford Burke, courtesy Desert Rose Press. P. 184: © Book Club of California, courtesy Desert Rose Press. P. 185: © Philip Whalen, courtesy Desert Rose Press. P. 186: © Stephen Mitchell translation, courtesy Desert Rose Press.

Index

Italicized page numbers refer to illustrations.

Passions in Print was set in Requiem, a typeface designed by Jonathan Hoefler of the Hoefler Type Foundry of New York in 1991 and completed in 1997. Requiem is a family of typefaces in the Renaissance style inspired by the work of sixteenth-century writing master Ludovico Vicentino degli Arrighi.

The book was designed by Deborah Flynn Post and set in type by Angela Taormina. It was printed and bound at Tien Wah Press of Singapore. Endsheets were reproduced from an original Willard Clark woodcut print (ca. 1938).